# ALL IN THE TELLING

# ALL IN THE TELLING
## a somewhat true story

## Saul Rubinek

Copyright © 2025 Saul Rubinek

All rights reserved. No part of this publication may be reproduced, distributed, or transmitted in any form or by any means, including photocopying, recording, or other electronic or mechanical methods, without the prior written permission of the author or publisher, except as permitted by U.S. copyright law.

Published by:
Redwood Publishing, LLC
Orange County, California
www.redwooddigitalpublishing.com

ISBN: 978-1-966333-21-0 (hardcover)
ISBN: 978-1-966333-22-7 (paperback)
ISBN: 978-1-966333-23-4 (e-book)
ISBN: 978-1-966333-24-1 (audiobook)

Cover and interior photographs are property of author
Front cover design: Saul Rubinek
Book design: Michelle Manley, Graphique Design Co.

For speaking engagement inquiries or to buy books in bulk, contact the author's representative Opus Entertainment at cbmgt@aol.com.

For Rachel

"The past is what you remember, imagine you remember, convince yourself you remember, or pretend you remember."

—Harold Pinter

# CONTENTS

| | |
|---|---|
| ONE | 1 |
| TWO | 29 |
| THREE | 51 |
| FOUR | 73 |
| FIVE | 111 |
| SIX | 125 |
| SEVEN | 133 |
| EIGHT | 141 |
| NINE | 157 |
| TEN | 173 |
| ELEVEN | 183 |
| TWELVE | 195 |
| THIRTEEN | 201 |
| FOURTEEN | 207 |
| FIFTEEN | 229 |
| SIXTEEN | 233 |
| SEVENTEEN | 259 |
| EIGHTEEN | 271 |
| NINETEEN | 291 |
| TWENTY | 299 |
| TWENTY-ONE | 303 |
| WHAT'S TRUE AND WHAT'S NOT | 319 |

# ONE

IT ALWAYS STARTS THE SAME WAY.

Dark. Black dark.

One vertical white bar creeps down, cutting through the black. Just one thick white bar. Which is bad but not too bad.

A second bar—just as white, just as thick—slithers down right beside the first, then another one, and another, and more of them fall straight down, all right beside one another, until the dark is imprisoned behind a row of thick white bars.

It's still okay because the white bars aren't touching. I don't know why that would be a bad thing, but the idea of them touching is fucking terrifying.

Then one fat horizontal white bar travels across deliberately touching the first white vertical bar, moving past that one to the next, touching them all, one at a time, and when that's done, another fat, white horizontal bar, unstoppable—does the same thing. And then more of them, each quicker than the last, until all the black is gone, ended by a sheer wall of pitiless white.

Which is when I wake up screaming.

It's a baby nightmare, before I can even walk or talk. I keep having the same exact nightmare. Like ten times a year. I don't always wake up screaming. But yeah, sometimes. Weird, it's usually after a stomachache. But I don't really know why.

Until today.

It's 1966. I'm eighteen. I have food in front of me on the kitchen table—my mom made me eggs and onions—but I can't eat much. Stomachache.

"You always have a bad stomach since you are a baby because that crazy woman in the refugee camp tried to kill you."

My mom, Frania. She's in her mid-forties, busy filling and labeling Tupperware. She's dressed up—not fancy, but she's always put together—a little makeup too, even for morning chores. And she says what she says pretty casually, like, oh you know why you get stomachaches—right?—because of the attempted murder thing.

"Ma! *What?!*"

"I never told you?"

"No! Somebody tried to kill me?"

"Not just specially you. She tried to kill all the new babies there."

She has an accent, a Jewish accent people would say, but it's actually Polish Yiddish by way of twenty-eight years in Poland, six in Montreal, and thirteen more in Ottawa. Her English is better than my dad's. My mom always wanted to be a modern woman, and getting her accent and her English grammar under control was one way to fit in as an Ottawa Jewish housewife.

"Ma, what are you talking about?"

"In the refugee camp in Munich was a woman, a Jewish woman, she took care of the newborns."

"She tried to kill ...? Ma, what did she actually do?"

"She did plenty, don't worry. She went from one crib to the next, all the new babies were in one big room, and she was force-feeding cream, heavy cream. For little babies this is like poison. For days she did this. Oh, you all got plenty sick. You were the worst, you almost died," she says, her back to me, labeling another Tupperware container with today's date.

What's going through my eighteen-year-old brain is *what the fuck!* What comes out is "Why?"

"She was a survivor from Auschwitz. She thought the world was a bad place for children, so she was trying to save them from being alive. With cream. Don't ask me. She was a cuckoo."

"Ma, Jesus, why didn't you tell me about this?"

"First of all, don't say Jesus. Anyway, now you know the reason you have your bad stomach."

No kidding.

I watch her moving around her spotless Danish Modern kitchen. She doesn't think this is a topic worth interrupting the organization of her freezer.

"Makes me wonder what else you didn't tell me."

"Listen, some things I don't want to remember."

I'm not mature enough to understand that might be an invitation for "What things?" so I say the teenager thing: "But, Ma, this was kind of an important event in my life!"

"Don't be so dramatic, you weren't even two weeks old, you didn't know from important events."

"Maybe I did, Ma. Maybe I *did* know." The pieces are falling into place. "We were all in cribs?"

"That's right. All iron cribs."

"Iron. Did she wear a uniform?"

"Who?"

"The cuckoo woman."

"She was like a nurse, all in white. Why you're asking?"

And right then, right at that moment, I thought: *What if, even at two weeks old, I could feel something really bad coming at me? Through the black iron bars of that crib, a white shape, coming closer and closer, reaching in through the black bars until everything is a sheer wall of pitiless white. Or maybe not pitiless. Maybe it's a compassionate wall of cuckoo white.*

The day I figure that out, the nightmare stops.

---

If I could go back in time and relive any of my days before I was eighteen, especially before I was seven when the nightmares came pretty regularly, would I notice something that happened that day, something weird enough to spark the nightmare? And if I knew what I know now, that it was the crazy woman trying to kill me, would I be alert to something that happens that day, something violent or maybe something as simple as bars on a gate or a woman wearing white?

Very soon after we arrive in Montreal in 1949, my dad gets a job working all day in a factory, and my mom stays in our two-room apartment, sewing piecemeal for extra money. When I'm five, my mom gets a half-day break from taking care of me because a bus picks me up on the street to take me to kindergarten at the Peretz Shule, a Yiddish-language immersive school for children of immigrant Holocaust survivors.

The school is supposed teach the humanist and social-justice ideals of the Yiddish poet Isaac Peretz. Fat chance of them getting much of that into my head, because when I get home from school at noon, my mom sends me out to my other school — the street. I only know a few English words, but because of how much time I spend on that street, I speak some weird combination of Yiddish and street French called *joual*, a French-Canadian working-class argot. I guess I speak *Friddish*.

Our street in 1953, Clark between Mont-Royal and Villeneuve, is working-class French Canadian Catholics and Jewish immigrants. Mutual hatred and suspicion. We Jewish street kids, ranging in age from five to around twelve, call the French Canadian kids *Frenchies*, and they call us *maudit Juifs* ("damn Jews")—which is even worse, we find out, than *maudit Anglais* ("damn English").

The French Canadian working-class families have it tough in 1950s Montreal. They see us as outsiders stealing their jobs. Oh, and of course, as Christ killers. Our families, newly arrived from having survived the Holocaust, have the images just behind their eyes of the murder of loved ones, and the collective generational memory of centuries of pogroms, so they see these working class Catholics as a much milder, more easy to deal with kind of Christian bigot. But we kids don't see it that way. We have no historical perspective. We have fists. And rocks.

The older kids do the fighting. The younger kids are the armorers, providing the older kids with weapons—chunks of brick, stones, and anything else throwable, like broken glass. Best of all is when that artillery is wrapped in spit-drenched balls of newspaper.

I have a secret friend—a five-year-old *Frenchie* kid, Jean-Claude. We only play together when it's just the two of us, no other *maudit Juifs* or *Frenchies* anywhere around or we both would be in deep shit. I don't have any memory at all about how and why we first start to pal around. I don't even remember what games we play or where we play out of sight of other kids, but I do remember the two of us having fun together, and him teaching me how to swear in joual and me teaching him how to say mean things in Yiddish.

The day for five-year-old me is mornings at the Peretz Shule and afternoons on the street. I never see girls my age out there unless they're with their mothers, going somewhere. The girls are kept inside, I guess. I don't know why. It's a mystery. We boys play tag and explore back alleys for treasure, like colored marbles or cigarette butts long enough to be smokable. We hold racing contests with complicated rules that change daily, down Clark Street to Mont-Royal or up to

Villeneuve. We buy candy at the mid-block variety store if we find or steal some pennies, and best of all, we dare each other to run across Clark in front of cars and risk getting hit, which triggers automatic yelling at us by some old Jewish or *Frenchie* grandmother sitting on a chair outside her building.

And every now and then, for reasons we kids under six can rarely fathom—a fight. The fights are already happening in the back alley behind the buildings by the time we younger kids know it. We see a few older kids running, *maudit Juifs* or *Frenchies*, or both, running silently—no yelling, no shouts, no sound at all—and that's the signal, the silent running, that a fight is on. So we right away run to our stash—we have places under stairs and in busted garbage cans or in weeds between the buildings where we stockpile our ammo. Loaded up, we race after the older kids to the battleground. I remember it as thrilling and fun. There are never more than six or seven kids on each side of the fight, the oldest hardly ever more than twelve. We throw stuff and yell at each other. Sometimes I see Jean-Claude on the other side of the fight, doing the same thing as me, making sure his older pals have shit to throw. We see each other across the battle lines and yell insults as if we're enemies. When we see each other the next day or whenever, we don't talk about these fights, ever.

One time, an ambulance and the police have to be called. An old Hasid with *peyes* is on his way to shul with his grandson, Mendel, a mean, foul-mouthed thirteen-year-old who always picks on us smaller kids. One of the older *Frenchies*, a nasty, pimply little jerk called Pierre, throws some dog shit at Mendel, misses, and hits the old Hasid's fur hat. Pierre takes off fast but Mendel is faster and jumps him, right in the middle of Clark Street—in the road, not in the alley behind where the fights are supposed to happen. Mendel sits on top of him and bashes his face over and over until there's blood gushing out of

Pierre's mouth and nose. I don't remember what I was doing right before I saw the shit hit the Hasid's hat, but I'll never forget all that blood. Even today, if I hear the name Mendel, I think of blood.

We kids, *maudit Juifs* and *Frenchies*, swarm, intermingling in a circle around Mendel and Pierre, and we literally stop traffic on Clark. I am right in the middle of that circle, all of us just standing there gaping at Mendel beating the crap out of Pierre. Then we start screaming for our guy, and in seconds, the circle turns in on itself, hitting, yelling, scratching, biting, and pounding each other. And then my secret *Frenchie* friend, Jean-Claude, is right in front of me, his fists up and ready to smack me, and mine ready to smack him. We stare at each other in shock, and we both back up and turn to smack some other kid.

Then I forget all about Jean-Claude because for the first time, I'm not an armorer. I'm a warrior. And I like it. Until I get a fist slammed into the side of my head. I fall down, my hand clamped on my right ear, and when I take my hand away it's covered in blood. That's when I hear, only out of my left ear, either a police siren or an ambulance. I don't remember which came first, I only remember thinking, *Whatever it is, oh no, it's coming for me.* So I get up fast, run to the nearest alley between two buildings and watch from the shadows.

I see a big white car that has a bright red cross on it, and a couple of guys get out, run over to Pierre, pick him up, and put him on a stretcher—a thing I've never seen before, and they carry him into the back of the car, and take off. I remember thinking, *I guess a car with a cross isn't here for me or for any other injured maudit Juifs.* I don't remember much else, except two very big guys in black uniforms, police I guess, walking around doing not much of anything, and then they get in their black-and-white car and drive away. By that time, all the kids have vanished. They are already gone when the ambulance guys pick Pierre up off the ground. Mendel and his Hasid grandfather for sure have disappeared.

I can see myself standing in front of our building, yelling "Mama! Mama!" up to the second-floor window, where she's sewing. I can see her opening the window and looking down at me, and I know I must have held up my bloody hand and that the side of my face by my right ear is bloody too. The next thing I remember is her in front of me, saying over and over, "*Vuss iz geshayn?*" What happened? I don't know how to answer that, I just remember feeling okay because I can hear out of my right ear again. I remember her scrubbing a wet yellow towel all over my face, and her stern look as she inspects my ear, my face, my hands, my neck. Then she holds me at arm's length and stares at me, and asks again, "*Vuss iz geshayn?*" I finally tell her some *Frenchie* kid hit me. She keeps staring at me for a long moment and says, "*Got hot dir gegebn tsvey foystn.*" God gave you two fists. Then she turns me around and gives me a gentle shove back toward the street.

There aren't a lot of days I remember really clearly from back then, but that day with Mendel and Pierre and the blood is one of them, so if I could relive that day somehow, it wouldn't surprise me to find out my nightmare came to me that night.

Halfway through first grade at the Peretz Shule, when I'm six, we move to Ottawa because my dad and another survivor he met in the Föhrenwald refugee camp somehow got the money together to start their own business, a ready-to-wear clothing store. Why that particular business and why Ottawa, I have no idea. My parents suddenly yank me away from everything and everyone I know, and I find myself at Osgoode Public School. I am the new kid in the class—a stranger, the one everybody stares at. These new kids have new rules that I can't figure out because I can barely speak English. I don't know what's right, what's wrong, what's funny, or what's not. I've lost both my friends and my enemies.

I hate being there. I'm not scared. I'm angry. I know there's something I'm missing, I feel it, something I can't name. Something that will make my anger feel—not *better*, that isn't it—something that will make it feel ... right. Then I find what I've been missing. A fight.

I don't know how long I've been in my new first-grade class, but it sure isn't more than a few days, when the teacher—a skinny woman with red hair, whose name I can't pronounce—sneezes. Immediately, because I was trained this way, I say *"Gesundheit!"* which is the Yiddish way of saying "Bless you." Just as immediately I hear a kid laugh, and the laugh is loud and ugly. I whirl around, ready to kill. I see a fat kid with yellow hair in the back row. His laugh has turned into a snigger, but when he sees me staring at him, he stretches out his arm and points straight at me with a dirty finger. I guess it's the look on my face that turns his snigger back into a laugh, but now it's even louder, a braying-donkey sound, and the rest of the class starts laughing too, but thinking back I guess they were probably laughing at the fat kid's stupid braying laugh as much as they were laughing at me.

I wait for him at recess. With a chunk of brick. I don't give him a chance. As soon as he walks out the school door into the yard, I slam the brick into the side of his head. He goes down, out cold, blood everywhere. On my block, on Clark Street, if you let a kid laugh at you without doing anything about it, you're dead meat. You might as well put a sign around your neck, *Kick me, I don't fight back*. It's a rule we all know as clear and simple as red means stop and green means go. *"Got hot dir gegebn tsvey foystn."* God gave you two fists. So I stand there looking down at him, and I remember clear as day thinking I should probably sit on top of him and slam the brick a few more times into his face. But I don't. I'm hoping for someone to come along, somebody like my mother, who'd say *"Gut getun."* Well done.

That doesn't happen. The rest of what happens is blurry, but I definitely remember realizing I'm in trouble. I figure this is bad luck because I wouldn't be in trouble if there were *maudit Juifs* or *Frenchies* around. Honestly, I have absolutely no memory of what happened to the fat kid with yellow hair. I never even found out his name. All I know is I never see him again. He didn't die, I know that, because, well, I think somebody would have mentioned it.

Anyway, pretty soon some teacher pulls me into a big office with a desk, and a small man with a bald head—I've never seen him before—stares at me with big blue eyes through his round glasses and I remember thinking, *His eyes are way too big for his face.* The teacher holds on to my arm so hard it hurts and tells the small man what happened—I suppose, but I don't really know because I can't understand the teacher's fast English. All I remember is the small man's big, shining bald head and his big, round blue eyes. I've never before seen eyes that blue or a head that bald. The small man pushes me onto a bench in the hall outside the office. Teachers keep sneaking around to get a look at me. Some kids, too. I remember thinking, *It's too bad they can't call my mom because she'll tell them I was only doing what was right.* But my parents don't have a phone.

The next clear memory I have is both my mother and father sitting in front of the small man with the bald head's desk, me on a chair behind my parents, and the small man listening to them, staring at them with his big blue eyes. Both my parents are speaking English—my mother's, much better than my father's—but whatever they're saying isn't working very well because the small bald man keeps shaking his head, *No no no.* Then my mother talks faster and now she's crying, and my father stands up to lean over my mother and hold her shoulders. And then my father says the word *Holocaust.* After that my mother says the word a few times. And then the small man's blue eyes get even wider behind his glasses, and he stops shaking his head.

The next thing I remember—this must be days later—my father takes me into a church. It looks like a church but really it's not, not anymore. We go around the back of the place and through a big wooden door. Inside it's dark and smells like musty perfume and something else, maybe sweat. There's a bunch of other people there, mostly women, and every single one of them is with a little girl, some of them my age, some a bit older, all of us standing on a platform lit up by rows of lights hanging over us, in front of a huge dark room with hundreds of chairs with nobody sitting in them. A tall woman with gold frizzy hair who smiles a lot with very red lips and very white teeth is standing with her back to the empty, dark room with all the chairs, speaking to everyone, but I don't understand any of it. It's only later I find out where I was—on a stage in front of an empty theater. For the first time in my life.

After that, things are blurry again until probably a few days later, or maybe it's just later that day. I'm in a large green room with twenty girls and two other boys, and the woman with frizzy gold hair tells us her name is Faith Ward and that we should call her Faith.

My fists are clenched. I'm waiting for the first wrong look, the first ugly laugh, and the first punch. It doesn't happen. Instead, Faith teaches us how to make up stories and tell them to each other by pretending to be the people in the stories. When she talks to us, her voice is deep and musical and so beautiful I could listen to it forever. It doesn't take very long for my fists to turn back into hands—and, in a way, for the rest of my life, I never leave that room.

It's a natural thing for my father to suggest I go to children's theater school. For sure, there's no such thing as therapy for violent six-year-olds in 1955 Ottawa. My parents don't know why, but the

Ottawa Little Theatre's school for children is free for boys, a huge bonus. But I soon find out why: boys are called all kinds of names for doing theater—sissy, pansy, fairy, fruit—so there aren't a lot of us willing to take that crap just to be in a play. Not that any kid at Osgoode Public School dares call me any names. They know what happened last time one of them laughed at me. The truth is, if they had picked on me, I probably wouldn't have done anything to them. Not anymore. I would have made a story out of it in Faith Ward's theater class and we all would have acted it out.

There's another reason it's a natural thing for my father to think theater school might be good for me. When he was sixteen, my father was an actor in Yiddish theater in Poland. Hitler put a stop to all that.

Somehow, even when I am a toddler, I know my father is a performer. It's the first memory I have of him: My father acting out stories by playing different characters and making friends and neighbors laugh, and making them cry. And my mother watching him with loving eyes and laughing and crying and clapping along with everybody else. So of course he sends me to children's theater school after I bash a kid's head in with a brick. Naturally.

I know this: By the time I actually play a part in a play in front of an audience, after around six months in Faith Ward's class, when I'm seven, my nightmare still comes, but a lot less often. A lot less.

And then, when I'm eighteen, and find out from my mother why the nightmare started in the first place, it just goes away and stays away.

Thirty-eight years later, the nightmare comes back.

---

I'm fifty-six in 2004. I'm in Los Angeles on a cool autumn morning, standing in front of an eighth-grade class of kids, most of them thirteen, pretty much half and half girls and boys, and all of them waiting to be entertained, and maybe something more, I can see it in their eyes, hoping for provocative, for stimulating, or if they're lucky, something funny or even offensive, but they all look like they're expecting something cool.

I've got dark circles under my eyes because I didn't sleep much last night. The nightmare came back, and I woke up screaming.

"Hi. I know most of you guys, but for those I don't, I'm Saul, Hannah's dad."

Hannah is in the front row—thirteen going on twenty in a lot of ways, especially the calm, wise way her deep blue eyes are watching me right now, and amused too, but I can also see the thirteen-year-old excited for what's about to happen.

"Mrs. Schmidt, thanks for letting me talk to your class today."

She's sitting behind her desk, Mrs. Schmidt, the Waldorf School's elementary class teacher. The way this school system operates, she has these kids starting in first grade and stays with them all the way through to this eighth-grade year. Next year, in high school, all that will change, but right now Mrs. Schmidt knows these teens almost as well as their parents, and in some cases, better. She smiles at me with what looks like encouragement, but it could be sympathy, because, like I said, I have dark circles under my eyes, and I know I must be giving off a nervous vibe.

"And I owe your parents thanks, too, for saying yes to this."

I hold up the DVD case I brought with me. The title is *So Many Miracles*, and the cover has a photo of my mom and dad in their sixties, sitting together at the base of a concrete pedestal under a monument of some kind, my dad touching my mom's face tenderly, like he's consoling her.

"Five years before Hannah was born, eighteen years ago, I made this film. In Poland."

I look at my daughter, who looks more anxious than she did a few seconds ago. "By the way, Hannah, thank you too," and to the class, "because Hannah also had to say yes, so I could show you this. I think your teacher told you the film is about what my parents went through during the Second World War, during what's called the Holocaust."

I look over to Mrs. Schmidt for confirmation. She nods. I turn back to the class. "Let me start by asking you, how many of you think what happened to my family is a more dramatic story, a more important story than what happened to your family? Show of hands?"

Most of the class raise their hands.

"That's what I was afraid of. Even though the school and your parents said yes about me doing this, at first I really did not want to show this film to you. I was worried that you'll think I'm saying that what my parents went through is somehow more important than what your parents or grandparents went through, what your people went through. And that's not true. Not true."

I have more to say. I prepared more to say. That's gone right out of my head. Every single teenage face is showing interest—curiosity, even. I better get to it. I take the DVD out of its case and slide it into the machine already set up beside the TV.

"Someone please get the lights and the blinds." A couple of students do that, and the room is darkened. I press Play to start the film, and go to the back of the class to sit at an empty desk.

The film music starts. There's a shot of my parents walking on a hilltop overlooking the town of Pińczów, and I hear my voice say:

"When my parents were young, they survived the German occupation of Poland. During the war, they were hidden for two and a half years."

The class watches my mom and dad as they walk together, arm in arm, on the hillside.

"Can you imagine, fifty years?" my mom says.

"I never dreamt ... I couldn't even dream I would be again here," my dad answers.

My mom: "No. I didn't dream about it. You know what? We are very fortunate, and God loves us. That we survived, and we could come to the places where we were so happy together ..."

My dad says, "That's *Romeo and Juliet*." My mom laughs.

I sit in the dark, listening to my own voice narrate the film.

"When I was a little boy, I thought that everybody's parents had nightmares and screamed in the night. I thought that was normal. Everybody's parents were like that."

I see myself on-screen, in my thirties, sitting on the same hillside, watching my parents.

"But as I grew a little older, and I heard stories about what happened to them in Poland, I found out where their nightmares came from. And I knew not everybody's parents were like that."

I found out where my nightmare comes from. That doesn't stop it from coming back. I'm watching the class watch the film. There are lies in this film. My parents lied to me, and now I'm lying to my daughter, Hannah. Maybe that's why last night the nightmare came back. I don't know. But I know this: If not for lies, there would not have been a documentary film in the first place.

It started as a con. And my parents were the mark.

---

I didn't just con my parents. My other mark was Kate, right after we started living together when I was thirty-six, in 1984.

The lie is born one night when Kate and I are in bed together. She's four years younger than me. She calls herself "black Irish." Dark hair, dark eyes, fair skin. She's wide awake, her bedside lamp on. My light is off, and I've got my back turned away from her. I hope she thinks I'm asleep, because I'm trying to avoid a question she asked me a couple of minutes ago.

"Saul?" Kate is persistent.

Okay, no use pretending I'm asleep. "What was the question?"

"Your mom and dad."

"Oh, right. It's all good."

"What are their names again?"

"Frania and Srulek."

"You told them we're living together?"

"It's totally fine."

Blatant lie.

Two years before going to Poland with my parents to make the documentary film, I met Kate. Five months after that, we started living together.

I'm an actor living in Toronto. Kate, in her early thirties, is an actor, a playwright, and a theater director. My parents live two hundred miles away in Ottawa, and I'm their only son. We're close, and I call them every week or so, but I never mention that I'm with Kate, not when we start dating, not when it seems serious, and not when Kate and I start living together. My mom and dad know *absolutely nothing* about her. Zero.

Right at that moment, if you'd asked me the reason why, I couldn't have told you. I never had a strategy about this or a thought-through reason. Instinct, maybe?

"What did your parents say about my not being Jewish?"

Stalling for time to come up with something that sounds reasonably positive and also might end the discussion, all that comes out of my mouth is, "Huh?" Then, "You know … it's cool, they're not very religious."

"What does *that* mean?"

"I mean it's not a big deal. They don't go to synagogue regularly, they don't have separate cutlery for meat and dairy. They're not strict about stuff like that."

"They actually said my not being Jewish isn't a problem for them?"

"Not a big deal," I say and quickly change the subject. "How was your day? You were gonna tell what's-his-name, the lighting designer, to go fuck himself."

"No, he apologized. When do I get to meet your—"

*Fuck.* I have to get her off this. "You said he's lazy, and he's not worth the trouble, and—"

"I was wrong. He's worth the trouble. Saul. When do I get to meet your parents?"

"Oh. I guess, you know, when they come to Toronto to see me in a play or something."

"Could you turn over, please, so we can talk to each other?" She's been calm so far, but now her voice has an edge to it.

I turn, taking my time. I look at her, trying for casual innocence. I even try a yawn.

Kate studies me for a moment. "You didn't tell them I'm not Jewish."

She's absolutely right about that. What she doesn't suspect, yet, is that my parents don't even know she exists.

I've taken too long to respond. As a new lie begins to form in my mouth, she says, "Don't even bother. Why not?"

My brain is too slow constructing a plausible response. She says, "It is going to be a big thing for them. I knew it. Is it a big thing for you?"

I pretend to be offended. I'm actually pretty good at that. "Of course not!"

"Then why not tell them?"

"It didn't really come up." Which is a kind of fucked-up truth.

"Didn't they ask?"

"Not really." Another fucked-up truth.

"What *did* you tell them?"

An outright lie is called for. "Just, you know, that I'm, I'm happy and I'm in love."

"Nothing about who with?"

"Not a lot of specifics."

She stares at me for a beat. And then: "My name?"

I can't even imagine what lie could work to answer that. "Um …"

"Oh my God! If you care about them and you're serious about us, then you have to tell them we're living together and who I am! Kate Lynch. And that I'm not Jewish."

"Just your name oughta do it."

———

"You're an idiot." This is my older sister Rachel's go-to comment whenever I tell her about stupid shit I've done.

"Could you not, please? I really need help."

I'm driving my old Honda Civic. Rachel is turned sideways beside me, all the better to stare at me, her face arranged in equal parts judgment and amusement.

"I didn't know you and Kate were living together. Since when?"

"I wouldn't call it living together. She moved in, like, only a few weeks ago."

"Those of us on planet earth call that living together. You in love with her?" She's like that, Rachel. Zooming straight to the point.

"Yes, but—"

"Wow, okay, you have to tell Mom and Dad. Why haven't you already? What do you think they'll do?"

Since I haven't even bothered to ask myself those questions, all I've got is: "I dunno. Nothing good."

Rachel turns away from me. I glance over and see she's shaking her head slightly, like *Oh my God, I can't believe he's got himself tangled up in this insanity.* She's a beauty, Rachel. She's a few years older but when you look into her eyes, she's a hundred years older. She takes after my mother, same deep-brown eyes, same curly, almost black hair. Tallest in the family, but that's easy to do since Mom and Dad are five-two and I'm only five-six. I'm lucky to have her as my sort-of rabbi. She is always there when I need her. I don't always get the help I want or expect, but she's always there for me, way more than I've ever been there for her. But she's never asked me for anything. I mean never.

"Does Kate go to church?"

"No! You think I could be with a practicing Christian?"

"Why not?"

"I couldn't be with a practicing Jew either. Anyway, Kate is an atheist."

"Mom, Dad, she's not Jewish, but the good news is, she is an atheist."

That makes me laugh. She's good at that. Especially when I'm tense. "So what do I do?"

"Are you and Kate talking about marriage and children?"

"Not really, no."

"Not really? Or *not*?" She's sitting sideways again, staring at me.

"Not." That's true. I have become adept at avoiding the most important topic about the future of our relationship. I'm pretty sure I don't want children, and I'm afraid that if Kate does, that could end things between us. So I don't want to get into it. And, conveniently, I figure if she doesn't bring it up, then maybe she doesn't want children, really.

"Kiddo," Rachel says, "you have to tell Mom and Dad. The longer you wait, the worse it'll be. But you have to tell them in the right way."

"There's a right way?"

"There's a sneaky way. Get Dad onside first."

"How?"

She thinks about it. Whenever she's strategizing, she closes her eyes. I know when she opens them, she'll have the answer. It takes almost a full minute. She opens her eyes. "Paint him into a corner. Steer the conversation toward antisemitism. He'll dive right into a lecture about—"

"INTOLERANCE!" We say it at the same time, making both of us laugh.

"And that's when you tell him about Kate."

"Brilliant."

---

I'm in my parents' living room. This is the room for serious conversations. You'd think that would be the kitchen, but my mother won't let my father smoke in the kitchen. Whenever my father becomes rabbinical, he smokes cigarettes, Matinées, one after the other, that come out of a bright yellow pack. My mother hates it, but she can't get him to stop. He will, eventually, when lung cancer almost kills him, but that's fifteen years in the future. Right now, we're in the rarely used living room reserved almost exclusively for "company"—meaning people we don't know well, or *goyim*. Or this, a serious talk.

The couch, a long deep-purple design in keeping with the rest of the Danish Modern furniture theme, is covered in plastic, which is, I know, a sitcom joke about immigrant families but no less true. My mother takes off the plastic for "company," but not for family. The wall-to-wall off-white carpet is, of course, spotless, and the room has a fireplace—a real working fireplace, never used, in which my mother has placed, for some unfathomable reason, not fake wood, no, she's put a carved ebony figurine of a naked African warrior with a spear in there. It's beautifully carved, but why she thinks the fireplace is a good place for it is a mystery never questioned, and the bigger mystery of why not actually use the fireplace in winter for, like, burning wood, is a ridiculous question that deserves only a look that says: *Are you crazy, we have central heating, and who needs the mess with the ashes?*

I've told Kate about this trip to Ottawa to tell my mother and father that she's not Jewish. Of course, what I haven't told her is that I'm going to tell them about her for the first time.

My dad stubs out his umpteenth Matinée into a large crystal ashtray on the white marble-topped coffee table. The thing is already full of butts and ashes. He's pacing. He likes to do that when lecturing. I'm sitting on the couch, following Rachel's strategy that I wait for the exact right moment.

"He made a law about intermarriage, Alexander. A very smart law. There is a reason why they called him 'the Great.'" He lights another Matinée with his silver Ronson lighter. "The law said the governors and the soldiers of every Greek-conquered territory had to marry with a woman of the local population. You know why?"

I do, actually. "So that their—"

"No," he says, interrupting me. He's in the midst of a Socratic rhetorical rant that requires no answers. "No. To prevent revolution. You see? Because Alexander's law forced intermarriage, the children in the occupied territories would never have a reason to overthrow the government. Genius."

"That's what I was—" I try to tell him that's what I was going to say, thinking, wrongly, that will get him onside more quickly so I can pounce with Rachel's strategy. But he doesn't want to hear explanations, answers, or commentary while he's in mid-lecture.

"Tolerance has to be taught, not by theory, not by religion, but by blood. By wanting your child to have a better life. If some of the blood in your child comes from another tribe, it also has your blood, so it's hard to hate that child, and hard even to hate the other tribe."

He takes a breath, or rather, he inhales some smoke. So I take the opportunity to start a new branch of the conversation that will lead where I want it to go.

"I think that—" is as far as I get.

"All right, you could hate, you could throw that child out—they do, some people, slaves to religious dogma or extreme nationalists or ignoramuses, but listen, after one, two, three generations, the hate would vanish. You know why there are Jews today?"

Did I hear him right? I wait for him to go on. But he actually wants an answer to this one. "Jews?"

"Antisemitism. That's why there are Jews today." And he waits for me to see the light. I see no light. I see he's still waiting for my response. I don't know what the hell he wants from me.

"Today?"

"Sure. Listen, I'm telling you, if not for antisemitism that threw us into ghettos, century after century, that forced us to be separate, to marry between ourselves, what would keep us Jewish?"

Incorrectly, I think he wants an answer. "I think—"

"Tradition? Our Torah, our Talmud, all right, good point, there would still be Jews. But not many. You see what antisemitism did? Made us proud, made us strong, made us to keep our identity even in the face of inquisitions and pogroms and genocide. But give to us a few centuries of tolerance and peace, and believe you me, it would not be such a big deal to marry the neighbor's daughter."

This is precisely the moment I've been waiting for.

"Absolutely! That's exactly right. Okay. Dad, listen, I … I think that today we've come to a point in our history where there can be harmony and we—"

Apparently, not the right moment. He stares at me. "*Harmony?!* Are you crazy? Only a few years ago was the Holocaust! I said after a few *generations!*"

"Of course, no, you're right, I mean, here, in Canada, harmony in Canada." I know I can mollify him with the word 'Canada.' He has a whole prepared speech about the glories of this new land that doesn't visit *pogroms* on Jews at Easter.

"When I came to this country, I kissed the ground."

I know exactly how to use that to get to my point. "I know, right, you did, because Canada is … So, listen, Dad, I fell in love. With a … Canadian." Okay, maybe I don't know *exactly* how to use that to make my point.

He has no idea what I'm saying. Like I suddenly started speaking Egyptian. "A what?"

ButI'monaroll.Downhill."ACanadian.Woman.Kate.FirsttimeI've ever been in love. We're living together, and it's amazing. I feel like—"

Now he sees where I'm going. "What you mean 'living together'?"

"We're both—"

"Kate? Kate what?" Which shuts me up. I wasn't ready for him to come up with that question this fast. He stubs out his Matinée and does not even look at me when he asks, "Jewish?"

I'm flailing now. "Her great-grandparents came originally from Ireland, and we have so much in common with the history of that *persecuted* part of the world because they—"

Now he looks at me. "You're living with a *shiksa?*"

Trembling, he picks up the heavy crystal ashtray, lifts it over his head, dumps it—ashes, cigarette butts, and all—on his own head.

Insanely, my first thought, as I see ashes all over my mother's purple couch, is that she was right about the plastic cover. My father carefully puts the ashtray back on the coffee table, grabs the collar of his shirt with both hands, rips the fabric apart, walks over to the living room wall, right underneath a framed triptych of three ages of me—as a fat and happy baby, an overweight bar mitzvah boy in a prayer shawl, and a standard actor résumé shot in my thirties—faces the wall, his back to me, and starts rocking, intoning the Kaddish, the Hebrew-Aramaic prayer for the dead.

I'm in shock, Rachel's strategy gone all to hell. He's chanting, "Yisgadal v'yiskadash sh'mei rabboh, b'allmoh div'roh khir'usei ..."

I go swiftly from staggered to pissed off. "You're saying *Kaddish*?! I'm *dead* to you now?!"

"I'm praying for *myself*," he says, facing the wall. He continues chanting.

"*You're dead*?! I fell in love with Kate and that *killed* you!?"

"...v'yamlikh malkhusei, b'khayeikhon uvyomeikhon uvkhayei d'khol beis yisroel ..."

"You're behaving like a bigot! We're not in fucking Poland!"

Of course, since new bad stuff piling on top of old bad stuff is a major theme of the Jewish experience, my mother chooses that moment to walk into the room, just in time to hear me shout 'bigot!' at my father, who is facing the wall, rocking back and forth, chanting the prayer for the dead.

"...b'agalah uvizman kariv, v'imru Amen."

My mother is horrified. "*Vuss is geshayn?!*" Yiddish for "What happened?"

"*Er lebt mit a shiksa.*" Yiddish for "He's living with a shiksa."

My mother cries out in agony and weeps. My father begins part two of the Kaddish.

"Y'hei sh'mei raba m'varach l'alam ul'almei almaya ..."

I'm exhausted. I drive away from Ottawa immediately after the catastrophe, arriving back in our Toronto apartment late, around midnight, and a whole day earlier than Kate is expecting. In fact, I have arrived back the same day I left. As I come in the door, I don't see Kate. Hopefully, she's asleep, and I can sneak upstairs and pass out. Maybe by morning I will know what to do. Or I can get Rachel to tell me what to do.

No such luck. From the kitchen, Kate's voice: "How'd it go?"

"Great!" I say, the first thing to pop into my head. On the drive back from Ottawa, I actually thought I would tell her the truth about everything. Ha.

Kate comes into the hallway in a robe and slippers, holding a glass of white wine.

"Why are you back a whole day early?"

I lie, "They have visitors, and my bedroom is taken. I didn't want to spend money on a hotel."

She gets right to it. "Your parents are okay with my not being Jewish?"

I need to think. I take her wine glass and have a long sip. "They weren't overjoyed, but it wasn't a big deal" is all I can come up with.

"What did they say exactly?"

Oh shit. "Huh?" I say as I head for the kitchen so she won't see my eyes. I get the white wine bottle from the fridge, and a wine glass, and pour myself a full one. By this time I've figured out something to say that's not a barefaced lie: "Would they have been happier if I was with a Jewish woman? I guess."

"They said that?"

I can see she's not thrilled with that answer. I say, "No, no, it's just a guess."

"You said 'not overjoyed.'" She is, I told you, relentless.

Stalling again, I go with "Huh?" and hold out the wine bottle. "More?"

"I'm good," she says.

We both sit at the kitchen table. I drink, pour myself more, and try to end this discussion on a positive note. "Bottom line: they're just happy I'm happy."

But she won't let it go. "Really? That's what they said, or it's 'just a guess'?"

"Believe me, my parents don't hide how they feel."

That makes her sit back and think. She sips her wine. "I wish *my* parents were as open about their feelings." Her voice is quiet.

"It has its pluses and minuses," I tell her, not looking at her in case she reads my mind.

After a moment, she sits up, brightening. "Well, great! Right?"

"Great!" I say, summoning enthusiasm from the depths of my acting chops.

Kate comes over and wraps her arms around me. I haven't moved. I'm still sitting there, tightly holding my wine glass, my head now pressed into her bosom.

"Don't you feel better now?"

---

I feel like shit. Rachel is right here when I need her. We sit side by side on a bench in the park right across from the building where Kate and I share our rent-controlled two-bedroom apartment.

"I knew it could be bad," she says. "I didn't know it would be biblical."

"Deuteronomy." I'm hoping for a laugh, but I don't get one.

"What did you tell Kate?" I don't answer that, which tells Rachel all she needs to know. She turns to face me directly. "Saul! Tell her the truth!"

"Kate, my father dumped ashes on his head and said the prayer for the dead in Aramaic, but the good news is, I'm not dead to him, no, the prayer for the dead was for *himself*, and my mom cried, not cried, it was more like the ancient wail of Hebrew women when invaders destroyed the temple of Solomon, and I lied to you about it because I thought it might hurt you badly to know that's how my parents feel about my being with a shiksa, which is what they called you—a *shiksa*—a word that does not just mean a non-Jewish woman since it comes from the Hebrew *shekets*, and really means an abomination, an impure object of loathing."

Rachel looks back down at the ground. "So lying was the way to go."

"Yep."

She closes her eyes, strategizing. Or it could be she's just out of ideas. She opens her eyes after only a few seconds. "Maybe they'll come around. They went through the same thing. Mom's family did not want her to marry Dad. He wasn't religious, he didn't dress like them, he didn't think like them. Mom and Dad were both so stubborn, in the end, Mom's parents just gave up."

"Hitler invading Poland might have had something to do with it."

# TWO

A MONTH LATER, we're having the first read-through for a new play, *Terrible Advice*. We four actors sit around a table, read the play out loud, and discuss script issues. We're not going to go into rehearsals for this for a few months but the director and writer want to have most of the script problems solved early.

I am not in a great space. I have not spoken to my parents in a month. That's longer than ever before in my life. I can't seem to focus properly on the work in front of me.

"When I wave my wand, I can send you back to any time in your life, and you can have an hour with your younger self."

That line is read by Caroline, playing the role of Hedda, a successful real estate agent.

Sitting at the table with us is the playwright, Jessica, perpetually depressed, our director, Martin, who is a cerebral and unnaturally calm man, and there's also our über-efficient stage manager, Connie.

Caroline, as Hedda, continues reading: "You get to talk to your younger self and say whatever you want."

I'm playing the role of Stanley, a college professor. "Your wand sends me back exactly as I am now, with everything that's happened to me?" I immediately think to myself, *What if I could go back and tell myself not to lie to Kate?*

Hedda: "Yep! So. The game is: When would you choose to go back to? And what would you say to yourself?"

Sandra, a strikingly beautiful woman, plays the role of my girlfriend, Delila. "Can I stay there and not come back?"

Hedda: "No! You got an hour to convince yourself of whatever. Jake?"

Stephen, his good looks going a bit to seed, plays the part of Jake, a failed musician who lives with Hedda. "Younger me will take one look at older me and kill himself." Which gets the kind of laugh from the rest of us that says we know he's right.

Hedda: "Honey, the point is, you could convince younger you not to *become* older you."

Jake: "If I was a person who actually knew what to tell me about how not to become me, I wouldn't be me, so—"

Hedda: "Chicken. Stanley?"

Me, as Stanley: "This is a game about regret, which I prefer to play privately." Which is, at this moment, also true about me.

Hedda: "The wand doesn't have to be about regret! *Somebody*, come on! I got a magic wand here, for Chrissake!"

Martin, our director, holds up his hand. "Can we stop here, please?" He turns to the playwright, Jessica, beside him. "Question. Hedda says the game doesn't have to be about regret. Nobody challenges her on that. But, Jess, if this is not about regret, then what is it about?"

Jessica takes a moment, looking at the script in front of her. "How about we just cut her line and go right into Saul's next line?"

Martin smiles. "I hate it when you go right to a solution before we have an argument." This gets a laugh from everyone. "Okay," he says. "Saul, you want to pick it up with your next line?"

As Stanley, I read, "Okay, Hedda. I know the exact day and hour when my life fell into hell. When I was ..." I stop and turn to look at

Martin and Jessica. "Wait. I just said I don't want to play 'regret,' and then, if we cut Hedda's line, I go right into playing the game? Don't I need ...?"

Jessica nods. "Right, something to convince you. Something to *make* you talk about a major regret in your life and share that with everyone. Saul, what would that be for you?"

I'm a bit taken aback. Too close to home. "In my own life?"

Jessica says, "What would convince you to talk about some big regret you'd rather not talk about?"

I say, "Something that would convince *me*, or convince Stanley?"

Martin suggests, "Maybe what would work for you could work for Stanley?"

"If it was me? A major regret? First of all, I'd make one up."

Jess is surprised by that. "A phony regret?"

"Just to get past the peer pressure," I say.

"And for Stanley?" asks Martin.

"It wouldn't take much," I tell him. "Stanley would tell the truth. Me, I'd lie." That creates a moment of awkward silence, until I add, "To be honest."

Which gets the laugh I was expecting, letting me off the hook.

---

"Hallo?" My mom has never quite mastered the pronunciation of *hel*-lo.

"Mom, it's me."

I'm alone in our Toronto apartment. My rehearsal is later today, and Kate is at work directing a workshop for a new play. It's the first time I've called home since the ashes-on-the-head day five weeks ago.

I can picture my mom using the beige push-button phone on the kitchen counter. My parents' Ottawa kitchen has the same

Danish Modern white wrought-iron glass-top table from when I was eighteen—actually, from when we first moved in when I was twelve. Same fridge, same stove, same floor and counters, all perfectly preserved by my mother's housekeeping diligence.

My mom tries to talk, but she can't get any words out. She's crying. Then she hangs up.

The next day, I try again. This time, my dad picks up the phone.

"Hello?"

"Dad?"

He doesn't say anything for about ten seconds.

"Dad?" I say again. He hangs up without a word.

Next day, I call again, and their answering machine picks up with my mom's voice: "Hallo, you reached Srulek and Frania Rubinek. Please leave a message when you hear the tone."

"Hi, it's me. I just want, uh, could you call me back when you get a chance, or maybe I'll call you later, but please—"

My dad picks up the phone, cutting off my message. He says, "To live, that is nothing. A dog lives. *How* to live, that is something." I wait for more. But there is no more.

"I don't know what you want me to say," I tell him.

"What do you want *me* to say?"

"Something that doesn't compare me to a dog?"

I don't hear anything for a few seconds. Then I get his answer. He hangs up.

---

Rachel sits beside me on our regular park bench.

"I wish you'd talk to them," I tell her.

"They won't listen to me. This is about you and them."

I hate it when she advises me immediately without even thinking about it first. "You're my sister!" I say. "I need you!"

Now she thinks before answering. "I'm here. I'm helping you."

"You're not! I'm *alone!* I can't sleep. I can't work. I can't talk to Kate. I can't tell my friends! If you could talk to them..."

"I can't."

The finality in her tone sets me off. "Because if you got in the middle of it, God forbid you cause them any pain. No, that's *my* fucking job. Have you ever, *ever*, done anything to piss them off? No. You're forgiven everything you do before you even do it. The golden child, born in the middle of the Holocaust, not your fault, nothing can ever be your fault. Not in their eyes. Never. You have no idea what it's like when they look at you with ... Forget it. You don't want to get involved, don't."

She sits there, waiting for me to go on, but I'm done, afraid of what will come out of me next.

"What do you mean 'when they look at you'? You mean because of Kate?"

"Long before Kate." I don't want to reveal anything else, but this is Rachel. I owe her the truth. "The way they once looked at me, I'll never forget it. Like, 'Who the hell are you?' Shock. Disappointment. Pain. Mostly confusion. Like, 'How could I have raised a son like you?'"

"When was this? How old were you?"

"I dunno, thirteen? You were long gone."

"What happened? Did you do something?"

"Do something? Like what, steal a car?"

"To make them look at you like that," she says, her voice gentle. She can see I'm hurting.

"Yeah, I did something. I did high school in the sixties, I did hockey and James Bond and Bob Dylan, and I did the Playboy centerfold, and what I did not do was be raised in a Polish fucking *shtetl*, boarding up the windows at Easter because there might be a *pogrom*."

Rachel watches me, quiet, knowing if she says the wrong thing, I may not tell her more.

"They looked at me like someone they don't understand, don't recognize, don't even *like*. Who does not honor his parents, the way they honored their parents. Their murdered parents."

Rachel looks away and closes her eyes. I know her closed eyes are not about trying to figure out a solution. "I'm sorry I wasn't there," she says, finally. Then, she reaches out and puts her hand on mine. "If I get in the middle of it right now, kiddo, then I won't be able to help if things get really bad."

"*Get* really bad?"

"We're Jews. Things can always get worse." She closes her eyes again, and I know that this time, there's a plan being hatched. She opens her eyes and says, "What's the one thing Mom and Dad can never say no to you about?"

"Food?"

"Idiot. Your career."

---

"Hallo?"

I'm in my apartment, Rachel sitting beside me since this is her plan. She's got her head right next to mine, close to the phone receiver so she can hear.

"Mom? Please don't cry."

"Who's crying, not me," she says, but there are tears in her voice. At least this time she's actually talking.

"Okay, Mom, good, listen, you know I've done a few interviews in the papers, especially since I've started to do some television, and I'm getting better known as an actor, so I—"

She interrupts me with "We are very happy for you."

Then we hear Dad's voice say "Who?" He must have just come into the kitchen. We hear Mom sigh. "Hang up," he tells her.

I continue: "Mom, I've been contacted ..." I look at Rachel for help. She nods, encouraging me to keep going. "... by a publisher who is interested in my writing a book about ..." Rachel gestures 'everything.' "... your life—yours and Dad's."

The mention of a book stops Mom for a moment. "A book? About what?"

"What book?" we hear my dad ask her.

"About you and Dad," I say. "They, um, want me to write it."

Mom covers the phone receiver, but not successfully, because we hear her say "He wants to write a book."

"About what?" he asks.

She passes the question to me. "About the Holocaust?"

I look to Rachel, who makes another all-encompassing gesture. "Not only about that," I say, "but also about your life before the war and—"

"Everybody read already *The Diary of Anne Frank*," she tells me. "Who needs another book about the same thing?"

"It's not the same thing," I say.

"Somebody is paying him for this?" we hear him ask.

So she asks me: "A publisher is paying you to write this book?"

"Yes," I say without thinking. "It's ...very important for me." I look at Rachel, who points to the phone, herself, and to me. "For *us*. Important for all *of us*. A very big publisher."

She covers the phone receiver again, and says, "They are paying him."

"Who is paying?" he asks.

"A big publisher."

"Who?" he persists.

Exasperated, she says, "You talk to him." He must have shaken his head, because we don't hear an answer. "Who is this publisher?" she asks me.

I look to Rachel. She mouths a word, but I don't get it. She thinks for a moment, then mimes a kind of waddle, her arms stiff at her sides. "*Penguin!*" I tell my mom. "Penguin Books of Canada!"

"Ohhh," she says, impressed. "That's a big company." She tells my dad, "Penguin Books of Canada." We don't hear his response, but then she says, "So what do you need from us?"

Rachel and I high-five.

---

The first weekend off from rehearsals, I drive to Ottawa. My mother answers the door and gives me a silent hug, not a bad sign. I don't see my father, and I decide not to ask.

"You are hungry?" she asks me. "I made tuna salad, and I have the rye bread you like without seeds."

I don't talk much as I eat my tuna sandwich. My mother fills the time with telling me about her problems as the new president of the Ottawa branch of Hadassah, a women's Zionist fundraising organization with chapters all over North America. She's always had a talent for organizing stuff, and listening to her, it seems she is also adept at dealing efficiently with bureaucracy.

All through my childhood, my mother suffered from terrible bouts of migraines that could incapacitate her for days, but she says now that she's been so busy with Hadassah, the migraines have been less frequent. Years later, I realize that she probably suffered from some form of PTSD ever since the war, a condition no one ever diagnosed.

After I finish eating, she takes my plate, washes it immediately, dries it, and puts it back on its shelf. She sits across from me. "So... let's start," she says.

I put a small cassette recorder on the kitchen table halfway between us, and start recording.

"Wait, wait, wait," she says. "Stop it."

I press the Stop button. "What?"

"I'll do whatever you want, but your father..."

"Don't worry about him, Ma. Is he even here? I haven't seen him."

"He's here. Listen, this girl..."

"Kate."

"Her parents know?"

I tell her the truth: "They know we're living together. They're fine."

"Christians?" She looks at me with some anxiety.

"Kate is not religious," I say, hoping that will calm her down.

"The parents?"

"They go to church sometimes. So?"

"Oy," she says, shaking her head.

"Ma, you hardly ever go to synagogue."

"So what I don't go, that makes me not a Jew?" Meaning, I guess, she's no less Jewish than Kate's parents are Christian.

"That's not what I meant," I say.

"So what you meant?"

I'm not even sure what we're talking about anymore. "I mean that just because Kate's parents go to church that doesn't make them Christians who don't want their daughter to be with a Jew."

"That's what she tells you."

"I met them," I tell her, thinking that will stop this debate.

That does stop her, but only for a moment. "You are talking about getting married?"

"No." This is true.

She sighs, slightly relieved. "All right." She points to the cassette machine. "Start."

Now I'm the one who wants to keep the debate alive. "But what if we were? Talking about marriage."

"You are?" Anxious again.

"No, but if we were, so what?"

'No' is all she needs. "I don't want to talk about it. Start."

"I didn't bring it up. You asked me about her parents."

My father isn't there to talk about this, so the least I can do is try to find some kind of common ground with my mother. That's why I'm here, after all. Not to write a damn book that has no publisher because the book is not real.

"Start."

There's no point trying to get anything else out of her on this subject. Not right now. I have not thought much about how to get this book charade going. I think of something and press Record. "So … just start by telling me about your life before the war."

"It was nothing special. We were a happy family. Life was very nice."

I wait for more. She waits for another question. "Okay, Ma, I'll need some, you know, details."

"So you'll ask, and I'll answer."

"You say life was good?"

"Pińczów was such a little town, I could not live my way that I wanted to live, to be more free."

Now I'm curious. "Free how?"

"I only could go out with girlfriends. To go out with a boy? Religious people, like my parents were? Never. That would be like today, I don't know, you go and convert."

"So life was not all good."

"If you didn't know any better, this was a good life. But I think I knew better."

I hear a soft footstep, and I can see my dad hovering in the living room, listening.

"How did you meet Dad?" I'm hoping he'll want to correct something Mom says or add something, anything to get him involved.

"You know this story already," she says. "So you should just write it."

"I know some of it, not the details. And besides, this needs to be in your own words." I come up with this last bit on the spot. I haven't thought about what this fake book "needs" for a second, until just now.

"My words?" she asks me.

"Yes, they, uh, Penguin wants this to be in your words, yours and dad's."

"Why?" She's not being difficult, she's just curious.

"It makes it, you know, more real."

"Alright," she says, "but fix my English, and especially your father's English. Promise me."

"Sure. I promise. So how did you meet?"

"I didn't meet him right away. First, I saw him. At a wedding. I was sixteen years old."

"You were attracted to him?"

"Attracted? I fell in love with him right away. He didn't even know, the poor thing."

I'd never heard this story. I'd never asked. "At first sight?"

"That's right. It's funny, I said to myself, that's going to be my husband when I saw him dance. At this wedding, there was an orchestra, Ben-Zion Klezmer—ha! That was some orchestra, he couldn't even play, but he played anyway, on a fiddle, with his two helpers. Mostly, people were dancing Hasidic style, you know, separate, not girls with boys. Then I saw him. My brother knew him a little bit. He told me his name—Srulek. And he lives in Łódź, but he came here to visit my grandmother."

"So you watched him dance, and that was it?"

"Not just that. First of all, he didn't wear a black coat, or the hat, all those Hasidic things. He looked modern. And he was dancing so beautiful with other girls—a tango, a waltz, a foxtrot—I was so jealous, I could bust. Anyway, what could I do? I was so heartbroken, nobody asked me to dance, so I went home."

"So how did you meet?"

"My brother Chamel helped me. On the outside, Chamel looked like any Hasidic boy, but he was such a learner, he wanted to know everything. So he wanted also to learn how to dance like Srulek. He was so intelligent, Chamel. You know that they kept him alive in the concentration camp to the last minute? He had typhus, and they cured him because they needed him in the office."

My dad calls out from the living room: "Not Chamel! It was Srulcie, her older brother!"

Okay, I got him. Something has made him finally get involved in this thing.

Mom calls back: "What are you talking about? They didn't kill Chamel in Majdanek at the last minute, when the Russians came?"

My dad finally makes an appearance at the kitchen entranceway. "Srulcie wanted to know how to dance. Not Chamel."

My mom puts her hand to her mouth. "Oy! That's right. I got mixed up. We were six children. Three boys, three girls. I was the oldest girl. The youngest boy was Yossel. Chamel was in the middle, a little older than me. Srulcie was the oldest boy, and it was him, Srulcie, he was the one who wanted to learn how to dance. He was the musician in the family. My family's store was selling shoes, and Srulcie was always all day long upstairs, cutting leather. Any second he had to rest from work, he would grab his violin. My sisters and me, when we were downstairs working in the kitchen, we could hear him up there playing. He had a special tune he always played. You know how many times I wanted to remind myself that tune?"

She tries to hum the melody, but she can't remember it. Her eyes fill with tears about to brim over. "One of these days, it's going to come back to me."

I've never heard this story about her brother before. I'm so taken by her telling me this, and by her being so emotional trying to remember the melody, I am silent.

My dad comes further into the room and puts a comforting hand on her shoulder. She makes a few false starts trying for the melody, then stops.

"Do you know the tune?" I ask my dad.

He takes a moment to decide whether or not to speak to me. "Her parents didn't let me in the house."

My mom quickly changes the subject back to: "Anyway, Srulcie wanted to learn to dance, so Srulek said, 'Listen, why don't you bring one of your sisters, and then you'll learn, at least, how to hold a girl.' So Srulcie rented a room from a man he knew, Yankel Roit, a smart cookie—with him, you could always make a deal. And then my brother brought me. Srulek brought a record player there, and first, my brother was dancing with me, and Srulek was making suggestions. I asked him if my brother is holding me the right way. He said, 'Yes, if you're contagious.'" She laughs.

My dad smiles, which is a good sign. He's warming up. Maybe I can actually get him talking?

"Then Srulek took my brother's place. You know what? It was like we are born to dance together. And that's when he started to fall in love too. And that's why my parents later said my brother is to blame. My parents didn't want me to marry him, it was going on a war, it was terrible. They saw Srulek's picture on the front page of a magazine, and they found out he was an actor, and that killed everything. He wasn't even allowed to come into the house. I met him all the time outside. Because he was an actor. With an actor, it's just like to marry, let's say, a Christian. They said, 'An actor? What kind of life will you have?' I told them, 'He's not an actor, it's just a hobby!' No use.

"Everything was by matchmakers at that time. And I have to say I was a very beautiful girl. The girl's parents had to pay a dowry, but for me they wanted to pay my parents. They wanted only a rich man for me. I deserve a rich man. I said, 'Money is here today and gone tomorrow.' I wouldn't listen, I was in love with Srulek. I saw handsomer men, but I saw he had such a heart of gold, and that was why I fell in love."

My father immediately says, "Then why did she let them matchmake her with somebody from Wiślica?" He asks that question looking at me, but it's directed at her.

"Wiślica? I never said a word to that man and I never even saw him."

He's still looking at me. "She told me, verbally, that they were matchmaking her with a rich guy from Wiślica, and he wanted to give ten thousand złotys to her parents." He glances at her. "Right?"

"So?"

"So he came to the store to see you."

"I never saw him in my life."

"You told me he was fat."

"No, I never saw him! The fat one's *father* came from Wiślica, yes. I didn't even know it's his father, but I never saw *him*."

"Then how do I know he was fat?"

"Because he is alive. Maybe after the war somebody told you that he's fat."

"How do you know he is alive?"

"You're driving me crazy!"

"But okay, let be like you say: you never met him." He turns to me. "That fat man's father came to look at her, and he liked her right away. And he wanted to give ten thousand *złotys* for her to marry his son. Who was fat, she told me, with a red, round face."

"The *father* had a red, round face."

He ignores that. "I was jealous of everybody. But the main thing: I was the lucky guy. You have the best mother in the world, and I have the best wife in the world. And I am sure after my death you will find out what kind of parents you had. But I wouldn't be able to enjoy it."

He sits at the table beside my mom. Finally.

"All right," he says, with a sigh of resignation. "What do you want to know?"

"What I really want to know—"

"Turn off." He means the cassette machine, which has been recording all of this.

"What? Why?"

"First, turn off." I press Stop. He speaks slowly, hitting each word deliberately: "I am not going to talk about you-know-what."

I hit every word deliberately too: "Maybe that's exactly what we should talk about."

"Finished." He gets up abruptly and leaves the room. My mom looks at me with an expression that says, *What did you expect?*

I know exactly what Rachel will say when I tell her.

---

"Idiot." Rachel and I are on our favorite park bench. "We knew Mom would be easy. Dad is the one you have to get talking."

"So I go back?"

"Yes! Of course you go back! Listen, he won't be able to resist. He'll want to tell stories."

I sit there, sulking. I dread the pressure of trying to get him back to the table, but I know if I don't, there's absolutely zero chance of finding a way to get him to be okay about Kate. And Kate has been pestering me about meeting them.

Reading my mind, as usual, Rachel says, "What does Kate think you're doing?"

"She thinks I went to Ottawa because I'm writing a book about Mom and Dad."

"You told Kate this imaginary book story too? Did you tell her it's being published by Penguin?"

"No, she'd know that's bullshit immediately."

Rachel stares at me. "Kiddo. Kate believes you're writing a book. Get ready."

"For what?"

---

"Will you let me read it?" Kate asks me.

We're in bed. My lamp is off, my back to her. I've been pretending to sleep. "Uhh ... what?"

"Oh, sorry, I thought you were awake."

"Uh, yeah, no. What?"

"I was wondering if you'll let me read what you're writing about your mom and dad?"

"You mean ... now?"

"I mean, if you want me to?"

*Fuck.* "I … of course I do. I just, you know, I just started, so I don't even know what I'm doing yet."

"Sure. No pressure. Whenever. How's it going? The writing. You've been back a week."

"It's a lot. It's going okay, but, you know, I've got to go back a few times. Lots, lots more to do."

"I'd love to help."

"Of course," I manage to say.

"It's a great idea. Have you thought about a publisher?"

Oh God. I have to get this to stop. "Way too early for that. Right?"

"Not necessarily," she says with some enthusiasm. "I know a couple of literary agents who might jump at this."

"Really?" The thought makes me want to throw up.

"If you need any help, let me know."

"Of course, yeah."

"How much of it is new to you? Their stories."

"Heard them all my life. Some of them."

"Really. Wow. You never told me. About any of it."

I realize I haven't. I decided to tell her the truth about this. "I get the stories mixed up. Most of their friends when I was growing up were survivors. They tell each other the same stories over and over."

Kate thinks about this for a moment. "I know your parents are survivors, but whenever I asked, you never want to talk about it."

I'm immediately defensive, for no reason, except that I think if I don't argue right now, she'll manipulate me, somehow, into telling her the truth about my bullshit.

"You never tell me about your grandparents in Ireland." I say.

"You never asked. And they're from Scotland, by the way. Great-grandparents were from Ireland. And they weren't being hunted."

Fuck. I hate that I get that wrong. So I try to be right. About something..

"They probably were hunted if you go back far enough."

"You know what I'm talking about," she says. "You never talk about being Jewish. Ever. Did you even have a bar mitzvah?"

"Yeah, because my father cried. I still don't know if he was acting."

She waits for me to keep going, so I have no choice. I'm not thrilled to be confessing this stuff.

"When I was thirteen I was already an atheist. And I hated religion, any religion, and everything to do with religion. I didn't want my parents to have an accent, I didn't want to hear any more stories about Poland, or about antisemitism, and I didn't even want my stupid Jewish name so if anyone asked me when I was a little kid I'd say my name is Bill."

"Bill?"

"Bill Clark. Bill Clark is Canadian and not the fucking son of Holocaust survivors."

Kate looks at me as if she's seeing me for the first time. "But your father cried so you had a bar mitzvah?"

"And that's the last time I was in a synagogue. I said to him 'okay, if, if I have a bar mitzvah it means I'm an adult after that, right? — and being an adult means I'm responsible for my own actions, right? — so after my bar mitzvah you can suggest — not demand — I should do my homework, you can suggest I watch too much television, or stay up too late, or I should go to synagogue, or I should go anywhere or do anything. I get to decide everything for myself or the whole bar mitzvah thing is bullshit so I'm not doing it.'"

"And he cried?"

"No, he said I should be a lawyer. *Then* he cried." She's quiet, thinking. This, I can tell, is now going to be an in-depth conversation, one I will not be able to escape.

"Can I ask what made you want to write about this now?"

The one question I absolutely cannot answer. So I go to my standard response in these situations: "Huh?"

"It started when I said you have to tell them about my not being Jewish."

"I guess, yeah." I have to admit that or sound like an idiot.

"Definitely. That seems to be the trigger."

"Yeah. Maybe. I dunno, really. Just, the idea kinda popped into my head. Anyway ..." Hoping that this can now end. God, please?

"Are your parents happy you're doing this? Reluctant? Eager?"

"All of the above, I guess."

"What I've heard," she says, "what I've read, is that people who were in a concentration camp, not many of them talk about it."

"They weren't."

"Weren't what?"

"In a concentration camp. They were hidden for two and a half years. By farmers. They were together. They were in love, they survived together, they consider themselves lucky. Easier for them to talk, I guess."

"And their son wants to tell their story. That must matter to them."

"Yeah." I decide to open the door a tiny little bit. "We argue a lot. Me and my dad, anyway."

"About?"

There's the opening. Now I should tell her the truth. But the memory of my dad dumping ashes on his head stops me dead in my tracks. "Oh, my dad can find an argument in an empty room."

She laughs. "And his son doesn't even need a room."

"Yeah, ha!" I laugh at myself, being a good-natured sort of guy who would now like to go to sleep and pretend none of this is actually happening.

"Was I the trigger? For starting you off on this?"

"Is that bad?" It's the right thing to ask her, but the question, I know, is one I should be asking myself.

"No," Kate says. "Bad is that I've never even spoken to them. And you've been to my parents' house what, a dozen times? And we play board games once a week with my brother and his boyfriend. And we went to a hockey game—okay, only once, with my very normal sister and her way-too-normal husband and their way-too-well-behaved kids. And all I know about your family is, your parents are survivors of the Holocaust, and just now I'm finding out they weren't in a concentration camp. Oh and I know that you spoke Yiddish and French before you spoke English. And that's about it, except I weirdly know a lot in detail about every play you've ever acted in. But boy, you are a keeper of a lot of secrets."

I say absolutely nothing. I feel terrible. Not terrible enough to come clean though.

"Is some therapy required?" she asks me.

Kate's given me an out—and herself too. An out we can both laugh about.

"Oh," I say, "therapy, definitely!"

"Okay then. That's settled."

"Yep."

"Yep."

We laugh, but it's a weak laugh. Then both of us are silent.

---

Kate is shaking me awake.

"Wake up, honey. Wake up."

"What? What? What happened?"

"You screamed. Nightmare?"

"Screamed? You mean, out loud?"

"You don't remember anything?"

I sit up in bed. "No." But I remember it all. Black turning to terrifying white.

Kate turns on her bedside lamp. "You want me to get you some water?"

"It came back," I say, not realizing I just said that out loud.

"What came back?"

I'm still half asleep. "Yeah, water, would you mind? That would be great."

"Sure." She gets out of bed and leaves the room.

I fall back onto the bed, eyes wide open, in shock. I thought that when I figured out the nightmare started because of the crazy nurse in the refugee camp, I killed the fucking thing for good.

Now, for the first time since I was eighteen, it's back from the dead.

# THREE

I AM BACK IN OTTAWA to try to get my father on tape for my imaginary book. My mother says she convinced him to talk to me as long as I don't bring up Kate. I have no game plan about what's supposed to happen after I get back to Toronto, except that Kate has asked to read some of the damn thing, so I'm going to have to write some of the damn thing. At least a few pages of it. I can delay that for a while, but not for long.

I'm in their kitchen again, and I haven't seen my father since I arrived. I've already downed two cups of tea and a tuna sandwich on seedless rye. I hear footsteps coming upstairs from the basement where my dad has a workshop to fix all kinds of broken mechanical stuff from around the house. He walks into the kitchen, washes his hands at the sink, then sits across from me. My mom takes that as a cue to sit beside him. She gives me a quick look that's a warning to keep the subject off Kate.

He starts with "So?"

"So," I say, "I have questions about history. Your history."

"Ask."

I press Record.

He looks skeptically at the machine. "It's working?"

"Yes."

"Are you sure?"

I press Stop, then Rewind, and play back the previous few seconds.

He says, "I can't even hear it. Penguin is your publisher, they can afford to give you a better machine."

Mom chimes in, "We're going to sit here all day? I have things to do." Clearly, she's frustrated with both of us, and worried our tempers and stubbornness will sabotage everything.

I press Record again, and start with "How did it feel, what was it like to be … hunted? You were both in hiding for how long?"

"Twenty-eight months," my mother says.

"How did it *feel*?" My father looks at me as if a question like that has never been asked.

"Tell him," my mom says, nudging his arm with a finger.

"It is an impossible question," he says to her, not even looking at me.

"Tell him the farmer and the king story," she says to him.

"He knows that story." He's still not looking at me.

"They have to have the story in our own words."

Now he looks at me. "Why?"

She answers for me: "The Penguin wants it like this. Just tell him the story."

"The farmer and the king?" I ask. "I don't know that story." That's true. I don't.

"No? It's a Talmudic parable. A good one," he says. "A long time ago, a king ran away from a revolution. He came to a village, to a Jewish farmer. 'Listen, some revolutionaries are running after me and want to kill me because I am the king. Can you hide me?' The farmer said, 'Sure, why not? I can put you in under the straw and cover you with a sheet.' The king said, 'Good idea.' It didn't take long, the revolutionaries came and looked everywhere, and they pushed their swords in the straw to see if somebody's there, but the king was lucky, and nothing happened.

"Soon the revolution was crushed, and the king was again king. He said to the farmer, 'I will never forget what you did for me. Here is my card. If you ever need anything, come see me.'

"The farmer couldn't sleep a half a year, it was bothering him something very much. Then he remembered the king's promise. The farmer went to the palace, but they didn't let him in. So he showed them the king's card and they said, 'Oh, okay, right this way.' It was an elegant palace, with ministers and court people all around and the king sitting on his chair. The farmer was shy. 'Do you remember me, Your Majesty?' he asked quietly. The king said loud, 'How could I forget?! You are my savior! What can I do for you?' 'Dear king, you told me that whatever I'll ask, you will give me. Since that time, I cannot sleep, it bothers me so much. Please, your gracious king, tell me: How did you feel? When the revolutionaries came in and pushed their swords in the straw where you were hiding?'

"Naturally, the king got mad. He said, 'You could have anything you ask, but instead you embarrass me in the presence of so many important people about how I was hiding? I pronounce on you a sentence of death.' The farmer cried, and he begged for his life. But the king said, 'Nothing will help! Because to humiliate a king in a public place is the worst crime!' The farmer cried, but forget about it, the king ordered to put up a ... what you call it?"

"A scaffold," my mom tells him.

"A scaffold. It took two days and they said, 'Your Honor, King, it's ready.'

"He said, 'Yes? Take out that farmer.' They put the farmer on the ..."

"Scaffold," she tells him again.

"Scaffold. And the hangman tied the rope on his neck. The king said, 'My privilege and pleasure will be to hang him myself!' The king went up on the scaffold, he took the farmer's face in his hands, and he whispered in his ear: 'Like *this* I felt.'"

I can tell he's pleased with his parable. He watches me carefully for my reaction.

"I don't think I would have survived," I say.

"What?" His voice is sharp.

"The Holocaust. I don't think I would have lived."

His face turns to stone. "Never, never, never do you say that. Not to me. Survive, not survive, save, not save, be good, be bad—you don't know until that minute when you are in it."

---

Back in my own living room, I sit in front of my typewriter and the cassette recorder. Rachel is in a chair beside me. Kate is out, at a rehearsal for her workshop.

My dad's voice on tape: "I did not want my father to know I am playing theater, it would have hurt him very much."

I press Stop and then type what I just heard. Rachel reads over my shoulder, which is getting annoying, and I forget what my dad said. Rachel prompts me, "It would have hurt him very much."

I type that, then press Play again. "Playing theater was, to him, ..." I hear a noise and immediately hit Stop. "Was that the front door?"

"Kate?" Rachel asks.

I look at my watch: Two forty in the afternoon. "Oh no. Can't be."

We wait, but there's no one there.

"What're you worried about? So Kate sees you writing the book she thinks you're writing. So what?"

"Right, right, right. Yeah. Fuck. I'm a mess."

"No comment," she says.

I press Rewind then Play. "Playing theater was, to him, first of all, to go away altogether from decency. He never was—listen ..."

I press Stop. Rachel watches me type for a few seconds. "If you want Kate to believe you're writing a book, you can't just transcribe this word for word. You have to clean up repetitions, tangents. You actually have to write the damn thing."

Like she just threw a bucket of ice water on my head.

---

After Rachel goes, I work most of the night.

When I shuffle into the kitchen holding a few typewritten pages, exhausted from lack of sleep, eyes bloodshot, I see Kate already at the table with the remains of breakfast and coffee, reading the newspaper, looking maddeningly bright and perky.

"Well, finally," she says. "Good morning! Did I hear you typing in the middle of the night?"

When I worked on the transcripts, an amazing thing happened: My resentment toward Rachel for telling me I had to fucking write this book turned into a revelation. The music of my parents' language, their colorful phrases, their unique way of describing events started to appear as words telling stories on the page, rather than what I'd heard and taken for granted all my life. I realized that they each speak differently, each with their own rhythm. Maybe because I'm an actor used to working with playwrights, the job of cleaning up the language had become much more than that: I was consumed with illuminating their voices as characters on the page. And I wanted Kate not only to believe I was writing this imaginary book, I wanted her to *like* it.

"If you're going to read some of it, I had to clean it up a little."

"Oh, that's great! I was wondering if maybe you don't want me involved?"

"Of course I do."

"How much is written?"

I manage to keep my voice light. "Listen, I'm going to show you just a couple of pages. I'm not ready for prime time." Actually, I have typed up twelve pages, but I don't want to show her all of it. Not until I know how it's coming across.

I place two pages in front of her on the table. She picks up the first page. Excited. She reads silently for a few seconds. "You want to hear this out loud?"

I make a beeline for the coffeepot. "Nah, it's all based on tapes, so I already, you know ..."

"Okay," she says, and goes back to reading silently.

I watch her for a few seconds. "Kate, listen, that's not how I want the book to start. What you've got is from an early interview. I don't know where or how that's going to end up in the thing."

"No, it's fine," she mumbles, absorbed in what she's reading.

"Cool."

I watch her read. I drink my coffee. I get anxious. Then a dull throbbing starts behind my eyes. "Wait, Kate. Yeah. Out loud. You mind?" Anything to distract my brain from yelling at me.

"Sure. But I'm not going to try to do your parents' accents. Wait, do *you* want to read out loud *to me*? You can do the accents much better than—"

"No, no, don't worry about their accents. Anyway, what you've got there is just my father speaking. I just want to hear it, if that's okay?"

"Sure." She finds a place earlier on the page. "'One time, I had a performance at eight o'clock. I was—' Your father was a performer? What kind of—"

"You'll see."

"When your father cried because you didn't want a bar mitzvah you said you didn't know if he was acting, was that—"

"You'll see," I tell her again.

"Sorry, okay", she says, and keeps reading. "'One time I had a performance at eight o'clock. I was at home, sitting with my parents, my brothers, and my sisters on a traditional Friday night ... 'Um, *shabos*? Sabbath, right?"

"Right."

She continues: "'... at a traditional Friday night *shabos* dinner, and I saw it's already seven thirty. It was not conceivable to leave the table ...'"

Hearing this read out loud by Kate, I am aware of something that before last night completely eluded me, something that would have been obvious to anyone but me because of my desperation to keep daylight off the truth: What I recorded, transcribed, and rewrote is a way to share my experience of my dad actually telling me the story.

Kate reads: "'It was not conceivable to leave the table on *shabos*, in the middle of the meal, but I had no choice. I had to be at the theater on time. Listen, one year before, I already cut off my ...' What's this word?"

"*Peyes*," I tell her. "The side curls that Orthodox Jews have."

"Oh, right." She continues: "'...I already cut off my *peyes*. I was acting in the theater, so I cut them off. I was waiting for my father to ask me why, but he didn't say a word about it. I looked at my watch. It was already half past seven, and the play was at eight o'clock. What could I do? I was on *shpilkes*—how you say—pins and needles. Everybody is at the table, my stepmother—my own mother died when I was just a baby, and my father remarried—my father is sitting at the head of the table, and all my younger brothers and sisters are there, from two years old all the way up to me—seventeen, the oldest. There are nine of us kids. I just got up right in the middle of everything and left without saying a single word.

"'I came home very late from the play because we used to go out afterward, you know, how actors do. It was probably two in the morning. I came into the apartment very quietly, not to wake someone. All the lights were off, and from the darkness, I hear my father's voice: "A friend of mine told me he saw you in a theater, acting in a play. But if he was really a friend, he would not have told me. He told me to hurt me. So I didn't give him the satisfaction. I just asked him if you spoiled anything or did you play good? That was for him. This is for you. Sit down." He was sitting there in the dark, waiting for me to come home. He turned on a light, and I could see he was still dressed like he was at the dinner table. He looked not mad, just tired, and also sad. He said, "You have eight brothers and sisters. You are the oldest. Don't you know that they all look up to you? That they want to be like you? That you have to set an example for them? Until now, I didn't say a word, but tonight you left the table in the middle of *shabos* dinner to be what— a ..."' What are these words?"

I look at the page. "*Schauspieler* just means stage actor. *Tummler* is derogatory, a professional entertainer, a comedian."

She goes on: "' "you left the table in the middle of *shabos* dinner, to be what—a *schauspieler*? A *tummler*? How could I raise a son like this? What you are doing is indecent! A sin! You betray your family. Your people. Explain to me: How can you go so far away from God?" He had two eyes, your *zayde*, like an eagle. They could see right through you. So for maybe a minute, I couldn't talk. Then I said, "*Tateh*, I was in a play tonight. It was written by a great Yiddish writer, Sholem Aleichem. It happens in a *shtetl*, about a Jewish family, about the troubles between husband and wife, about their hopes for the children. Theater, if it's good, the audience sees themselves on the stage. They laugh. They cry. And for a few minutes, they don't feel so alone." Your *zayde* sat there, and he thought about it. Then he said, "Maybe it's not so far from God after all." '"

Kate puts the page down. "It's really good, Saul. Was that the first time he told you that story? Or you already knew it?"

"First time."

"So that must have been amazing for you both."

"Huh? Yeah. Amazing."

Amazing? Mostly, it was tense. I don't want to tell Kate about conversations I had with my parents. Especially ones that were uncomfortable. That's opening the doorway too wide. Besides, I want to leave her with *amazing*.

---

When my dad finished telling me about the confrontation with his father, I said, "And then he was fine with your being an actor? That's all it took?" He looked at me and then turned off the cassette. "Why'd you turn it off?" I asked.

"Because we are going to have an argument."

"No we're not. Jesus." I turned on the cassette again. "How old was he, your father, when that happened, when he caught you coming home from the theater?"

"I was seventeen, so he was, in 1937, in his forties."

"Not much older than me. Jesus."

He turned off the cassette again. "Please do me a favor: stop saying *Jesus*."

I turned the cassette back on. "After that one conversation, he was okay with your acting in the theater?"

"When I told him that night, I was acting already for over a year. A year! I told you, when I was sixteen, I cut off my *peyes*. He didn't say anything about it. You know who he was, your grandfather? A *dayan*. A judge. A judge for civil cases between the Jews, because no Jew wanted to take their troubles to the Polish court, to the *goyim*. He was highly, highly respected. And his oldest son cut off his *peyes*? So he knew I was doing something wrong for more than a year, and he didn't say not even one single word. That's the kind of man he was, my father."

"What kind of man?"

"He didn't go to me to say 'Stop what you are doing.' He waited for a year for me to go to him to explain."

"But you didn't go to him. You got caught."

"You don't understand what I am saying! *He thought!* He thought a long time before he said something!" He was exasperated with my inability to understand.

My mom said, "How about a nice cup of tea?"

"Thanks, Ma, that'll be great."

My dad leaned back in his chair, and said, "You should dress better."

I wasn't sure I heard him right. "What?"

"Penguin is publishing your book. An artist in public has to be dressed."

"I'm not in public. I'm in your kitchen."

"You are on television now, so when you are going out, people will recognize you. You have to be dressed."

"He's right," my mother chimed in.

"Okay," I said. "Thanks."

"You could come to the store," he added. "We got some new stock, beautiful suits. You could pick whatever you want."

"Thanks. Okay. Did your father—"

"We went out to a restaurant after a performance. We were always dressed tip-top."

"Got it, okay. Your father ..."

"He was a great man. I wanted him to be proud of me."

I waited for him to say more, but he was suddenly silent, in his own world. I let him be for a while, and I checked the cassette to see if it was still recording properly.

My mom placed a pot of tea on the table, also sugar cubes, lemon slices, and three teacups. And a few cookies, *mandelbroit*, almond bread, my favorite.

"Did your father ever come to see you in a play?"

He thought about that. "In 1939. Right before the Nazis. Twice he came. The first play was a drama. The second time, a comedy. He liked the comedy better."

---

We're in the final two weeks of rehearsal for *Terrible Advice*. I am not in a good mood. I'm anxious about the lies I have to keep spinning like plates in the air. If they stop spinning, they will crash to the ground.

We're in the rehearsal hall, the floor taped to mark out the playing area: a living room. We're one week away from moving onto the actual stage with the set, and a week after that is our first preview audience.

Watching the rehearsal, sitting behind a long table littered with scripts and notes, are the playwright, Jessica, our director, Martin, and our stage manager, Connie.

Caroline, Stephen, Sandra, and I are in the middle of playing a scene—all of us, of course, off book by now. We're drinking prop wine, and we're supposed to be a little drunk.

I've been having some trouble with this scene since the first read-through. On top of that, my bad mood is leaking into my work.

Caroline, as Hedda, leans back on the couch, and smiles broadly. "My magic wand can send you back to any time in your life and you can have an hour with your younger self."

As Stanley, I respond, "Send me back exactly as I am now with everything that's happened to me?"

"Exactly!" Hedda laughs loudly. *Caroline is making her drunkenness a little too evident, I think.* "So the game is, when would you choose to go back to? And what would you say to yourself?"

Sandra, as Delila: "Can I stay there and not come back?"

Hedda: "No! You got an hour to convince yourself of whatever. Jake?"

Stephen, as Jake: "Younger me will take one look at older me and kill himself."

Hedda: "Honey, the point is you could convince younger you not to *become* older you."

Jake: "If I was a person who actually knew what to tell me about how not to become me, I wouldn't be me, so—"

Hedda: "Chicken. Stanley?"

Me, as Stanley: "This is a game about regret. Which I prefer to play in private."

Hedda: "Oh, come on! If I really had a magic wand, and you could really go back and change something in your life?"

Me, as Stanley: "Okay, Hedda. I know the exact day and hour when ..." But I have no idea what the next line is. "Sorry." I look over to Connie. "Line?"

Connie, following in the script, says, "'when my life fell into hell.'"

"Well," I say, "no wonder I didn't remember. Too close to what's actually happening in my fucking life!" Which earns the laugh I was expecting from everyone. *Joking on the square,* I call it—a joke that's true underneath. Honesty without consequences.

I continue as Stanley: "I know the exact day and hour when my life fell into hell. When I was fourteen, my mother said at a dinner party that if she had it all to do over again, she wouldn't have children."

The others laugh in a shocked kind of way.

Hedda: "So you'd go back and confront your mother?"

Me, as Stanley: "She'd just say I take everything too personally."

Hedda: "How much more personal can she get, wishing you weren't born? Okay, everybody, confession: the magic wand game has in it a kind of a trick question."

Delila: "Trick?"

Hedda: "But not really a trick that would affect any of you. You guys aren't parents. You can pick any time to go back and change shit. I have my daughter, Moxie. I'd have to pick a time *after* I had Moxie. Because if I change *anything* before then, Moxie wouldn't have been born."

Me, as Stanley: "My mother would be fine with that." The others laugh, but uneasily.

My bad mood now finds an outlet. "Can we stop?" I look over at the playwright. "Jessica, my next line. It's 'You're saying that no matter all the bad stuff you could tell yourself to avoid, having your daughter makes it all worth it. I get that.'"

Jessica looks even more depressed than usual. "What's the problem with the line?"

"It's a bit on the nose, isn't it?" I ask without diplomacy. "Do we really need the whole preamble? Can't I just say 'I get that.'?"

Jessica doesn't answer. She lowers her head, anticipating an argument. Martin, our director, notices that Caroline doesn't look happy. "Caroline, would that line change work for you?"

She says, "My next line is 'Wow, Stanley, you shoulda been a dad.' I don't know how I'd make that leap from Stanley just saying 'I get that.'"

I say, "How about if I say, 'I *really* get that.'"

There's an awkward silence, broken by Connie. "We should take fifteen now, guys."

As the rehearsal breaks up, people get coffee and chat, but I stay on the living room set in a world of my own, a world of plates wobbling in the air, ready to fall.

---

I climb wearily into bed beside Kate and hand her a few typewritten pages.

Ever since the first few pages, she's been eager to read more. This has galvanized me. Kate's excitement reading what I've written is real, and that's making me feel that not everything I'm doing is perpetuating bullshit. Something is being communicated. Maybe something worthwhile.

"You sure you want to do this? Did you have a bad day? You've hardly said a word all night."

"Rehearsals on my mind, that's all. I'm not connecting to the role the way I should."

"Maybe this is not the best time for you to hear me read aloud about your parents escaping the Nazis."

"That's exactly what I need to take my mind off the fucking play."

"The Holocaust as a distraction. How bad can things be?"

"You have no idea."

"All right." She reads out loud: "'They made a law for when we Jews were allowed to be on the street. One time, maybe a year and a half before the roundups ...' Wait. Is this your mother speaking?"

"My father. Sorry, I should have made that clear."

There's no real plan, no strategic order to my questions, so the stories jump around. An incident about what life was like before the German invasion could be immediately followed by them telling me about something that happened when the Germans were in control of all aspects of daily life in the town of Pińczów. I've been asking questions haphazardly, just to keep things rolling. I just want my parents to keep talking to me. Somehow, at some point, I hope a door will crack open, even a little bit, and the subject of Kate might become possible.

Kate reads, "'They made a law for when we Jews were allowed to be on the street. One time, maybe a year and a half before the roundups, I was in Pińczów staying with my grandmother. I was rushing home from a date with Frania. The curfew for Jews was seven o'clock, but I was fifteen minutes late. Right at my grandmother's door, a Gestapo caught me.'"

"Kate, wait. Let me read this story. Otherwise, we'll be stopping and starting a lot because there's quite a bit of German and Polish in it."

"Okay, great," she says, and hands me the pages.

I start to read, "'Right at my grandmother's door, a Gestapo caught me. He yelled, "*Warum bist du auf der Straße?!*" Why are you on the street?

"'I said, "*Ich bin gerade draußen, wo ich wohne.*" I am just outside where I live. He hit me with his closed hand, and I fell down.

"'He screamed at me, "*Es ist Juden verboten, sich zu dieser Stunde auf der Straße aufzuhalten!*" It is forbidden for Jews to be outside at this hour!

"'The Gestapo was yelling at me, but I could see he wasn't mad, he was acting mad. It was orders. Kill, don't kill, but the important thing was, make an example for the Poles so they will be scared to do anything. And also this: make the Poles to be collaborators. He was waiting for a crowd to gather. Sure enough, the Polish police captain, a man called Kopecz, he came running outside to watch. Right across from us was the office of the Pińczów Police. Then started coming a bunch of our Polish neighbors. Kopecz was the cheerleader. He shouted out, "*Błagaj o życie! Zaoferuj mu złoto!*" Beg for your life! Offer him gold!

"'Every day they saw a Jew begging the Germans to let him live, offering money, jewelry, anything. It was, for the Poles, like watching a sport. I didn't say a single word. I just looked at the Gestapo, plain in the eyes. So he hit me in the face. I fell down. Blood was running on my face. He yelled at me, "*Warum bist du nach der Ausgangssperre draußen?!*" Why are you outside after the curfew?!

"'I got up on my feet, and I said, "*Ich war mit meiner Verlobten und ich habe die Zeit vergessen.*" I was with my girlfriend, and I forgot the time.

"' "*Das ist keine Ausrede!*" That is not an excuse! He hit me again, and I fell down. One more time, I stood up and looked at him. Then he took out his gun.

"'Kopecz yelled, "*Błagaj go, a może cię nie zabije!*" Beg him, and maybe he won't kill you! He was laughing his head off.

"'The Gestapo hit me on the head with the gun. Hard. I fell down, blood was pouring like a river down my face. I looked up, I saw my grandmother looking down from her window, crying.

"'Again, I got up on my feet. I could hear Kopecz yell, "*Wkrótce będzie o jednego Żyda mniej!*" Soon there will be one Jew less! All the Poles standing around were laughing.

"'I was dead anyway, so I didn't say another word. I did not want to give the Poles the satisfaction. I just looked at the Gestapo straight in the face. Then he just turned around and went away. I don't know why he let me live. Maybe he liked that I didn't beg. Maybe he was late for dinner, who knows, maybe he got bored.

"'I went upstairs to my grandmother. She threw her arms around me, crying. She was sure I was going to be shot. And then she cleaned the blood away, and she tore a piece from a sheet and put it around my head. Before I even had a chance to change my clothes that were covered in my blood, there was a knock on the door. Standing there was that same Gestapo. It was not more than half an hour later. He took off his hat. He was very polite.

'"*Entschuldigen Sie bitte, dass ich Sie störe. Ich muss mit dem jungen Mann sprechen.*" Please excuse me for disturbing you, he said to my grandmother. I must speak to the young man.

"'She let him inside, and he said to me, "*Als ich Sie auf der Straße befragt habe, habe ich Deutsch gesprochen und Sie haben auf Deutsch geantwortet.*" When I questioned you on the street, I spoke German, and you answered in German.

"'I looked at my grandmother. We were worried about what's coming next. He said, "*Es ist notwendig für mich, mit einem Polack zu sprechen. Ich benötige einen Übersetzer.*" It is necessary for me to speak with a Polack. I need a translator. "*Bitte übersetzen Sie für mich?*" Please, will you translate for me? "Please," he said—"*bitte.*" What could I say?

"'When I went outside with him, my blood was there on the sidewalk. We crossed the street and went inside the Polish police office. Captain Kopecz jumped up from his desk and stood staring at both of us. I had my grandmother's cloth around my head, and blood was starting to leak through. Kopecz didn't know what was happening. The Gestapo said to me, "*Sag ihm, ich brauche seinen Schreibtisch für mein eigenes Büro.*" Tell him I need his desk for my own office.

"'So I said to Kopeck, in Polish, "*On chce, żebyś oddał mu swoje biurko.*" He wants your desk.

"'Kopecz relaxed a little bit. He said, "*Powiedz mu, że może je mieć.*" Tell him he can take it.

"'I thought for a few seconds, then I said in German to the Gestapo, "*Er sagt nein, du kannst es nicht haben.*" He says no, you can't have it.

"'The Gestapo looked at me like I'm crazy. "*Er versteht, dass ich seinen Schreibtisch will?*" He understands I want his desk?

"'I said, "Er ist ein Polizeikapitän. Ich nehme an, er mag es nicht, Befehleentgegenzunehmen." He's a police captain. I guess he does not like taking orders.

"'You see, when the Gestapo was yelling and hitting me before, he was pretending to be mad. But now he was just plain mad. He went to Kopecz, stood in front of him, and gave him a hard slap in the face. Right away, blood came out from Kopecz's mouth.

"'Kopecz yelled at me, "Co do cholery! Nie powiedziałeś mu, że kazałem zająć biurko?" What the hell! Didn't you tell him I said take the desk?

"'I said, "Oczywiście, że powiedziałem." Of course I did.

"' "Więc dlaczego mnie uderzył?" Then why did he hit me?

"' "Czemu? Kto wie, dlaczego cokolwiek robią?" Why? Who knows why they do anything.

"'The Gestapo said to me, "Was sagt ihr?" What are you saying?

"'I said, "Er fluchte. Ich sagte halts maul." He cursed. I told him to shut up.

"'I could see the Gestapo was trying to control himself. He was so mad, he was getting red in the face. He said to me, "Sagen Sie ihm noch einmal, daß ich seinen Schreibtisch brauche." Tell him again I require his desk.

"'I had to think now what to do. I said to Kopecz, "Chcę wiedzieć, czy masz żydowską krew. Tak czy nie?" He wants to know if you have Jewish blood. Yes or no?

"'Kopecz looked scared to death. He said straight to the Gestapo the only word in German that he knows: "Nein! Nein! Nein!" So the Gestapo thought Kopecz was yelling "No!" about the desk. He pulled out his gun and hit Kopecz right on top of the head. Kopecz fell down to the floor, blood running down his face.

"'The Gestapo screamed at him, "ICH GEBE HIER DIE BEFEHLE, DU VERDAMMTER POLACK!" I gave you an order, you goddamn

Polack! Then he pointed his gun straight at his head.

"'This is the moment I was waiting for. I said, "Słuchaj, Kopecz. Może jeśli będziesz błagał, to cię nie zabije." Listen, Kopecz, maybe if you beg him, he won't kill you.

"'Kopecz got on his knees, begging, "Proszę, proszę, błagam, nie zabijajcie mnie! Nie jestem Żydem!" Please don't kill me! I'm not a Jew! Of course, the Gestapo didn't understand. He put the gun into Kopecz's ear. Kopecz started crying, and in bad German, he said, "Nein Jude, nein Jude!" Not Jew, not Jew!

"'The Gestapo looked at me like *Why is he saying that?* I just shrugged like I have no idea. "Proszę, proszę,!" Kopecz was still begging for his life, blood and tears running down his face.

"'Now I was afraid the Gestapo would really shoot him. And I had enough. I said, "Müssen Sie ihn um Erlaubnis bitten? Sie sind jetzt das Gesetz hier. Nehmen Sie, was Sie wollen." Do you have to ask him for permission? You are the law here now. Take what you want.

"'The Gestapo thought about it, and then he smiled, slapped me on the back like I'm his friend, and went out.

"'I helped Kopecz to stand up. He said, "Myślałem, że mnie zabije! Co mu powiedziałeś?" I thought he was going to kill me! What did you say to him?

"' "Powiedziałem mu, że jesteś dobrym człowiekiem i nie powinien cię zabijać tylko dlatego, że jesteś Polakiem." I told him you are a good man and he shouldn't kill you just because you are Polish.

Kopecz put his arms around me. He was covered all in blood. My head was bleeding again through the cloth, and now his blood was all over me. Both of us, all red. I tried to pull myself away, but he held me even tighter."

I've finished reading the story. Kate just sits there for a moment. "Wow," she says. "Not a good idea to get on your father's bad side."

No, I think. It isn't.

"It's amazing," she says. "You must have heard this story before."

"Maybe a long time ago. I didn't remember it."

"Really? Because it seems to me your dad must tell this story a lot."

"Well, not to me." But then I think, I don't know, maybe he has told it to me. So many of his stories have gone in one ear and out the other.

She is silent. Her face looks sad and anxious at the same time.

"Saul, who do you want this to be for?"

"I really don't know," I tell her. Not exactly a lie, but close.

Kate is silent for a little too long.

"Kate, what's wrong?"

After what seems to me an eternity, she finally says, "I know this is a big subject we've avoided. Children. Not fair for me to say 'avoided.' We just started living together, mostly because I was here all the time anyway. And it's cheaper. So we haven't avoided the subject, we just haven't got around to really talking about it."

She waits for me to say something but I'm in a kind of shock.

She keeps going. "What I'm seeing in these pages . . . your mom and dad, they're . . . in love. Still in love. It makes me think. . . . Maybe you're writing this for the children you may one day have?"

I don't know what to say. It's a big door she just opened.

"For me," she says, "maybe it's reading these stories, how close your mom and dad are, I don't know, but I know this: I want to be a mom. With you as the dad. What do you want?""Kate, can we think about this?"

"Can we think about this out loud?"

"Right now?"

"Look, if you say no, you don't want kids, I'm not going to go pack my bags. But I am going to ask if you're sure. And if you're not sure, then we should talk it through. But if you *are* sure, then you do need to tell me."

"I don't really know what I want. I don't even know how to talk about it. Maybe I should see a shrink."

"What would you say to a shrink?"

"That I'm terrified to have kids."

"Know what a good shrink would tell you?"

"What?"

"If you weren't terrified to have kids, you'd need a shrink."

We both laugh. After the laughter calms down, she says, "Let's take a breath. I'm tired. So are you. This can wait. Now that you know how I feel, it can wait."

"But not for long."

"Not for long," she says.

---

A few days later, as I drive to Ottawa, I should be thinking about how to talk to Kate about children, but no. I'm thinking about the questions I'm going to ask my parents because I am now becoming convinced I have to write this book, whatever it turns out to be. I feel there's something in my parents' stories that will reveal why they reacted so over the top about me being with a non-Jewish woman, some reason that I cannot yet grasp. I feel it's too easy to say the reason, obviously, is because of the Holocaust. I feel there is something else, something that is not *beyond* the obvious, but somehow *within* the obvious. "When you make the obvious mysterious, then the mysterious becomes unavailable." That quote, by the artist Walter Darby Bannard, has always fascinated me, but for the first time, I feel I'm experiencing what it actually means.

I have a long weekend away from rehearsals, so I stay in Ottawa for three full days, longer than I have since the beginning of the tapings. I feel driven. We record for eight hours a day.

When I get back to Toronto, I can't wait to work on the transcripts. In between rehearsals for the play, I work on the tapes for a few hours each day for a week. I still don't know whether to take Kate's advice to put myself into the writing. I sense she's right about this, but I don't know how to do it without revealing the lies—to her and to my parents—and I know I'm not ready to do that.

I hand twenty-three pages to Kate. I suggest she read them to herself this time, rather than aloud. This way, she'll finish faster. I'm eager for her reaction. I realize I am actually writing this thing.

# FOUR

## FRANIA

I turned nineteen in August 1939. Then, two weeks later, the war broke out. We heard on the radio that the Poles lost right away—I think after two days or so. We were so frightened. We heard what was going on in Germany, that the Jews were running out of there since 1933. What do you think—we didn't know?

My father had a policy that we should not stay together: "Together, we're going to die together." He was right. After just one day or two, he sent my oldest brothers, Srulcie and Chamel, to run away to Lublin to be with our grandfather, my father's father. The rest of us took all the shoes in stock from the store down to the basement, and we hid there too—figuring, first, if we have all the shoes we'll be able to live on something, and second, if there's fire, the basement will be safe, and maybe the Germans won't find us.

They came after three days, the Germans. We were sitting there in that basement, and we could hear German being yelled on the street: "*Komme raus!*" Come out! Oh, I'll never forget it. And we could see smoke is coming into the basement. The house upstairs is burning already, and we were choking. Then we heard a loud "*Komme raus! Komme raus!*" from the top of the stairs, but they didn't come down.

Maybe they were afraid somebody will shoot them from the basement. So we had no choice. There was a little kerosene lamp, my father closed it, so there shouldn't be fire in that full basement of shoes, and we went up—what could we do—with our hands in the air.

They made us run to the church on the corner, all the Jews who lived on the square. All the houses all around the square were burning. They chased us to that churchyard and put machine guns all around. And they were shooting at us too, even with the children there, just shooting, just for fun, and who caught the bullet was dead. I was too scared to even look around. Everybody was yelling, one on top of the other, like hay falling. I was so young. People were killed right beside me. When did I ever see something before like this? Never in my life. We were in that yard for three days and two nights.

The house, the store, was burned, everything was a ruin. My grandparents' beautiful house was on the same square as ours, and it burned right to the ground. A few months before the war, they were the richest in town, and now, overnight, they had nothing. They owned a flour mill, but the Germans didn't take it away yet. It wasn't working, but it was a place for us to live. It was a little outside of town. On the same property was a little caretaker's house, two rooms and a kitchen, that's all, and we stayed there, eight of us—me, my parents, my mother's parents, my two sisters, Shaindel and Malka, and my brother Yossel.

After a few days, I said I want to be in Lublin with my older brothers. My father gave permission, but Pińczów to Lublin was two hundred fifty kilometers east, on the other side of Poland, so he wouldn't let me travel alone. I went with a very nice boy. He was the same age as me, nineteen, and yet my father let me go because the boy was from a very Hasidic family.

It was very hard to travel. It took three days because the trains weren't yet functioning properly, so we went by horse and wagon, by train, by car if we could find a ride, whatever. You know, we sometimes had to sleep in the same room, but that boy was such a gentleman—I just can't tell you—from a very good family. When we arrived at my grandfather's house, it was all closed up. He had there a business together with the house: wholesale textiles, trimmings and linings for men's hats. Nobody was there.

My Aunt Topcie and her husband lived in Lublin. We went to their house, and there was my grandfather, afraid to stay in his own house because it was in the business section of the city. Also staying with Topcie was another aunt of mine, Sarah, but she was only a few months older than me. My brothers were gone. My aunts told me that after only a few days in Lublin, Chamel and Srulcie ran away to Russia.

The Germans were in Lublin everywhere—soldiers and guns. People were staying in their houses and walking faster on the street. One day, things were a little quieter, more back to normal. My grandfather said Sarah and I should go to his textile business to bring something back. I forget what it was. We went, and as soon as we opened the store, a man followed us in and started to take merchandise. We could see right away that this man was a Volksdeutscher. You know what this is? A German living as a Polish citizen in Poland but collaborating with the Germans. We could recognize them right away. He just took whatever he wanted without paying, like it's his right. We were too frightened to make trouble.

Well, he left, and we were just recovering from this when in comes two SS officers. Do we live here? No. Where? We had to give Topcie's address. They spoke to us in German, and because Yiddish is like German, we understood them, and we could answer. They yelled at us for a while—who remembers what—and then they started to pick merchandise for themselves, also for no money, just picked. Did anybody else take out merchandise from the store, they wanted to know. So we told them about the Volksdeutscher who came before them and took. Well, this made them mad, they were SS and had the right to take, but nobody else did. Could we recognize him? Yes. Something will be done. Meanwhile, they made a parcel of what merchandise they liked and said we have to come to such and such address tonight to bring them this parcel, me and Sarah. Can you imagine how much aggravation this was? To go, we were afraid. Not to go, we were even more afraid.

Nine o'clock that night, we took that parcel, me and Sarah, and we went to the address they gave us. It was a house where a Polish family probably lived before, but the SS used to kick the people out and take it over for themselves. We came in, gave them the material, and, you know, we were lucky that time to get out of there alive. A dog was there that looked three times as big as me. We were terrified. They made us stand there in that room while they looked at us, looked at us some more, and then one comes over to me, quietly: "If I want, you would now undress and dance naked on that table for me." I didn't say a word. I was just standing there like a fool. We stood a little longer, and then they let us go, just like that.

A few days later, two SS officers, different ones, came to Topcie's house and asked me questions about that Volksdeutscher that stole merchandise. But I knew I would be afraid to point a finger if I saw that man, he could come next day and kill me. The officers were very polite, explaining about order and right. We were there, listening to them—my grandfather, Topcie, Sarah, and me—all of us shaking. They took me out to their car and drove me around the whole day to different villages around Lublin to find that Volksdeutscher, to recognize him. The SS officers talked to me. They were very nice, my God, they even bought me lunch. Finally we came to a place, and I saw him.

Believe me, he turned white when he saw it's me, but I said, "No, I don't recognize him."

"Are you sure?"

"Sure I'm sure. I saw him, how can I not recognize him?"

I didn't see that Volksdeutscher after that, but if I would have said yes, I would have seen him, don't worry.

I stayed in Lublin four weeks. I missed my family and went back to Pińczów, again traveling with that very nice boy.

## SRULEK

In 1939, in the spring before the war, I was working in a Łódź factory as a mechanic of knitting machines. One day, a German worker—Herr Bittner was his name—a nice, quiet man, came to me and begged me to do something. He shouldn't be fired, he has three children at home. You see, Łódź was a city with many people of German descent, Volksdeutsche. Before the war, the Poles were sure Hitler will invade Poland, so from fear of spies, they started to throw out all the Germans working in their factories. I went to the boss and told him Bittner was a good man, his children wouldn't have what to eat if he threw him out. He said okay, but I have to take the responsibility for him, and I said all right. Later on, the factory had a money shortage and the boss fired me, but Herr Bittner was still working there.

I know now that many of these Volksdeutsche, in fact, were spies. On September 1, 1939, Hitler invaded Poland. We had a neighbor on our street, Narutowicza Street, a very polite German. When the Nazi bombers started to fly over our heads, from down on the street, we saw that German on the roof with a swastika flag. He was making signs to the planes. He was scared because the Poles could kill him, but he was living among Jews, and only Jews saw him do it—Jews too scared to do or say anything.

The Germans did two things to panic the people: First of all, a few months before the war, they took in all the change money, coins. There were German banks in Poland, and they made sure there was a shortage. Nobody could go out with a five złotys paper bill to buy something and get change. That, the Germans did for sure, made chaos. They also did another thing: A rumor came that the first thing the Nazis will do when they come is kill the Jewish youth. My father said, "I cannot conceive that people will come in and just kill for nothing." He never believed it. But when the Nazis first marched into Poland, we didn't know if it's better to run or to stay. My friend Itche Kashteinski wanted to run to Warsaw, maybe it will be easier for Jews in a bigger city. I wanted to go. My father said he could not run suddenly with seven small kids to Warsaw. My brother Chaim-David, almost the same age as me, was too weak, too much a dreamer to run. My father said to me, "Go, and let God bless you."

We started walking to Warsaw, Itche Kashteinski and me. On the way were thousands of people—Jews, Poles—walking, in carriages, on wagons, on horses, with parcels, carpets. Whatever they couldn't physically carry out from their house, they left behind. I saw—I still remember—a beautiful motorcycle, left behind. No gas. We went into houses for a drop of water on the way, into empty villages. Farmers were running away. We saw, even, meals still on the table.

Warsaw was already surrounded, and the German army was going by tanks, trucks, motorcycles, thousands of them, on the road to Łódź. We were walking on a field, a group of ten of us. The road was just a few yards away when suddenly, a bunch of motorcycles stopped, looked at us, then came and surrounded us. "What's your name? What's your name, you and you?!" People told their name and were let go.

They came to me, and I said, "Srulek Rubinek."

They looked at me and started to yell, "A Polish Jew?!"

I said, "Yes."

They called all around for the soldiers to come look at me. They caught a Polish Jew. They stared at me like I would have horns on my head. They didn't want to touch me, just walked around like visitors at a zoo. When they got tired of it, they left on their motorcycles without hurting us.

We were walking for two days. At night was not too bad, but in the daytime, the airplanes came down, shooting the people like cows. I was running, I saw people falling dead near me, but the bullets didn't catch me. The Germans later waited till hundreds of us accumulated. They surrounded us with motorcycles and pushed us into an open field. It didn't matter if you were a Pole or a Jew, everybody was scared of them. Right away with the Germans has to be order. They told us to sit down, all of us, with hands behind the head. We were sitting like this for hours, the sun was just cooking. Then, one by one, we were called, and they asked, "Jew, or not Jew?"

When it was my turn, it just came into my mind to say, "No." And my friend Itche also said, "No." All who said, "Yes," they put later on trucks, and who knows, but I think they took them right away to Germany for labor. Or worse. The rest of us, they let go.

The truth is, at the beginning of the war, the Germans could not differentiate who is a Jew and who not, because I saw them ask even a Hasidic man with a beard and side curls, with *peyes*, if he's a Jew. They didn't know if we had a specific face or something, not yet. But the Poles knew us, and the Poles turned on us, like we knew they would.

You see, every single Jew in Europe, you recognized in the eyes. In Europe, you knew it was a Jew even if he was blond with a small nose. The eyes. When I came to Canada, I was watching the boys when they came out of a Jewish club, the YMHA. I said, "They're not Jews." The eyes were free. In Europe, the eyes told you "I am afraid." Recently, I met in Miami a man, he was eighty-three years old, tall, walked straight, red hair. He was a fireman from Michigan. Did I get shocked! One morning, he took off the shirt for swimming, and I see he's wearing a Star of David around his neck. He was a Jew! I would never guess in a million years. He was an American-born Jew, and I felt from him the same freedom I felt in the eyes of the boys from the YMHA. It's true, I find the same thing with many Jews in America but not so much as with that fireman. Some Jews, even born here, you can tell they're mixing in a little bit in their talk, a Yiddish tune. But that man? He carried himself like a non-Jew, talked like a non-Jew. He never talked about Jewishness, just normally an absolute American. It just happens he was born a Jew, that's all. He was proud of Judaism. That was nice. He didn't know a thing about it, but he was proud of it: "I don't care, I'd stand up for anybody." I was looking at him with amazement, with jealousy. How can a man not be scared of anything? His face was so ... "I am!"

## FRANIA

In Pińczów, the Jews were allowed to walk only on side streets, not on main streets. Also another law: we had to wear armbands with a yellow Star of David. My two sisters and me, and my brother Yossel, would sneak onto the side streets. One of us was always running in front to see if the Germans were passing, then we were hiding in burned homes until we got to our burned house on the square and into the basement. We had hundreds of shoes there, you understand. We wanted to smuggle them back to the mill. They were worth a lot of money. The shoes were all in boxes, everything covered in dirt and smoke from the fire, so when we came out of there, we looked like coal miners.

We took the shoes out of the boxes, put them into big bags, and carried them back to the mill. Imagine: We smuggled like this every day, twice a day, for two weeks. And it was, from Pińczów to the mill, maybe three miles. I don't know how I did it—by nerves, I suppose. But we had something to sell and something to live on.

By the mill, near us, lived a man with his wife in a small house. He saw how we were making a living on those shoes. He got jealous, and he squealed on us. One night, just after supper, two German soldiers came in and said we have to give them the shoes. Well, what can you do? Right away they started to threaten with guns, so we started bringing out bags of shoes. While we were doing this, one of the soldiers—oh, a face like a murderer, I'll never forget it— started to stare at me, and I knew what he was getting at. He didn't do anything. He was scared, I guess, because, you know, they were not allowed by Nazi racial law to sleep with Jewish women. *Rassenschande* it was called. We weren't good enough to rape. He kept staring at me, I was so frightened. I saw it was eating him up, the frustration.

Suddenly, he grabbed my father and went outside, and just to bother him, aggravate, scare him, he started giving my father orders: "Run! Lie down! Run! Lie down!" It was October —muddy, cold, very wet—and my father had a weak heart, he couldn't stand up anymore. Finally, he dragged my father inside and started to come right for me. He was hot already, he worked himself up to it. My mother is sitting there, the whole family standing there. It didn't matter to him, he's coming right to me. I got so frightened. I was so sure he was going to rape me right there, my blood went cold, and I fainted. The other soldier, when he saw this, he started to yell that it was not allowed, and he took out his gun and said he'll shoot him if he goes farther. So the other one backed off. They grabbed the bags of shoes and ran away. They thought they confiscated everything, but half the bags of shoes, we had hidden in another place, so we still had half to live on. But from that incident, my father became very sick, and it lasted a long time. His heart was bad.

The flour mill began to operate once again, controlled by the Germans through an overseer. You've never seen such a gentle man, this German—in his seventies already, from the old Germans, aristocratic. It happened that he came by the next day and saw that my father is so sick. He asked what was the matter. My father told him the story, everything in detail. The old man said he's going to look into this—would I recognize that soldier? Oh, yes, I can't forget him. Well, the old man found him, and asked me to identify him. "Yes, that's the man." I don't know what they did to him, but they fixed him up, don't worry. I had my revenge.

## SRULEK

At home in Łódź, everybody was scared to go out. Every day we heard that somebody we knew was shot. Every day they published new laws against us: a Jew can't intermarry with Gentiles, or work at certain kinds of businesses, or go here, or walk there. Later came the order that Jews had to make themselves a Star of David armband.

In those days, there were long lineups for bread in our city. You could wait in line all day for one loaf. One day I went out early to buy bread for the family, and on the street, German soldiers grabbed me and took me with a bunch of other people to a train station that they made into a big warehouse, where I saw hundreds of people working. I saw thousands of kerchiefs—all kinds and colors—everybody standing at tables to fold them and wrap them in packages for shipment to Germany. So I was standing there, working all day long with nothing to eat till six o'clock. Then they threw us out. I saw a soldier sitting, counting everyone who went out. I thought to myself, I'm going to ask. He can say no. I have nothing to lose. I came up to the soldier and said politely, in German, "I would like to have a statement signed that I worked all day and authorization to buy bread without lining up." I remember that German was not a Gestapo, he was from the Wehrmacht, the regular army. He wore glasses. He looked at me curiously for a moment, thought about it, and said, "You know what? You're quite right." He made out the authorization for me. I was probably the only one who asked for it.

When I got home that day, everybody was waiting to see if I'll come home alive. In the morning, I went out very early, before the curfew allowed. You see, I went out always without the Star of David armband because even though the Poles were under curfew too, they were allowed out three hours earlier than the Jews, and whenever a Jew came to a bread lineup, it was already four, five blocks long. Every lineup had soldiers watching that it ran in order, straight. I took my paper with the authorization, went up to a soldier, and showed it to him. And you know, he pushed away everybody else, and I was the first to get bread. I ran home fast. But mine was a big family—lots of kids, all hungry. So I started thinking, *If it worked once, why shouldn't I try it in other places?*

Łódź is a big city, but I ran around that day to quite a few lineups, and every soldier, when I showed him my paper, took me to the front of the line. I brought home four, five loaves, and that was worth more than gold. Gold, you couldn't eat. The authorization was dated for one day only, but I carefully erased it, and every day for almost two weeks, I marked a new date, until my piece of paper wore out. Then I was like everybody else. Again, I would go out earlier than Jews were allowed—without my armband—to get bread for the family.

It so happened that one morning, I ran into Herr Bittner, the German who used to work with me in the factory, the man whose job I saved. Herr Bittner was now in the uniform of the Gestapo. He saw I'm not wearing the Star of David, and he started screaming at me that he doesn't know me anymore, times have changed, I'm breaking the law—better run away, or he'll shoot me right where I stand. I was astonished, shocked. I stood there, probably with open mouth. A man that I gave to eat, a man that I helped—if my boss would have squealed on me that I stood up for a Volksdeutscher to work in the factory, the Poles could have jailed me as a spy—now Herr Bittner sees me without an armband, and he's ready to kill me. That's the German personality for you. I believe that every nation has its peculiarities. As for the German, either he's on top of you, or he's under you. If under you, he's like a dog—wiggles his tail, and he's ready to shine your shoes. But when he's on top of you, he's the master of you and at your throat.

A few days later, I again went out before curfew allowed—without the armband—around four o'clock in the morning, even before the Poles were allowed out. There were a few of us hiding near a wall, waiting to be the first in the lineup for bread. Gestapo caught us. There were six of us, all Poles, nobody knew I'm a Jew. We didn't have time even to think. "Hands up! Face the wall!" I just stood there, the first one in line on the left side, looking at the wall, my hands up. It was so fast, I didn't even feel what happened, I just heard a bang, and the woman next to me fell down dead, that's all. And another bang, and one more—every second person, shot straight in the head. I didn't have the nerve even to turn my head to look. I thought, *I'm next.* Suddenly, they yelled, "Los! Los! Los!" Run! Run! Run! So the three of us who were left alive started to run. I didn't look where I was going, just ran. I found myself in a doorway to a courtyard. I went in, sat down on the ground, and just breathed. I couldn't come to myself, I was shivering, in shock, couldn't really grasp in my brain what had happened to me. And I sat there till the night was over and I came to my senses.

One thing I knew: I wanted to get out of Łódź. You can imagine, that shooting at the wall just sat in my brain. And now that I was scared to break curfew for bread, we all went more hungry than normal, and normal was already bitter.

One day, my father came home and said that he saw a young Jewish boy begging in the street, begging for a piece of bread. He said that boy looked familiar but he didn't know who it was. Well, it was my brother Yitzchak. Later, Yitzchak came in, and my father realized it was his son who was the beggar, and he started to cry. He just couldn't conceive that he walked by and didn't recognize his own son. He cried probably half a day.

I just couldn't take the pain, to see the kids hungry, crying. Wherever you looked in our house, there was someone else crying, crying. It made my father helpless. It was impossible to do anything about it. It took the life out of me, and I just knew I must leave. I must go to Pińczów. And the truth is, I was worried about Frania. We heard that Pińczów was burned, but we didn't know who was alive and who, not.

Finally, what decided me to leave Łódź was the forced work order. You see, the Germans very quickly set up a council of Jewish elders, a *Judenrat*, who passed on to the rest of us the Nazi orders. The *Judenrat* sent out lists of Jewish youth who had to report to work for the Germans, and when I saw my name there, I decided that I'm not going to do it. Why? The incident with Herr Bittner made an impression on me. Łódź was a city with many German nationals like him, and I felt that in such a large city, if we went to labor for them, they could do with us what they wanted. We might not come home at the end of the day.

I decided to leave. My father didn't want me to, all the kids liked me very much, they were hanging on my legs—but I couldn't help it. I said, "I'm going. I'm taking off the armband, my face is not typically Jewish, I speak a good Polish, a good German, and I'm going to see if maybe in Pińczów, I can do something to help. I'll be back."

My father walked down with me into the yard. He was not an emotional man, he was a good man, but he kept his feelings buried inside. I hardly ever saw him cry—only on Yom Kippur in the synagogue, one day a year, he would weep so powerfully, his whole body shook from it—but that day in the yard before I left, I looked at him, I was shocked, I wasn't expecting it, tears were pouring from his eyes like blood. "I won't see you again," he said. He could barely talk, tears were running into his beard. He put his hand on my head and blessed me. I started to cry too, and he put his arms around me and squeezed me and said, "May God save you and protect you from evil." I was numb. I walked out the gate into the street, and when I looked back, he was still standing there in the yard, crying.

I walked two hundred kilometers to Pińczów. Four days. On the way, I passed through the small town of Piotrków, and standing there in the middle of the way was a whole bunch of Gestapo. I wasn't alone—a lot of people were walking—but I didn't know who was a Jew and who was not, because nobody was asking questions. The Gestapo was stopping everybody—looking, asking, letting some go. Some, not. I saw also a lot of Volksdeutsche that just went by and said, "Heil Hitler," and they let them go, no questions. Well, you know, I was an actor, so when it came to me, I went by with my parcel, saying, "Heil Hitler!" So they didn't look at me, just let me pass.

I came to Pińczów, and I met a whole picture: my aunts, my uncle, my grandmother, in a hole. They had a house before, a store. Everything burned down to nothing. They were all sitting in a small room, nothing to eat, crying. Grandmother was there. My Aunt Surele was there with her husband and two small children and her younger sister, my Aunt Hadas.

My grandfather died a few years before, he was the lucky one—he was dead for normal reasons.

The life was terrible. There were restricted places in Pińczów where a Jew couldn't walk even. If he was walking, they were shooting him. We were treated like dogs. Worse than dogs—a dog could go where he wanted, but we could not.

After a while, my grandmother rented a very small store, just to make a living. Bread and coffee, that's all you could buy there. I had a few złotys. I bought a bike, and I rode back on the bike to Łódź—as a Pole, not as a Jew. My plan was to buy merchandise for the store because they couldn't get it somewhere else. So I was with my family in Łódź again for a few days. I bought merchandise and left. By the time I came back to Pińczów, my behind was with blisters from the bicycle. That, I could never forget. It was raining on the way, and I had on my shoulders a sack, between my legs, another sack and I was riding hard, I didn't want to stop. For a whole week, I had to lay down, I couldn't sit. Whenever I went with the bike, I came back always very sick, exhausted. But I didn't know another way to help out.

When I was in Łódź with my family, everybody was wearing the blue Star of David on a white background. Not on the arm, but on their front lapel, and also on the backs, so you could see if it's a Jew from behind or in front. That was the law. You had to do it, or right away be killed. I told my father I'll go back and forth another few times. Maybe I can help bring things or even bring the family to Pińczów. But I only went like this with the bicycle twice before they created the ghetto in Łódź, and I couldn't get through anymore.

It's strange, when I first went walking to Pińczów—that time when I took off the armband and my father stood crying—that's when I thought maybe I'll never see him and the kids again. But I did. Twice more, I came back on the bicycle. When I really was seeing them all for the last time,

I left with no special feeling, I was sure I'll be back soon.

Half a year after I went to Łódź with the bicycle, a Polish friend from Pińczów told me he is going to Łódź also, so I said I want to go together with him. Maybe it would be safer. It was winter, and we went in a sleigh. We made holes in the sleigh to hide money. Eighteen kilometers before Łódź, we came to the border. There was a new German border outside the city because, by this time, Łódź was connected to the German Reich. They renamed Łódź, *Litzmannstadt*. So at the border, the Gestapo kept everybody—asking, asking—and to me, they said they don't believe I'm a Pole. They let the other people go, including my friend with the sleigh with the hidden money.

They dragged me into the office. The Gestapo beat me and yelled at me to take off the pants, he wants to see if I am a Jew or not. I took it very slow because I knew it's going to be the end of me. Suddenly, there came in a higher rank of Gestapo, and he asked what is going on. They told him. He looked at me and said, "Is he a Jew or not a Jew? The hell with him, throw him out." They threw me out half-naked.

I walked back forty kilometers to Piotrków, and it was twenty-five below zero. When I got there, I was almost frozen to death. Finally, I got a train toward Pińczów. I acted like a drunk Polish peasant. I put up my feet and pretended to sleep. Soon, two Gestapo came into the train car, pushed my feet off the seat, and sat down right in front of me. I kept my eyes closed, and I snored a little bit. A few kilometers later, the train stopped. A few Gestapo came in with maybe ten, fifteen Jews as prisoners. One of those Jews—he was in bad shape, who knows what they did to him—was somebody I knew. I used to be in school with him. He looked at me and then he stared at me.

Suddenly, he started to yell in Yiddish, "Srulek, you know me! Help me! Tell my parents I'm arrested by Gestapo!" He didn't realize what he's doing, he was in panic. Everybody looked at me. I wasn't wearing an armband.

I yelled at my friend in Polish, "I don't know you, and you don't know me! I am not a Jew!"

But the Poles on the side started to look at me up and down. They said, "You know, you look like a Jew."

I swore at them like a Polish peasant—every second word I said was "Jesus Christ"—and I told them that probably they are Jews themselves. When I raised my voice, they settled down because I was too sure of myself to be a Jew.

## FRANIA

By springtime of 1940, we had a little money already from selling those shoes that we smuggled, and the flour mill brought in something too. We figured we'll try to build up our house that was burned. So my brother Yossel was the one who supervised it. He really worked hard because the other two brothers were in Russia—who knew if they're even alive.

We moved back into our house—my parents, grandparents, sisters, and brother—in the fall of 1940, so we were in the flour mill for around twelve months. The store was still burned in front, and we left it that way, but in the back, we built everything new. You know, when you build, you can make a place where to hide things. We still had left some soft leather to make shoes, and this was worth a lot of money. Some Poles helped us with the construction. We thought we could trust them.

Well, one day came the Germans, with a truck. They went right to that hiding place. I wouldn't say that it was the Poles who informed on us. You think there weren't Jews who gave one another away? If they saw that you have something to eat, the jealousy ate them. Listen, that's war: some people are nice, and some people are showing they are just like animals. So I don't know who or how, but the Germans came one day and took out everything. They cleaned us out so that we didn't have next day even a bread to buy.

So the bakery shop there—listen, they knew us, that we were such a respected family—so my father said I should go for two breads in the morning. I said, "I'm not going for the bread. How are you going to have money to pay? I'm not going." And I didn't. My father had to go by himself, I was too embarrassed. Every single day, we ate black bread—every single day, three times a day. We had a lot of potatoes, so my mother cooked a potato soup, and we had that with bread and butter. Three times a day, we ate this. Believe me, compared to later, life was sweet.

In the meantime, you know, I was going out with Srulek. He lived with his grandmother, but he didn't come to my house, I didn't dare ask him. He never came inside the mill when we were living there either. My parents knew that I'm going with him, and they didn't like it, but I saw him anyway. I couldn't help it.

His grandmother had a little grocery store. He was working there, helping out, sitting there all the time in that store, so I used to go and the whole day I was sitting there too. Or we saw each other on the street. We were walking the side streets, you know, just like thieves, we were going.

A lot of Jews were running to Russia. So Srulek said, "Now it's a good time, we could get away. Everybody's going. We could smuggle into Russia."

"Not me. I won't do it. My conscience, I wouldn't be able to live with. I won't do it. I'll never do this to hurt my father."

It's funny—I didn't say "mother," but I said "father."

He said, "But you're going to save your life. What's going to happen to us in Poland? Now we're young, we could go."

"I'm not running away. They're going to say Shloime Baruch's daughter ran off with a boy. I would never do this to hurt my father. Que será, será—what's going to be, will be—but if I'm meant to be alive, I'll live—and we'll get married too." But when was that going to happen? I figured we're going to go together so long, my parents will say, "It's enough already." And that's what happened.

That summer, while the house was being rebuilt, my brother Chamel came back from Russia—without Srulcie, my oldest brother. Chamel left him there and came back himself because Srulcie wanted to stay. And probably when he *did* want to come back, it was already too late. Maybe they caught him on the border in Russia and said that he is a spy. The Russians did that to a lot of Jews. But really, who knows what happened? I don't know, maybe they sent Srulcie to Siberia. He was a very delicate boy, probably died from the hard work in the woods and everything. Who knows? We never found out about him. Never.

## SRULEK

Every day, the *Judenrat* in Pińczów had to give a contingent of people to the Germans for work: digging, fixing railroads. I got up in the morning, and we opened my grandmother's store, but sometimes the *Judenrat* sent me to work. I had to go, my name was on the list. If not, you couldn't go out—if they caught you on the street, who knew what they would do? The Germans would take a bunch of us first to one place for labor, then another place, and so on. I always stayed the last one in the group, and when it got a little bit darker, I slowed down. As I was at the end of the line and because I am a small size, I could sneak away and run home. I could have got shot, but I was trying always to run away. You see, we never knew what they'll do to us at the end of a day. I got scared I'm never coming home again.

## FRANIA

In the beginning of April 1941, a deep depression came on me. I wanted to get married, you know, very much. But I couldn't even talk to my parents—especially in the war, they didn't even want to hear about it.

Life was full of anxiety. There were different rumors: we heard they took out from a town near us all the Jews and nobody knew where they took them. If to work, why don't they write? Why don't we hear anything? My nerves were very bad. One night I woke up, and I started to scream, "I'm afraid, I'm afraid!" I was sleeping in the same room with Yossel, and I ran into his bed. So this was a sign that I am not well. After all, he was eighteen years old, and I ran into his bed? My parents were afraid that I could get a nervous breakdown or something. I remember that the next day, I was all day in bed. My parents were so afraid for me that they even sent for Srulek. It was the first time he was in my house. He sat with me by the bed, and naturally, I felt much better. I was sick maybe just a few days, and thank God it went away.

I remember, it was raining, it was a miserable day. Around two o'clock, I made up my mind to meet Srulek somewhere. My father came over to me and said, "So, my daughter, it's raining outside, and you were just sick, and now you're going out with Srulek again? What's going to happen with the two of you?"

I said, "What I want to happen is to get married!"

He said, "Now? In the middle of the war?"

"Yes, now. I'm going around already with him five years, and I don't care even if it's just for one night. I want to be married."

You know, if it would have been just up to my father, he would have helped a long time before. But my mother was very stubborn. She used to get so mad, her neck and chest got red, it was terrible. My father said, "All right, let's see. I'll come with you, and I'll have a talk with Srulek."

When Srulek saw from far away that I'm walking with my father, he got nervous. And I always told Srulek, "We will go so long till my parents will tell me it's enough and they let us be. I'm not going to do anything to hurt them, that's all." He very much understood this. Anyway, my father told me to go home, he wants to talk with Srulek. Okay, I went home—and my mother knew what was happening, but she didn't say a thing. I suppose she and my father talked about it already.

When my father came home, he said, "I talked to him. He's a good man, but if you marry, how are you going to live? We hardly have what to eat. What are you going to do?"

I said, "Look, Father, I'm not going to marry right away. I'm going to open myself a little store first, and if I'll see that I make a little something, we'll get married. But I want Srulek should be able to come into our house, so I shouldn't be so miserable. At least *this*, I deserve. I could have run away, and I didn't, so at least give me something!"

You know, right away, he was laying down stones in front of me: "What do you mean you're going to open a store? Where?"

I said, "Don't worry. I'll find something."

"With what money? You haven't got a cent, and I can't give you. We don't have enough for ourselves."

I told him I would go to my Uncle Itchele, my mother's brother who lived thirty kilometers away, in Działoszyce. He was very comfortable, he had money, he was dealing with grain, and he did very well. And he always had a soft spot for me.

I said, "Uncle Itchele will give me money, and I'll buy a little bit of what I need: some pieces of soap, kerosene, a little bit of thread—things the farmers need, just necessities—a little coffee, sugar. I'll buy from a wholesale place, and that's how I'll make a little money."

My father said, "How can you get a permit from the Germans?"

"Don't worry," I said. "I'll do everything."

The German headquarters for the area was in Busko-Zdrój, sixteen kilometers from us. It was like a resort town. I knew a family in Busko-Zdrój that used to live in Pińczów—the nicest people. He was a goldsmith, and the Germans were going to him all the time for rings and jewelry. He always liked me, so I said I'll go to that goldsmith in Busko, and with his contacts, he will be able to get for me a permit. Otherwise, you couldn't get it, you had to have a little side way to do it.

The first thing, I had to see if I can find a store somewhere. There was a butcher shop, it was closed up, a widow owned it. The whole store was only so big, like maybe twice this kitchen—not even twice. And the walls, like in a butcher shop, were completely red. The widow told Srulek and me she's going to rent us that store. She was a very good woman, she knew that we wanted to get married. Well, everybody in Pińczów knew that Shloime Baruch's daughter is running around with a young man, an actor. You know what this means? A scandal. I can't even explain to you how bad this was for a girl from a religious family. But that was the way of life.

First I had to go to Działoszyce, to my Uncle Itchele. But you needed a permit just to be allowed to travel to another place. I wrote to that goldsmith in Busko, and he took out a special permit for me to be able to go out from Pińczów. I went on a wagon with a horse, and in Działoszyce, my uncle didn't say a second word, he took out five hundred złotys and gave me right away.

I didn't get much for the money: I had to pay the widow rent right away for a month, me and Srulek had to fix up the store a little bit—I had to paint over that red, and we went to that wholesale place to buy two kilograms of sugar, five pounds of salt, flour, some shoelaces, kerosene, salt, soap, some cotton, some thread, needles—just what the farmers might need right away. I remember, in the beginning, we couldn't buy much, so when we made that store, I put on the shelves empty boxes, so it should look like we have some merchandise. But I don't have to tell you how friendly I am and how friendly Srulek is. When a farmer came into my store, he never walked out fast. We told him stories, and when we didn't have the thing, Srulek ran fast to the wholesale place and bought it while I kept the customer there with stories. And everybody got free a little bit of vodka and a cookie. And they wouldn't leave, they just loved us. So the farmers would tell one another, and we had a lineup! After three months, that store was growing so fast, I didn't have where to put my merchandise anymore, and the farmers, they were just crazy about us.

There was a woman—Zofia Bania was her name—she was a farmer's wife. You know, the farmers brought into the town eggs and butter, and then when they sold it, they bought kerosene, a piece of soap, shoelaces, things they need. They didn't eat what they grew—they ate just rye bread—and everything they had, they took to town to sell. Very poor farmers. A farmer there didn't have even a floor, it was just mud.

Zofia Bania came once to the store. I remember, she was short fifty groschen, which was less than a quarter. She didn't have enough money, but she needed the goods. Srulek said, "I'll lend you the money." There wasn't such a thing in Poland that you lend—credit. Nobody did it. And during wartime? Forget about it. You could be not alive next week. And here she comes in, and Srulek says to her, "You'll come next week, and you'll bring me some butter or some eggs. I'll take it off then. You need the things, so you're not going to go home without it. How you're going to manage during the week?" She couldn't forget that, that he trusted her. She could never forget it. In fact, if not for her, we wouldn't be alive today. So it's a two-way street.

## SRULEK

One time, came into our store two Wehrmacht soldiers. At seven o'clock you had to be at home because of the curfew. And they were sitting and talking because they were lonesome. They couldn't talk to the Poles, it's such a different language. But Yiddish is like German, so to the Jews, they could at least talk. They were quiet soldiers. They talked about their family in Germany. We asked them what they're doing with the Jews. They said, "We don't know anything."

In the meantime, I saw it was after seven. I couldn't throw them out. I told them we are scared to go home after curfew and they should take us home.

First they said, "Oh, no, we're not allowed."

I started to talk to them, to appeal to their understanding, and they said, "You know what? We will go behind you. You'll go forward. We will see." It just happened nobody caught us, that's all.

The most troubles we got was from the Poles, from our neighbors that for our whole lives, we lived side by side. They used to come in the store and grab things and run away. "You're going to die just the same, what do you need it for?" And if we went out for a few minutes after the curfew—let's say somebody was a little bit late—the Poles brought the Germans and said, "He went ten minutes after the curfew." The Germans didn't bother so much, but the Poles were watching us like hawks.

It was hell. So if you are in hell, you cannot think normally. You think of two things: how the day is going to go by and what to eat. The worst thing is a human being when he's hungry. Cannot think.

I could not escape because I was with Frania. I could escape by myself—my friends in Łódź asked me to go to Russia—but I didn't want to go without her. People thought that in Russia, they will save themselves. But it was very hard to separate families. You could not do it just like that. An accident could happen, and that's it: you're dead, and so is your family. People think an accident is happening to somebody else, not them. The head was so blocked, you couldn't really think straight. You are thinking minute to minute, not what's going to be a day after. You only hoped the night would come. All day you were thinking about the night. Because only in the night was it a little bit easier to breathe. Every day you were expecting—every hour—something terrible will come, because every day the Germans issued new orders. And every day was something worse. Maybe today the war will be over—maybe tomorrow, two weeks, a month, two months—because England is going in. America will go in. And especially, we thought that Russia is strong. We never thought the war is going to take six years. We were only wondering if, in the morning when we got up, will there be some new orders? Where am I going to be taken to work? What's going to happen?

Every day we went to work, and we didn't know if we'll come home at night. So what could you think? Every day we were thanking God the day is over.

## FRANIA

After three months in the store, my father saw that I am doing so well, we planned a wedding. You know, if you're in the religious way, before you get married, the girl has to go for a *mikvah*—a ritual bath—otherwise, the rabbi doesn't give permission to get married. Well there, it's not like here, it was so filthy. And there was an old woman sitting there—and to me, a young girl, she looked like a witch. You first of all have to cut your nails, a religious way, the toenails too. So I did it myself before, I didn't want anyone else should ruin my nails for me. At that time, my hair, I wore with one curl on top. It was stylish, and it suited me so nice. I had a long bobby pin, and if I put it in, that curl was standing. So if I'm going to the *mikvah* there, I'll have to dip three times and say the blessing. I'm going to lose that curl.

First of all, the old lady checked my nails, and cut two of them herself, they didn't please her, and they were bleeding. Second, when you get into the water, you're not allowed to have a thing—all naked, the way God made you—so you're not allowed to have a bobby pin in your hair. I took it out, and I was holding it tight in my hand, so she shouldn't see. I figured, the minute when I'll get out of the water, I'll stick it in right away so I won't lose that curl. It was so filthy, that water—oh! All those old Hasidic men used to go in there, and they splashed around there good. Anyway, I had to dip three times. Well, I dipped already three times, and when I went out, I was so alert that I remembered my bobby pin and stuck it in fast, but the witch, she noticed! She said, "It's not kosher." I had to go all over again. It was bad enough once to go in that water. I had to do it twice.

A week before the wedding, Srulek's grandfather—his mother's father, Michael Zawadzki—he was a rabbi in Busko-Zdrój. He sent a courier, saying that Srulek should come to Busko to see him. He should take off his armband and come. Imagine—he asked him to risk his life! Srulek took off the armband, took a bicycle, and went to his grandfather. My heart was beating. He went to Busko, and the rabbi gave him the wedding ring that I still have. He said, "This belonged to your mother, and I want you to marry your wife with this ring. Remember that whatever is going to happen, she should not lose this ring. She should always take care and watch that nobody should take it away. God will help, and you'll both be together alive." Those words.

Srulek brought the ring back, but it was big, and we had to go to a local goldsmith. His name was Kugiel, and he was a little bit of a crazy little man. We asked him to make it smaller, so he took the measurements and said to leave it.

I said, "I can't leave it."

He started to yell, "What do you mean, you're not trusting me? You can just leave altogether!"

I said, "Look, Kugiel, let me tell you why. I want to tell you the story." I told him how Srulek traveled without his armband, risking his life to get the ring. "The rabbi said not to leave it out of my sight, and so you have to do it right away."

Finally, he settled down a little bit, but he was still mad. We stood there while he made the ring smaller. I really watched out for that ring, whatever happened. I still have it right here, on my finger.

We got married in my house. I'll never forget that day: I woke up at seven o'clock, and it was raining, a storm. September usually is beautiful, but there was such a storm, it was so dark, like night. And eight o'clock, the same thing. And nine o'clock, the same. It never stopped. And here I had a nice little dress and a little veil, you know, to go down to the wedding. My grandmother comes to me, and she says, "Don't worry, at one o'clock, when you'll go under the *chuppah*—the wedding canopy—the sun will shine for you." That's what she said, and that's what happened.

I had a pink dress, a beauty. You know, I'm a good dresser, but I went special to another town, Kielce, to have that dress made. It was dusty pink, made from a light wool. I could picture it now. Well, the sun came out, and it was a gorgeous day. And that day, a postcard came from Srulek's father, wishing luck. That was very unusual because at that time, the mail wasn't regular—believe me—and in Łódź was already a ghetto. That's why it was such a miracle that this postcard came.

We got married, and we lived with my parents. They gave us one room, and we lived there. In the morning, we went to the store. Right after we got married, I said to Srulek, "You know what—I think I'm going to start baking little rolls, cookies. Because the farmers come Sundays to town for church or to visit sick people, friends, or family. So we're going to be making a fortune on these cookies and the rolls I bake." They let me use the bakery next door to make those rolls and cookies, and we were selling like hotcakes.

Three months after I got married, I got very sick. I had typhus. There was a small epidemic of it. Six people—I remember them all—got taken to the hospital, and the minute they went there, they died. We had a family doctor, a little old man, such a nice man. He said he's not going to take me to the hospital, but you're not allowed to be at home if you have typhus. He said, "I'm going to say it's something else: scarlet fever. We're not going to take her to the hospital, because there she has no chance." I was very thin, I probably didn't weigh more than ninety pounds. My father was the only one allowed in the room with me. He didn't allow anybody else inside the room. Srulek wanted to see me, he had to go to the window to look in.

I remember, there was a table there, the whole table was full of medicine. Then I started to lose my hair. The doctor begged me I should shave off my head, and I didn't want to. I made a mistake, because I wouldn't have such thin hair now. But I would lose everything if not for my brother Chamel in Lublin, because he was sending the best medicine to rub into my scalp. I was so sick for three months that I had to be carried on the chair on pillows.

At that time, the trouble started with my youngest brother, Yossel. We didn't have any money, and Yossel—he was then seventeen—he wanted to smuggle things from one town to the other. You could smuggle things like peas or potatoes, things like that. Jews weren't allowed to go from city to city. The minute they caught you outside Pińczów, they could shoot you right away.

Anyway, Yossel went with his friend Zavel on bicycles to smuggle. I remember, my father used to say, "Yossel, this friend is not for you." My father told him that Zavel's father was a horse dealer and that he has got the character from his parents, because he is brought up in that house. But Yossel wanted to make some money, he wouldn't listen. He had a bicycle, and they smuggled already twice. What made it even more dangerous: Yossel had to take off his armband to go smuggling, but he didn't look Jewish at all. He looked exactly blond, like Shaindel—like a Gentile. His friend Zavel, you could see he's Jewish from his features. Yossel could have smuggled by himself.

Anyway, the Germans caught them, and Zavel told the Germans right away, "This is my friend, he is Jewish too." My father warned Yossel about that boy. They put them both in jail, and they wanted to shoot them both right away.

Shaindel—what she did, it's unbelievable. She was going everywhere with money she got from Chamel in Lublin. She was very intelligent, she had a way how to do things, you know. Personality. First of all, you had to go to the German authorities for a paper that allowed you to travel from one town to the other. You couldn't just go out of town, especially as a Jewish girl. So she got this permit, and she traveled to a main office in the town of Radom. From there, they gave orders to the smaller towns. She got to the secretary of something, some important man, a German, and she paid him a lot of money. That man promised her that when the execution papers of Yossel and Zavel came up, he would put them on the bottom.

Shaindel made such contacts with the jail people in Pińczów that Yossel could send out letters, and we could send in some food to him. I'll never forget when he wrote once in a letter that each time he heard the key in the cell door, he thought, *That's it, they're taking me out to be shot.* Imagine. A few weeks later, they took him to Kielce, forty kilometers away from Pińczów. After that, a few months later, they took out all the Jews from Kielce for deportation to the camps, so naturally, they took out everybody from the jail too. Anyone that had a death sentence was handcuffed, and the feet too. A lot of people were jumping the train, some are alive today. Some got shot, it's true—but who could run away fast sometimes lived. Yossel, the poor thing, how could he jump if he was tied up? He couldn't. So he was taken away on the train to Majdanek and killed. Never mind killed—at Majdanek, they burned.

## SRULEK

We were in the store around six o'clock in the evening, and we wanted to close up. The murderer of the city comes in. This was a German everybody recognized. If you saw him on the street from far away, you ran the other way. He killed every day two, three people in the street, mostly Jews. He took out his gun and shot, just for fun, and laughed. This German came into the store, and when I saw him, I got white. I asked him very politely in German, "What can I do for you?"

He said, "You will give me two batteries for my flashlight." He gave me the flashlight.

I turned around, and I just could not put the batteries into the flashlight, so much my hands were shivering. If you showed that in a movie, people would say it's exaggerated. The fear told me now is the end—because we knew him, what kind of man this was.

He yelled at me, "You dirty Jew! Why can't you do it!?" He took it from my hands and did it himself, and he started to curse. Then he looked around to see what else he could take and walked out. It took probably ten minutes, but those ten minutes were ten years.

## FRANIA

By April 1942, I was already pregnant. The Germans came to our store, more than once, to check on us. You weren't allowed to sell cigarettes or flints for lighters. If they would find this, right away they would close you down. They could shoot you too. You had to risk it—what could you do? You couldn't help it, you made money on those things, and without the money, you couldn't survive. So Srulek made a little wooden chair with a seat that could open like a lid, and there inside was everything hidden. There was one SS, when I saw him coming into the store, I was just shaking. Once when he came in, he spent the whole time sitting in that chair.

Later they put in a commissar, like an overseer, into our store. Imagine—into that tiny little store! They saw that we're selling so much, there was always a lineup outside, so they put in a commissar. The commissar had control: we made so much, and he took so much. We had to remove those things hidden in the chair, but we were doing so well with other things, we didn't need to sell contraband.

By the spring of 1942, people started to say that soon they're going to take the Jews out of Pińczów. They asked my father to be on the *Judenrat* committee in Pińczów, and he didn't want to. He was lucky they didn't force him, because if you were on the *Judenrat*, you had to do all the filthy work to your own brother and sister. You know what happened in Warsaw? There was on the *Judenrat* committee a doctor and his wife, and the SS told them that they had one week to give up ten thousand children of such and such an age. How could they give up ten thousand children? They found him and his wife both dead in the morning. They committed suicide.

### SRULEK

Bad news travels fast. We didn't know exactly what is what, but we knew people vanish, that's all. Vanish. People escaped from the concentration camps, and they tried to tell people about what is happening to the Jews. They were going from town to town, going into the synagogues, telling anybody who would listen. "*Men brent Yidn! Men veln unz ale hargenen!*" They're burning Jews! They're going to murder us all!

### FRANIA

Everybody thought, *Impossible! They must be crazy!*

### SRULEK

Most didn't want to believe. But I believed.

## FRANIA

Chamel gathered the family together in our house. There was me, my parents, and my two sisters, Shaindel and Malka. I was already seven months pregnant. Chamel said to us, "Listen, in a small town like here in Pińczów, we can do nothing, but in a big city, Jews work in the government for the Germans. In a big city, maybe I can do something."

Chamel went to Lublin, where we had relatives. He started working for a German factory. He made a lot of money there and sent quite a bit to us. You know, he was so intelligent, I told you, he had such a terrific head on his shoulders, the Germans made him there the main accountant. He was doing bookkeeping. He had forty shoemakers there, sitting making shoes, and he was the whole manager of this, you understand? Let's say, when a transport of leather came, right away, he sold it to somebody on the black market. The Germans didn't know anything, that's why he had so much money. He would always send money to us with Polish couriers. No matter how hard the times got, Chamel always found a way to send money for us. And that's the way we lived. Just every day, from day to day, we were waiting for the Messiah to come. My brother Chamel wrote letters from Lublin, saying he wants to take us out of Pińczów, to get us to Lublin, where he could help us better. But we didn't know things were going to happen so fast, that soon the Germans would take out all the Jews to the concentration camps. After a few weeks, Chamel sent us papers—false papers—that we are Lublin Jews.

## SRULEK

And he made the papers with a special J on them. Frania's father read to us the letter from Chamel: "'Here in Lublin, they had already the deportation from the ghetto, but if your papers have this letter J, this means you are a Jew the Germans want to keep: Jewish police and their families, government workers, accountants. But I don't have papers for Frania. Not yet. If you are pregnant, you cannot have a J on your papers.'"

## FRANIA

My sister Malka started to cry. "He should make you the papers anyway!" I said to her, "Look at me, Malka." My stomach was already big with the baby. Malka put her arms around me and said, "You could wear something big to hide it!" I said to her, "And when I have to give birth? Then what?"

## SRULEK

Chamel said we should come to Lublin by train, two hundred fifty kilometers on the other side of Poland in the east. He said we should come only one at a time, one every week, so no one would notice. So no one will squeal on us.

## FRANIA

For me, he can put that special J on my papers in two months, after the baby is born.

## SRULEK

We didn't know if we have two months. So I started to dig a bunker.

## FRANIA

For the whole August 1942, he was digging it. The way he made that bunker, your father, it was a masterpiece. At the bottom of the stairs, in the burned part of the basement in my family's house. And the cover was made with clay and pieces of wood and dirt, so it was impossible to see it.

### SRULEK

The first night of Rosh Hashanah, we were sitting upstairs in her family's house, at the table.

### FRANIA

Two days before, my grandparents went to be with my Uncle Itchele in Działoszyce. In that town, they already had a deportation of Jews, so my grandparents thought they would be more safe there. Just one week before, my mother went by train to Lublin, so I was already in charge in her place. I had to cook, everything was ready on the table for Rosh Hashanah.

### SRULEK

Suddenly, right when we are lighting the candles, from outside, we hear *"RAUS! ALLE JUDEN RAUS! RAUS! RAUS!"* All the Jews out! We ran to the window, and we could see the Germans were gathering all the Jews from in town and from out of town. Everybody was pushed into that big square, that garden in front of the house.

### FRANIA

We left everything on the table, and we ran fast down to the bunker—me, Srulek, my father, and my two sisters. Srulek made the bunker deep, so we could stand up in it, but we also put there little chairs. We didn't have any food—we just ran straight down there. We didn't know for how long, we just thought that when night comes, we'll run away through the woods to another town, and later Chamel would take us to Lublin. The main thing: we shouldn't go with that deportation.

We closed ourselves up, and we lit a candle. And we waited. Then, from outside, we could hear the Poles yelling on the square, "*Gdzie są Greenfeldowie?*" Where are the Greenfelds? Our family name. You could hear them right outside: "*Gdzie są Greenfeldowie?*" My grandfather owned the flour mill, so who didn't know us in Pińczów?

## SRULEK

We had false papers, but the Poles would tell the Germans right away who we are.

## FRANIA

So they came looking for us, the Germans. They ran down the stairs, right on top of us, they were standing. You were afraid even to breathe. We could hear them talking right over our heads. They were looking for probably not more than two minutes, but you can imagine: every second was for us an hour. Then they left. And we were sitting in that hole for hours. Hours. Forever. For what? What do I have to look forward to?

## SRULEK

After a few hours, it was quiet. I wanted to see what is happening, so I opened the bunker cover, sneaked up the stairs, and looked between the stones in the wall. The whole square was Jews. Maybe a thousand people. Mostly quiet, except for people crying. And babies crying. I heard a gunshot. A scream. I heard yelling in German, but I couldn't hear exactly what. I saw big trucks all around. Motorcycles. Germans on horses, riding around, hitting people. And the Polish neighbors looking out of their windows. Some yelling. I could not hear what. And then I saw my own grandmother standing frozen, terrified. Standing in the front, I saw a man with half his beard torn off, and then I realized that is my grandfather, the rabbi from Busko-Zdrój. His face was covered in blood, his clothes, torn. I didn't even recognize him. He was in his seventies, my grandfather, and not a well man. They made him walk sixteen kilometers all the way from Busko.

### FRANIA

Srulek came back after fifteen minutes. Oh did he cry. He couldn't stop. We asked him, "What did you see? What did you see?" He couldn't talk. You know when he told me what he saw on that square? After you were born. That's when.

### SRULEK

I did nothing to save them. Nothing.

### FRANIA

What could you do, Srulek? Get shot?

### SRULEK

Four in the morning, we hear the sound of boots coming down the basement stairs. Then was a knock on the bunker ceiling. We hear a voice, saying in Polish, "Come out, it's quiet now. It's over." I opened the bunker. There was Kopecz, the Polish police captain. You see, when I made the bunker, I thought, *How long will we have to stay in this hole? When will it be safe to come out? Who will help us?* I had to trust somebody who is not a Jew, so I asked Kopecz. And he said yes, he'll help. Why? Because Kopecz believed that I saved his life.

#

KATE FINISHES THE PAGES. It's late. We're sitting side by side on the couch in our living room. I pour us both mint tea. I wait for her to say something about what she just read.

"It's fascinating. There are things in here that I've never thought about before. Polish farmers save your parents. Polish neighbors tell the Germans to hunt your mother's family. Kopecz, the police captain, wants your father dead, then helps him live. It's so complicated, the relationship between Poles and Jews."

"A thousand-year complicated relationship," I tell her. "It was always one step forward but then two steps back. The Catholic Church has a lot to answer for. People with power always have a lot to answer for. It's always been about power, money, fear. And lies, like the 'blood libel' lie."

"The myth that Jews need the blood of Christian children to make matzo for Passover."

"Which people still believe now, today."

"Jesus."

"Him too. We're also Christ killers, even though the Catholic Church officially said no, we're not any more guilty of that than anybody else."

"When did the Catholic Church say that?"

"Council of Trent, mid-sixteenth century. Didn't do any good. Nobody could read their fucking edict."

"What does your father say about all this?"

"A lot."

---

My father says to the cassette recorder, "I don't know who will be interested in it, but I'll never forget, when the Germans made the roundups, how much our Polish neighbors enjoyed it. It was for them like a holiday. They're taking away the Jews. 'Better tell me where you hide your gold, because you're going to die just the same!' The same Poles who lived side by side with us our whole lives."

He's getting emotional. My mother tries to cool things down. "Who wants a cup of tea?"

"Yes, thanks, Ma."

"You could understand it from the not educated, from the farmers, plain religious people who couldn't stand it that the Jews killed Lord Jesus Christ. Every single Sunday, they were reminded about it."

"Srulek, you'll have a cup of tea?"

He ignores her, wanting to make sure the cassette recorder is getting all this. "My grandmother's house was connected one wall with the church, and during Easter, we closed ourselves in very tight. If not, whoever went out, if he didn't get killed, he came home with blood because they were hitting and yelling, 'Christ killer! Christ killer!'"

"Maybe we should stop for today?" my mother says.

We sit there, not talking for a minute. Then I ask him, "What if it was the other way around? Would you risk your life to save the Poles?"

"I told you already. You do not know what you will do until—"

"Until the minute you're in it, I know, but would you risk your life if the situation was the other way around?"

He doesn't answer me right away. My mother stops what she's doing, she wants to hear his answer too.

Finally, he says, "If I would risk my life and the life of my family to hide them? Maybe not, no. So I cannot blame the Poles for not risking their life. If it was the other way around, nobody knows what they would do, but I want to believe I wouldn't betray them the way they betrayed us. They did it not just for money or to steal. They betrayed us even if they got nothing for doing it. Even those Poles who were a little more educated and didn't listen to every single word from the church. 'This one is a Jew! That one is hiding there!' For nothing, for no reason at all."

"Why?"

"Why?" His smile is about my naivete and has no humor in it. "Why is not a question. You know the story about the bicycle riders?"

"The bicycle what?"

"Riders. An old Jew is running from the Gestapo, and they catch him. They put a gun to his head, and say, 'Tell us, Jew: Who started the war?' The old Jew is no fool. 'The Jews,' he says. 'The Jews started the war.' The Gestapo laugh. 'That's right! Jews started the war!' Then the old Jew says, 'And the bicycle riders.'

"'Why the bicycle riders?'

"The old Jew says, 'Why the Jews?'"

I turn off the cassette recorder. "What if you ask me who started the war?" I ask him.

"War?"

"Between you and me."

"No," he says, starting to get up from the table. "I told you, I will not talk about this."

"Nobody knows what they'll do, you say, till the minute they're in it. Well, this is the minute. And you and me, we're in it."

The kettle on the stove starts to whistle.

---

I'm pacing in our living room in front of a desk that holds both my typewriter and the cassette recorder. I'm listening to the most recently recorded stuff. I hear my voice: "Nobody knows what they'll do, you say, till the minute they're in it. Well, this is the minute. And you and me, we're in it."

"Is that you on tape?" Kate is standing in the hallway. I didn't hear her come into the apartment. I wasn't expecting her back this early in the day.

The sound from the cassette is my mother's kettle whistling. I quickly turn it off.

"What were you talking about?"

"I was just commenting on something my father said."

"Oh, keep playing it."

"I'd rather you wait till I write it up."

"You have new pages for me?"

"Working on it as we speak."

"I'm dying to finally meet them." She takes a moment, then says, "Saul, don't they want to meet me?"

"Of course, of course they do. You know what? I'll ask when they plan on coming to Toronto, okay?"

"To see your play! Of course!"

I hadn't thought of that. *Fuck.* I was going to delay with some new excuse.

"You open in a week, right?" Kate asks.

"Previews in a week. Opening is four days after that. But, you know, come to think of it, Kate, I think they might be going to Florida early this year."

"Florida?"

"They go every year."

"They'd miss your play?"

"They don't see everything I do."

"But this time, it's not only a new play, I'm new too."

"I'm sure they'll try to come. Let me check."

Kate looks at the cassette player. "I'd love to hear their voices, at least?"

I can't think of a good reason to say no. I think about what's next on the tape, and I'm pretty sure there's nothing else about Kate.

I press Play. We sit on the couch and listen to the tape. We hear the kettle whistling, and then it stops. There's a sound of some dishes rattling as my mother starts preparing tea.

And then we hear my mother's voice:

### FRANIA

We got out of that bunker in the middle of the night, and we went through the woods. The best thing now is to run, run to another town—to Działoszyce, where my Uncle Itchele lives. And my grandparents are there too. Imagine, for me, pregnant, to go through woods thirty kilometers to Działoszyce. But what could I do? I'm not going to die here.

We started to cut through the woods—me, Srulek, my father, Shaindel, and Malka—Srulek knew exactly how to go. Suddenly, two Germans—I don't know from where they came—"*Halt!*" Can you imagine? They put their flashlights in our face and looked at us. "Where do you think you're going? Who are you?" They wanted to kill us right away. After the Jews were already taken away, if they found a Jew left over, they shot you.

### SRULEK

We took out our J passports and showed them that we are from Lublin, not Pińczów. It just happens that we were here.

## FRANIA

One was standing with his rifle ready to shoot us that minute. But the other one, it's my impression he was sent from God. I could recognize him now, a beautiful face he had, a good face.

He said, "We have no right to shoot Lublin Jews."

The other one, the bad one, said, "There are four papers for Lublin Jews, but here are five Jews." He saw I am the one who does not have papers.

I thought, *I'm dead.*

But the good one, he said they have to take us back to the Pińczów jail. The bad one, even though he saw I am pregnant, when we started to walk back to Pińczów, he took his rifle and hit my legs and feet. I was already in my seventh month, and I fell over. Then he hit me again. He made me all full of marks, blue marks. Only me, he hit. Just me. So the other one yelled at him, he shouldn't do it, and he tried to stop him. One was an angel, and the other one was just a devil.

## SRULEK

They took us to the Pińczów jail. And who was in jail? Other Jews also made different hiding places, and after they took out all the Jews, if they still found somebody, some of them, they shot right away, and they took some to the jail. Why to jail? If there's going to be, let's say, a deportation in another town, they'll take those Jews there.

We were sitting in jail, we didn't know what's going to happen with us, and on the second morning, they came in: "*Raus!*" They put us all on a wagon. They caught quite a few Jews after the deportation—fifty, sixty people. There were probably ten wagons with horses. Polish farmers were the drivers. Where do you think the Germans got the wagons? They go to the farmers and force them to give it for nothing. The farmer on our wagon told us the Germans are taking us to the jail in Stopnica. My Aunt Hodel lived in Stopnica, so we thought that if we could get out of the Stopnica jail, we'll have somewhere to go.

## FRANIA

In Poland, the roads were very bad—and everywhere, deep ditches. We were already out of Pińczów. Suddenly my father said to Shaindel—I'll never forget it—"Shaindel, jump!"

In front of us were wagons, and in the very front was two motorcycles with Germans. We had wagons behind us, but they were all Jewish people and all from our city, they wouldn't give us away. And the farmers, you think they liked the Germans? In the very back was a truck with German soldiers. We were on a big curve in the road. The motorcycles in the front and the truck in the back would not see our wagon for maybe another half a minute.

My father said to Shaindel, "The Germans can't see us now. You just jump and go right into the ditch. Save your life!"

Shaindel said, "No! If you are all gone, I'm not going to have anybody. I won't do it!"

My father said, again, "I'm telling you—jump! Why should we all go from this world? At least one will be alive."

And why did he ask her? Because she looked like a shiksa. She never looked Jewish, never. But she said no. The road was narrow, and there was a big ditch there, very deep—and she didn't realize that her own father will do a thing like this: while the Germans couldn't see, in that few seconds, he gave Shaindel a push and threw her off the wagon. That's guts. You think about it.

## SRULEK

When we came to Stopnica, they locked us up in jail to wait for the deportation.

## FRANIA

This jail, I'll never forget in my life. We were probably two hundred people—there were some already from before too—in two little rooms. I couldn't breathe there, I thought I'm going to faint. There was a window, but it was high and on a slant. So Srulek and my father were holding me up to the window so I shouldn't slide down, and I was getting some air there through the steel bars. We were sitting there two days, and it was just impossible. Why? Because there wasn't a bathroom, so everybody was making on the floor. Can you imagine sitting there in that shit—excuse my expression. It was impossible, it was unbearable.

Soon they're going to take us to concentration camps, but we knew one thing: if you're young, if you're still healthy, they take you first to work, they don't burn you right away. Everybody wanted to work because meanwhile, you have a hope that the war will finish and you'll still be alive.

My father had a beard, and a beard makes everybody look older. Anyway, in that dirt there, in that filth, Srulek found a bottle and broke it. I'll never forget this moment in my life. With that piece of glass, he shaved my father. He was shaving him, and we were all crying, the tears were just coming down. We wanted him to look younger, so they should take him to work, they should not murder him right away. In the middle of that filth, Srulek shaved all his beard off. You know, my father looked probably twenty years younger, and he was so handsome, I'm telling you.

There was a Polish officer at the jail, he was a higher rank than a policeman. And I say the same thing: it was an angel sent from God. You know, if you have faith, you believe it. That officer saw me pregnant, my father and my husband holding me up to that window, that I cannot breathe and so much filth there on that floor. When he came, always he said these words: "How are you, children?" Just like that—like a father coming to see how his children are. Srulek gave him the idea that if we don't get out, we are all of us going to be sick with typhus and that will cause an epidemic. That's what they were afraid of, the Germans. If it's an epidemic, they're going to catch it too. Let us out, we'll wash, at least we'll be clean. And when they deport the city, we'll go anyway. That's what the Polish officer told the Germans, and I suppose the Germans saw that it's logical. In the morning, they let us out.

We went right away to Srulek's Aunt Hodel. When she saw me, she gave me a big pot with hot water she warmed up on the stove, and I got undressed and washed up. I felt like alive again. You know, when you're in the dirt, you don't think. And Srulek washed up, and my father, and Malka. Then Srulek's Aunt Hodel cooked potatoes with red borscht, I'll never forget the taste, how good this was.

You're clean, you're not hungry, you start to live again and to think, *Why should I wait for the deportation?* We wanted to save a little bit our life, to stretch it. Maybe there is still something we can do. We ran to a phone and called Chamel in Lublin. He told us Shaindel was already together with him in Lublin. That she was alive was a miracle.

Chamel said the first thing for us to do was to go to Działoszyce. We should not go with the deportation that was coming soon in Stopnica. In Działoszyce, they had already a deportation. He told us my Uncle Itchele was still in Działoszyce, and with him, my grandparents. And also the Germans left the *Judenrat* and a few Jews with their families. From Działoszyce, Chamel said he would be able make arrangements to take us to Lublin.

## SRULEK

It was sixty kilometers from Stopnica to Działoszyce. We couldn't just go to any farmer for a horse and wagon because instead of taking you, he could take you right away to the Germans, and for each head, he'll get two kilograms of sugar. We called her Uncle Itchele in Działoszyce, and he sent a farmer he trusted with a horse and wagon. He came at night, right to the door. It was an open wagon full of hay.

## FRANIA

Srulek and my father hid in the straw. Malka and me, we sat on top with the farmer. If the Germans would see a farmer and two women, they wouldn't stop us, but with the men also sitting there, it would be too dangerous. This farmer took us by side roads to be even safer. In the middle of the woods, all of a sudden, a few Poles—hooligans—came running out: "Stop the wagon!" And they started to search what we have. Right away when I saw them running out of the woods, I knew that I have to save my wedding ring. I took it off and put it under my tongue. But they took my watch and a little brooch, and from Malka, they took things too. They didn't look in the hay. This was very lucky. We came to Działoszyce, straight to my Uncle Itchele.

Itchele had a wife and two daughters, but they were already gone. They were taken right away in the first deportation, so only Itchele and his sixteen-year-old son, Leibick, were left. And my grandparents were staying there. Itchele was their son, my mother's brother. When we arrived, we right away called Chamel.

## SRULEK

Chamel had all his family's money in cash and in gold. He gave it all, everything, to Shaindel. He gave her a new identity, to be a shiksa, and he's sending her to live in Warsaw. She would be like the bank. If she heard from one of us we need help, she could maybe do something. Chamel wanted to make arrangements to bring all of us to be with him in Lublin. First he wants to bring Malka, so both the sisters can go to Warsaw together. Next, Frania's father.

## FRANIA

But me, I couldn't go. I didn't have that J on the papers. So that's that. I have to wait for the deportation. And that was the luck that Chamel couldn't take me. Because if I went to Lublin, I wouldn't be alive now—and neither would you, my son, because from the Lublin ghetto, they took everybody to Majdanek, and everybody was murdered there in the gas chambers.

Kate and I sit in silence. The tape hisses.

"Is that all?" Kate asks me.

"No," I tell her. "Just, nobody said anything for a while."

There's almost thirty seconds of silence, except for the sound of tea being poured and a spoon stirring sugar. Then we hear my father's voice:

## SRULEK

Frania's father took me aside and he told me, "It is a time that you have to think without emotion. We know probably nobody of us will stay alive. Run. She is my daughter, and I love her, but if you're going to hold on to her, you're going to die together with her. You look like a Gentile, you were traveling without the armband so many times, and nobody would dare ask if you are Jewish. Run away. Take off the armband and save your life. Run."

I told him, "No. If I wanted to save my life by myself, I could have saved it before the war, my friends wanted me to go with them to Russia. But I am in love with Frania, and she is carrying our child, and later on, if I'll be alive and she is not—no! I cannot do that, and I'm not doing it, and don't talk to me anymore, that's the end of it."

## FRANIA

So my father came to me. "My daughter, you know how much I love you. You cannot run anymore. In a few weeks, you will give birth. I talked to Srulek, he doesn't want to listen to me, but if you talk to him, maybe he will listen. The minute they have the deportation, right away they separate husband and wife. You're not going to be with him even one minute. What good will it be if he is going to be dead too? Persuade him, talk to him, he should run away, he should save his life. Look, I saved Shaindel's life, I threw her down from the wagon. You think I don't know how you feel?"

I saw my father is right, he talks sense. So I did it. I went to Srulek.

"If you stay with me, you're going to die together with me. And not even together."

He looked at me for a long time, and then he said, "Would you do it?"

I said, "How could I do it? I cannot run."

He said, "Just tell me, if it was the opposite, would you do it if you could?"

So I didn't answer. What could I answer?

So he said, "That's all. I don't want to talk about it. Enough." And he walked away, and that was that.

Silence. The cassette tape hisses and then runs out. The cassette machine clicks off.

Kate sits in silence for a moment. "I feel I just met them." Then her face lights up. "How about this: What if I go with you to Ottawa next time?"

I suddenly have a deep understanding exactly how a deer feels in the headlights.

What comes out of my mouth is "Um..."

Misinterpreting my "um," Kate says, "Sleeping together in the same room at their house wouldn't be a thing, right? I mean, they already know we're living together. Or we could stay in a hotel?"

"My parents hear that we're staying in a hotel, I'll never hear the end of it." True.

"Right, they wouldn't want to split us up, that's sweet. Okay I'm going to bed. When's the next Ottawa trip? Oh, wait! I could meet them sooner! They'll come to Toronto for your play, right?"

"I'm not really sure exactly what their plans are. But you know what? I'll call them tomorrow. and find out what's what."

"Saul, what if I talk to them on the phone? That might help, right?"

*Fuck.* "You know what's better Kate? Better is if I go to Ottawa to talk to them in person to convince them to come."

"Okay, you know them best, but please make sure to tell them how much I want to finally meet them."

#  SIX

I HAVE TWO FULL DAYS OFF from the play, so I drive to Ottawa.

The minute I pull into the driveway, my mom comes out the door. "Come in for dinner," she says, "but leave your suitcase in the car. You have to go to a hotel, or maybe you can sleep on the couch."

"What's wrong?"

"Nothing is wrong. My sister Shaindel came from France."

My Aunt Shaindel steps out the front door. I haven't seen her since 1966, when I was eighteen.

---

Summer of 1966, I was going to Europe for the first time, on my own. My plan was to go to Paris at some point and visit my Aunt Shaindel and her husband, Jean, for the first time. I'd also meet their son, my cousin, Gérard.

My dad was waiting in the car in the driveway, ready to take me to the airport. As I was about to leave the house with my guitar and my suitcase, my mom stopped me at the door.

"Listen—my two sisters are fighting, and I don't want you to get in the middle. You know that after the war, my sister Shaindel married Jean—a French guy, a Catholic, a lovely man—and they had a son, your cousin, Gérard. My younger sister, Malka, also lives in France with her husband, a Jewish man. They never had children. Malka is very angry because Shaindel never told Gérard she is Jewish. Gérard doesn't even know his mother's name is Shaindel. She changed it to Zosia. Malka was not allowed to tell him the truth even though Malka knows Gérard since he was born. Why is Malka now suddenly mad about it? I don't know. And who am I to judge? If not for my sister Shaindel and what she did to help the family during the war, none of us would be here now. Anyway, there is a fight between my two sisters, so when you meet Gérard—he is seventeen, almost the same age as you—just be quiet about being Jewish, you don't have to talk about it."

"Ma, my name is Saul Rubinek, and I look like *this*. I think he's going to figure it out."

"If he does, he does, but you don't bring it up."

When I got to Paris, I stayed with Aunt Shaindel and her husband, Jean, and Gérard. None of them could speak English well, so my high school French got a workout. Shaindel, who I had to call Aunt Zosia, *not* Aunt Shaindel, was tall and blond with sharp blue eyes. She had a no-nonsense air about her, practical and unsentimental. Her husband, Jean, was quite different: warm, and full of jokes. Gérard was thin, blond, nerdy, and a little aloof. But he seemed happy to see me, especially since he also played guitar, and I could teach him some Bob Dylan songs.

The second day I was there, I made a decision. Fuck it. I'm telling him the truth.

Gérard and I were alone in his bedroom, sitting on the floor, facing each other with our guitars. I was teaching him the chords to *The Times They Are A-Changin'*.

He was trying out a chord pattern I had just shown him. "I go G *à* C *et après encore* G?" he asked me.

"G to E minor, then to C, then G." The door to his room was open, and I could see Shaindel in the kitchen. I didn't want her to hear what was about to happen, so I got up and closed his door. "Gérard, we're first cousins because your mother and my mother *sont sœurs*—they're sisters."

He was concentrating on the chord pattern, not even looking at me.

"Gérard, did you hear—*as-tu entendu*—what I said?"

He finally looked up at me. "*J'ai d'autres cousins*—other cousins, I have—*du côté de mon père*—my father side."

"Ah, *oui*. They're Catholic, right?"

He shrugged. "*Je suppose*." He looked back down at his fingers on the neck of the guitar.

"Your father, *ton père*, he goes to church? *Il va à l'eglise?*"

"*Non*." He played a chord change and looked up at me. "*Est-ce correct? A minor ou E minor?*"

"E Minor. I'm Jewish, you know."

Gérard was still absorbed in getting the chord change right. "Okay, cool."

"I mean, my parents, both of them, are Jewish. *Ils sont juifs*. From Poland. Polish Jews. *Juifs Polonais*. My mother is Jewish, and your mother is her sister. Their maiden name is Greenfeld. So, *tu es demi-juif, toi*. You're half Jewish."

I waited for that to sink in. He looked up at me briefly. All he said was "*Eh bien. Oui*. Cool. So … *comme ça?*" He started singing and playing the song. He seemed really pleased that he was getting the chord pattern right.

I was shocked that being told he was half Jewish had absolutely no impact on him whatsoever.

The next time I see Aunt Shaindel, eighteen years later, she's walking out the front door of my parents' house in Ottawa. Her blond hair has gone gray, but her blue eyes look just as sharp.

"My fault!" she says. "I steal your bedroom!" Her accent is Polish with a French twist. Then she turns to my mother, and says in Polish, "*Mówiłam ci, żebyś mówiła mi Zosia.*"

My mother says to her in Yiddish, "*Du kenst toyshn deyn nomen ober du kenst nisht toyshn ver du bizt.*" I understand the Yiddish: "You can change your name, but you can't change who you are."

Shaindel ignores my mom and walks quickly over to me and gives me a big hug.

"You still speak Polish when you have secrets," I say to her.

"*Mais tu parles encore français?*" she asks.

"*Oui,*" I say, "but my French is not good. *Pas bien.*"

She says, "*Ce n'est pas un grand secret. J'ai dit à ta mère, que je n'aime plus qu'on m'appelle Shaindel. Je préfère Zosia.*" It's no big secret. I tell your mother I don't like being called *Shaindel.* I prefer *Zosia.*"

"What did you tell him?" my mother asks Shaindel.

"A big secret," Shaindel says and winks at me. "Go in the house," she tells my mother. "I have more secrets."

My mother stands there for a moment, worried. Shaindel gives her a sharp look. My mother sighs and goes inside.

Shaindel holds me at arm's length with a big smile. "*Dix-sept ans!*"

"Eighteen years," I correct her. "You look—"

"*Vielle!* I am old woman. Your mother, she invite me, and I decided to come. Since cancer took away my Jean, I do not visit anyone."

"I'm so sorry about Jean."

She nods sadly. "*Eh bien.* Tell me: you write a book, *ta mère,* your mother say."

"Uh, *oui.* Yes. A book. It's not finished."

Shaindel studies my face. "*Dis-moi la vérité. Quelque chose ne va pas entre toi et tes parents, je peux le sentir.*"

I know what she said, but to stall, I say, "I'm not sure I understand. Sorry."

"Tell me the truth: something goes not right *entre* you *et tes parents*. I can feel it."

I tell Aunt Shaindel everything. About my being with Kate. About Dad's ashes on his head. The prayer for the dead. Mom weeping. Everything. Shaindel is furious.

"*Mais c'est impossible!* I will speak to them about this tonight."

"No! Listen, we've spent months *not* speaking about this!"

"So it is time, no?"

Good question. I say nothing. I don't really want to stop her.

That night at dinner, she lays into them. In Polish. I don't understand a word of it. But it's a very harsh-sounding monologue. My parents say absolutely nothing.

Later, when I'm alone with my mother, she tells me that Shaindel told them their attitude about Kate is embarrassing. Shaindel said, "Don't you dare tell me it's because of the Holocaust. It's because you live here, in Ottawa, with bourgeois Jews. You're afraid about what your friends will think. So your son fell in love with a shiksa, so what?" She said to Mom, "You fought our parents so you could marry who you love." And she said to Dad, "And you! You broke from an Orthodox life to become an actor! You both should be ashamed! You both loved my husband, Jean! My *Catholic* husband! Look me in the face and explain this hypocrisy!"

---

Two days later, when I'm back in Toronto, I tell Rachel what happened.

"I'm surprised Mom told you what Shaindel actually said to them."

"I think she told me because she doesn't really disagree with Shaindel. I think the problem is actually Dad."

"What did Dad say to Aunt Shaindel?"

"Nothing."

"Dad loves to argue."

"Not with her."

"The first dinner in the history of our family where Dad didn't talk about the Holocaust."

"He did. Later. He got me alone and said, 'I want you to know something: Shaindel saved our lives during the war. She is probably the bravest person I've ever met. She risked her life for us and for her family. More than once. For that reason, I would never talk back to her. She calls me a hypocrite. Maybe it's true. I loved Jean, her husband. I never cared that he was not Jewish, not at all. He was a great guy—kindhearted and generous—and they loved each other. What else matters? Nothing.'

"I said, 'Well, Dad, something else clearly matters when it comes to me and Kate! You dumped ashes on your head! I've spent a year not talking about this—you forbade it—but it's enough. A year listening to story after story about all the terrible things that happened to you, and underneath it all, there's only one thing that matters: how much you and Mom love each other and how that love helped you survive. How can you be so against it when *I* find love? I found love, and when I told you, you said the prayer for the dead.'"

"Did he have an answer for that?" Rachel asks.

"Not right away. He just stood there for—I don't know—almost a minute, Rachel. Then he said, 'I was afraid of what will happen if you have children. Look what happened with Shaindel's son, your cousin, Gérard. She didn't tell him nothing about who he is, about where he is from, about her history, about her family. *His* family. She did it, I'm sure, so Gérard would not feel different, so he wouldn't have to hide who he is, like she's had to hide who she is.'

"I said to Dad, 'Kate and I aren't married, we haven't decided about children. But if we do have a family, Kate has her background, I have mine, and the children would be who they are. We wouldn't lie to them about where they come from. What are you so afraid of?'

"He said, 'Me? Everything. It could happen here, what happened in Europe. Any people ripe for it. Just look what people did to each other over the last three thousand years. I am not a religious man, but if you will come to me right now with a gun and tell me I must convert, if not you'll kill me, I would give my life. I would never be a traitor to my people. Their blood is my blood, blood that was spilled and buried for two thousand years.'

"I said, 'You think I'm a traitor?'

"'You asked, and I answered.'"

# SEVEN

I TELL KATE that my parents aren't going to come to Toronto because my mom's sister Shaindel is visiting. And then they're going to Florida. As good an excuse as any.

Kate listens to this news, that she won't be meeting my parents anytime soon, and says nothing. She just nods. She seems distant and a little cold. I don't pursue the subject, and neither does she. In any case, I'm swamped with the final week of play rehearsals, and Kate is distracted with directing rehearsals of her workshop, which is soon going to have a full production in Winnipeg.

Rachel is with me one afternoon as I set up the cassette player to listen to one of the last recordings. Kate is at work.

"Did Mom tell you the story about the wagon?"

"The wagon? There's more than one story about a wagon."

"The one to the Bania farm. She's on that wagon, traveling all day, sitting beside some farmer, pretending to be his wife, eight months pregnant. Dad is hiding in the straw behind her. No idea if the Banias will take them in or not. Did you ask her how she felt, what she was thinking?"

"I don't remember."

"Kiddo, you gotta ask these questions, or what kind of book is it going to be?" Rachel already knows—without my actually telling her—that I now am eager to write the book.

"Right."

"Play it."

I press Play.

## FRANIA

After a few days, a man came to bring Malka to Lublin. Then, right away after Malka went, Chamel sent for my father. If my father wouldn't have gone, he would be alive today because he would have been safe with us. But my father had a policy that it was such a war that you had to make sure whatever life you could save, to save. If you stayed together, you died together. And that's why he threw down Shaindel from the wagon.

Just before he left, my father wanted to ask my Uncle Itchele to try to arrange for a farmer to hide us. I said, "Hide with a farmer who doesn't know me at all? A farmer is going to hide my Uncle Itchele, they know him for so many years, they were dealing with him in grain—but with me, he's going to hold me a day, take the money, and then he is going to kill me. Or he is going to throw me out."

"Maybe," my father said, "but it's possible that the war will finish tomorrow." You understand, we just had that hope: it's going to finish tomorrow. Like a dream.

That's when we heard a rumor that Zofia Bania was looking for me: "Where is Frania Greenfeld? I want to save her." It was a rumor. A woman in Pińczów, at the market, told a farmer who delivered potatoes to Działoszyce. He told somebody who told my Uncle Itchele. So who knew what's true, what's not true?

When we heard that Zofia was looking for us, well, you had to be a diplomat at that time. You couldn't say, "Oh, I'm going to run to that farm!" You had to think about yourself. If you said something, right away you had another three people who wanted to go with you, so then the Banias wouldn't take in a whole army. We didn't say a thing, Srulek and me.

I said to him, "Why should we go to a farmer who doesn't know us? If we are hearing Zofia is running all over, that she wants to save us, shouldn't we go to somebody who is looking for us, somebody we know?"

You see, I remembered that Zofia was so grateful to us when one time we credited her a few złotys in the store, you understand? She remembered that, I was sure. But how would I get there, to their farm? And how do I know if she still wants me? My Uncle Itchele said, "I will send somebody on a bicycle to the Banias' farm. We will let Zofia know you are alive, and she should come here to Działoszyce. Then we will talk with her, and we'll make a decision."

He found a young fellow, a Pole. You see, he knew nice people, there were Poles that were nice people too, you know. Not many, but there were some, like any other nation. This young fellow never gave us away. He took with him a letter I wrote to Zofia, and he rode half a day—thirty kilometers—on a bicycle to the Banias' farm with a letter from us. He came back and said that he found Zofia working in the stable. She almost fell off the ladder when she read my letter and heard that we are alive. She said she will come tomorrow.

## SRULEK

Next day, we waited all day, but we didn't see her. She probably backed out, she changed her mind, she's afraid or something, and that's it.

## FRANIA

Meantime, in Działoszyce, it started already to get hot. That means people were saying "Any day, tomorrow, it's going to be the next deportation." Imagine—already I prepared myself to go with the deportation. Srulek didn't want to run away, he wanted me. So we already started to get ready. I remember, I took a kerchief, and I put in some sugar and some candies so I should have something prepared for the deportation when we go. And que será, será. What can I do? Nothing.

## SRULEK

First of all, we didn't have any news, only the German paper—the Polish paper was under the supervision of the Germans—so we didn't know anything. But the older Jews said, "We remember in the first war, the Germans took everybody to work. They didn't kill, it's just propaganda." But some people read Hitler's book *Mein Kampf,* and they said, "The Jews are not going to live." Other people said, "The world would not allow it." So everybody wanted to believe that they're being taken to work. Because the Germans did like this: They took people to the concentration camp and forced them to write letters home. And letters came: "We are working, and everything is all right." In fact, in Pińczów once, a letter came from a man, a water carrier, who was blind and couldn't read and couldn't write. From him, a letter came. So people said that he must have asked somebody to write the letter for him. You see, people wanted to believe that way, even though we knew the Germans were killing cripples and the very old. But to kill everyone? To kill millions? Impossible. We were counting on the fact that it's impossible for one nation to go against the whole world. First of all, we knew the Russians are against Germany, and now that they are in the war, it maybe will be over fast. Two days, one week, two weeks. The thing to do is just to wait it out.

## FRANIA

My grandmother and grandfather too, they couldn't help it, they were old people, they had to wait for the deportation.

## SRULEK

Frania's grandmother came to me, put her hands on me, and cried. She said, "Srulek, could you make a bunker for me and my husband?" I knocked half a wall out from her room, and I made the room smaller and built another wall. Then I made a wardrobe with a false back so you could get into that small room. I worked quite a long time on it, but I built it. I don't know what happened later. We heard, after the war, that Frania's grandparents died from hunger in a camp somewhere, we didn't know where. That's all that we heard about them. They were caught, that's for sure.

## FRANIA

When Zofia Bania didn't show up, we resigned ourselves already to go with the deportation. After another few days, I said to Srulek, "What do I have to lose? Why should I go with the deportation? Who knows what happened to Zofia, really? If she was running, like we heard, all over the woods looking for us, what do I have to risk? Here, I know I'm going right to the death camp. Pregnant, I'm dead right away. At least for one night, Zofia is going to let me in."

My Uncle Itchele had a very trusted farmer—the father of that young fellow who went by bicycle to Zofia. That farmer, an older man, brought a horse and a wagon with hay—and Srulek was buried in the hay, under the straw. The farmer brought me a big, full skirt of his wife's—a stomach I had anyway—and a wool shawl, a dark green, I remember, for my head. I looked exactly like his wife, sitting together with him in the front, and Srulek was hiding in the back under the straw.

Before I left, my grandmother gave me a bottle of alcohol, a vodka. In Poland, the vodka was ninety-six percent, very strong. When you have to give birth, at that time, it's very important to have vodka—that's what my grandmother told me. I didn't know. I was so naive. "But," she said, "don't show this to the farmer. Watch out for this like your own head because you'll need it."

My grandmother, before the war, she never gave me ten cents. I don't remember once receiving a gift from my grandmother. She told me the sun would shine when I got married. As long as it didn't cost her any money, she could say everything. But listen, with her hands, she gave me the alcohol, and maybe this saved my life. I saved that bottle. I knew that in one month, I have to give birth. If I would give it to the farmer, I wouldn't have it, he would right away drink it.

We left five o'clock in the morning, November the third, 1942—a Tuesday. The next day, November the fourth, they took all the Jews out from Działoszyce. One day more would have been too late.

It was already cold, and it was raining. The roads were so bad, the farmer took two big towels, made a knot, and said to me, "My child, put this around your stomach because the roads are so bumpy, it's very dangerous." He did it by himself, putting the towel around me. I wasn't even shy. The farmer said, "I'm not going to sneak on the side ways. I'm going to go with the main roads." By the main roads, you had to go through Pińczów, on the main street, where all the Gestapo were going. Through there, he went, just like he's not afraid. He's a farmer with his wife on a wagon, that's all. Can you imagine my heart? And Srulek under the straw?

We went right through Pińczów, and I saw all the Gestapo. I knew them, I recognized the faces, I knew them very well. It was a very cloudy day, a dark day. Maybe if it was sunny, somebody would recognize me. I was lucky, that's all. That old horse with the wagon, I could have walked faster. It took ten hours. It took forever. We went right through Pińczów to the village of Włochy, three kilometers away from Pińczów.

### SAUL

How did you feel, Ma? What were you thinking about?

### SRULEK

Listen, when you ask a question, how did she feel—

### SAUL

Please don't tell me the Talmudic story about how you'd have to almost kill me so then I'll know how she feels.

### FRANIA

I have nothing to lose. That's what I was feeling. Who could think at that time that the war will be another two and a half years? I thought it's going to be another two months, three months, a half a year, so maybe Zofia is going to keep us there. Maybe we'll survive there.

This village, Włochy, is like one street. Outside the village there was a hill and a big field, and after that was one little house— Ludwig and Zofia Bania's house. That was the good thing about it: that there wasn't a neighbor right next door. If it would be between the neighbors, she could never hide us there.

The Banias' house was, I would say, a half a kilometer from the village. By itself standing—one little house. So I think that this house was just built special for me.

The only thing what it was bothering me was that I was pregnant. My gosh, how it's going to be there when the time will come and I will have to give birth to that child? But I didn't want to think about it. You cannot think that far what's going to happen. You take it step by step. Day by day, you take it.

### SRULEK

It was already pitch-dark when we got there.

### FRANIA

I got off the wagon and knocked so Srulek would know he could now come out. Zofia came out from the house, and when she saw me, the way she ran to me and grabbed me around, I could swear that a mother does not greet her own child the way she greeted me. I said to myself: I'm going to survive this war.

### SRULEK

Ludwig, Zofia's husband, came out from the house. I was more than a little bit scared because he had a stone face. He didn't smile, didn't say anything, didn't do anything. Nothing. He just was standing there, looking at us. You know how they say: if looks could kill.

The tape hisses to a stop.

I look over at Rachel. "See?" I say. "I asked Mom how she felt." She has a faraway look in her eyes. "Rachel, you okay?"

"Not really. I know how this story ends."

# EIGHT

TERRIBLE ADVICE is a medium-sized hit, and I get decent, but not great, reviews. I never connect deeply with the character of Stanley. The whole rehearsal and performance experience has been overshadowed by my adventures in the art of lying. Lying in real life doesn't get you good reviews or applause—not for me anyway.

It's been a year since the beginning of this insanity, since my father dumped ashes on his head, since Kate asked if she could read my book, since I started actually writing it. I've been running on automatic: driving to Ottawa during breaks from the play, doing a few hours of taping, driving back, doing the play, working on the transcripts, handing new pages to Kate. Rinse and repeat. All the while, I was nursing the hope that the process would create an opening for me to come to an understanding with my parents about Kate, based on compassion, forgiveness, and love. Two weeks ago, when my Aunt Shaindel visited my parents, my father and I finally had it out about Kate, and any hope I have for a resolution based on love and understanding is, I now know, delusional.

I don't know how long I've been staring at the blank page in my typewriter. I should be making notes about the recording I just listened to.

I'm frozen. I got a call from my mother a few hours ago, a call that changes everything, but the enormity of it didn't sink in until about an hour ago, or however long I've been sitting here, motionless, in front of the typewriter.

For the past couple of weeks, Kate and I have had hardly any time together. Our work schedules have been so completely different that when I wake up, she's already gone, and when I get home late, she's already asleep. She has not had time to read any more of what I've written. And since the day I told her my parents are not coming to Toronto anytime soon, she's been distant whenever we do get a moment together.

This is one of the very few times we're both here, awake, at the same time. Kate is about to go to Winnipeg for a few weeks to direct a new play, so tonight is the night.

"Wine?" Kate's voice from the other room.

"Yes, please."

She arrives with two glasses of white and hands me one. "How's it going?"

I look up at her. I don't know what to say. Well, I do know what to say, I just don't have the immediate words to say it.

"Stuck?" she asks.

"You could say that."

She touches a small stack of typed papers beside the typewriter, all the pages I've written so far, about a hundred of them. "Seems to me," she says, "this is the only way I'm going to meet them. In your book."

I take a deep breath. "Kate. There is no book."

She's not sure she heard me right. "What?"

"There's no book. Right after you asked if you could read it, that's when I started writing it."

"No book?" Now she's heard me right. I want to tell her that there might be a book, because I finally want to write it, but I know I have to get the confession out first.

"Kate, I told my parents I was writing a book about them because … to have a reason to go see them."

"Why would you need a reason to …" In that instant, I can see in her eyes that it's all starting to become clear to her. "What did they really say when you told them about me?"

"It did not go well."

"My not being Jewish."

"I didn't know what to do! It was bad, they freaked out, I didn't expect it. It was like they wanted me to choose between them and you. I tried to choose both. I was ashamed, I was a wreck. I'm so sorry."

Kate sits on the couch. She downs the rest of her wine. "I can understand your trying to manage them. Why manage me?"

"I just thought, delay, delay, delay. Tell you everything's fine, give them time. I thought I could eventually bring them around."

"And did that happen?"

"No."

"So you were going to keep this going until … ?"

"Now. Right now."

"Saul, you've been lying to me for almost a year. The biggest thing going on in your life, and what's most important to you is making sure none of the truth gets anywhere near me. Why? What did you think I would do?"

"Think less of me. Think less of my family."

"Well that's bullshit," she says. "You didn't want to have a hard conversation with me. Which is a pattern, right? You don't trust me. Apparently. You won't even let me in on what you think about having children."

She waits for me to say something. Anything. Instinctively, I think saying nothing is better than the crap excuses forming in my brain.

"Saul, you don't have to figure out everything before you talk to me. We figure things out by talking to each other. That's what a relationship is supposed to look like. If we trust each other."

She takes a moment to calm herself. She looks at her wine glass. Empty. "Why are you telling me now?"

"I got a call from my mom. She got a letter from Zofia in Poland. Zofia doesn't have long to live, and she wants to see my parents again. So they want me to go to Poland with them. That's next month. Right after the play closes."

"They're in Florida?"

"No, actually, they're coming to Toronto to see the play tomorrow night. You're leaving for Winnipeg the day after that, right? My mom said they want to meet you tomorrow. She said enough is enough."

Kate stares at me and says nothing for an eternity of ten seconds. "Do they know you lied to me?"

"We don't talk about it."

"Do they still believe you're writing a book?"

"For Penguin. I wanted them to believe it was going to be published."

"But, of course, there is no Penguin."

"No Penguin."

"And you figured, what? You'll tell me the truth tonight, and then tomorrow when your parents meet me for the first time, with me standing beside you as if I've been a part of this whole conspiracy, that's when you'll tell your parents you've been lying to them for almost a year?"

"Not exactly." I don't know what else to tell her. I'm ashamed. I hope that's evident. I can't stand the silence between us. "Can we get past this?"

Silence again. She gets off the couch. "You trapped me. You

didn't trust me enough to tell me the truth from the start because you thought I'd have a bad reaction. Now you've decided to tell me, and I'm having a bad reaction. You want to get past it, what, right now?! No, we fucking can't get past it. Since you've had a lot of practice, maybe you can get past it all by yourself, but leave me out of it. I'll meet your parents tomorrow, Saul, but after that... I don't know. I'm going to Winnipeg, so after that, I won't see you until you get back from Poland. We both have a lot to think about."

"Will you give me a chance to make things right?"

"I really don't know." She touches the typewritten pages on the table. "You should finish the imaginary book. It's real now."

---

My mother calls me to say they've arrived in Toronto, and that night, after seeing the play, they come backstage. Kate is already there, waiting for them.

"Hallo," my mom says. "You are Kate?"

"It's nice to finally meet you, Mrs. Rubinek."

"Frania, call me Frania. Here is my husband, Srulek. His name really is Israel, but Srulek is like a nickname."

My dad holds out his hand. Kate shakes it formally. "Nice to meet you," she says.

"And you," he says. He turns to me. "You were good in the play. I have some suggestions, but we will talk about that later."

"Sure. Later. Listen, let's sit and talk for a minute before we go get something to eat?"

I usher everyone into my dressing room, where we can have some privacy. I close the door. Everyone takes a seat.

There is an awkward silence for a few seconds. "Well, listen," my mother says, "what can I tell you? We figured, it's time."

"I've heard so much about you both," Kate says.

"Sure. And you probably are reading the book?" my mother asks.

"Yes, I—it's ..." Kate looks at me. We have a plan for when I'm going to reveal everything. It's supposed to happen when we all go out to a restaurant after this.

"Saul doesn't let us read it till it's finished," my mother says.

My father is suddenly animated. "You finished it? When they are going to publish it?"

I look at Kate. She is trying to telepathically tell me *Not now*. But I think this is the time to do it because, as you now know, I'm an idiot. "Okay, Mom, Dad, about the book. Listen. I have something I want to—"

Kate interrupts me. "How about we not do this now. They just got here."

"Do what?" My mother looks at Kate and then at me.

"Mom, Dad, now that we're all finally together, I want everything to be out in the open. Listen ..."

"Maybe after we eat?" suggests Kate.

"Okay," I say. "You're right. After."

"Well, now I'm worried." My mother says. "What is it?"

I look at Kate. She gestures, her arms wide, like *Go ahead, it's your party*.

"I lied about writing a book. There never really was a book. I'm sorry." I wait for a reaction, but my parents just sit there, staring at me. I plan to tell them that now there really might be a book since I now want to write it, but first I have to tell them about why I lied. "I just wanted to have a reason to keep seeing you both."

My father says, "A *reason*?"

My mother says, "What do you mean, there is no book? You made all those interviews. And Kate just said she read the book." She looks at Kate. "Right? Yes or no?"

"Right. I did. A lot of it."

"Because Kate wanted to read some of it, so I had to write some of it. But now I—"

"I don't understand 'had to write it,'" my father says. He doesn't seem at all upset. Just confused.

My mother gets it. She turns to my father and says, "Because he lied to her too." And then to Kate: "Right?"

"Yes," Kate says.

"About the book, he lied?" my father asks my mother.

She says, "Because he wanted to have a reason to see us."

My father, now completely at sea, looks at me. "You needed a reason?"

My mother is getting frustrated with my father's obtuseness. "Come on, Srulek—what's the matter with you? You wouldn't talk to him because he's living with a shiksa." She turns to Kate. "It's not a bad word, *shiksa*, just a not Jewish woman."

Kate says, "It is actually a very bad word, I think." And she looks at my father. "Right?"

My father ignores that direct question and turns back to my mother: "I never said I wouldn't talk to him." He looks at Kate. "What did he tell you about us?"

Kate takes a deep breath. "He said that when he told you I'm not Jewish, you were both totally fine with that."

I watch my mother and father think that through. Then both of them, at the same time, get it. They both say, "Aha."

Then my father looks at me and says, "So Penguin is not going to publish the book?"

"No."

"You know what?" my mother says to me. "You have chicken feathers in your head. If you ask me, you overreacted to the whole thing."

I'm speechless, but just for a moment. "I overreacted?"

My father says, "I don't know what is worse, that she is not Jewish or that Penguin is not going to publish the book."

No one knows how to react to that. "A joke. It's a joke," he says. So we dutifully laugh. Weakly.

"It's good, the book?" My mother's question is for Kate.

"It is. I told him to finish it."

"So he could still show it to Penguin, right?" my father asks her.

I decide to enter the fray. "Actually, I now think that I do want—"

My mother interrupts me. She now much prefers to talk to Kate. "You tell him to go to Penguin. He's not going to listen to us."

"I will."

After a brief and very uncomfortable silence, my father says, "About the word *shiksa*, you are right. It does not just mean *Gentile woman*."

"I know," Kate says.

He smiles, which is unexpected. "Say what you want to say."

His smile lets her speak frankly: "*Shiksa* is a word that doesn't say anything about who I am, just who I am not. I looked it up. *Shiksa* means I'm a defiler of Jewish men, an object of sexual and moral disgust."

"No, no, no. Maybe in the old world. It doesn't mean that now."

"No? How did you mean it?"

He is silent. Then he smiles again. "You know? I like the way you argue."

She smiles too. "I work in the theater. Words are my life."

"I worked in the theater too. I was an actor."

"I know," she says. "It's in the book."

"I promise you," he says, "I will not use that word again." He holds out his hand again, and they shake on it.

"Tell me, Kate," my mother says. "You were mad at my son for lying to you?"

Kate is not used to this kind of direct conversation. In her own family, she is used to innuendo, subtle shifts of tone, and, at all costs, avoiding emotional confrontation.

"I'm still mad at him," she says.

"You want to be mad, be mad at me and my husband."

I try to enter the conversation: "I don't think—"

"You stay out of this," my mother says. "I am talking to Kate."

Kate says, "I understand why you both reacted the way you did more than I understand his lying to me."

"If you understand, do me a favor: explain it to me. Me, I want to blame the Holocaust, but my sister Shaindel told me that's *głupie gadanie*, Polish for—excuse me—*bullshit*."

Nobody speaks for a few seconds.

"All right," my mother says. "Listen, I know we were going to go out to get something to eat, all of us, but we drove in early this morning, and the play is good, but I have to tell you, it's long, maybe a little too long. And I didn't like all the swearing. Anyway, I'm tired. I want to go to the hotel and sleep. Maybe we could see each other tomorrow?"

Kate says, "I'm leaving for Winnipeg tomorrow, so ..."

"Ah," my mother says. "Well, then, another time."

After Kate and I get back to our apartment, we barely speak. She tells me it's good she finally met my parents, but I know it was not good. It was stiff, and awkward, and mostly about the damn book, and not at all about us, about me and Kate.

When she leaves the next morning, she says, "I really hope things go well in Poland."

"I hope so too. Call me when you get to Winnipeg?"

"Saul, I think we need a break. We both need some time. We'll see where we are in a couple of months, when I get back from Winnipeg and when you're back from your Poland trip."

I know at that moment that it's over between us.

---

Later that morning, Rachel and I are sitting side by side on our bench.

"You told Kate the truth?"

I nod.

"You told Mom and Dad the truth about everything last night?"

I nod.

"And now you're going to Poland?"

I nod again.

"Good times," she says.

"Want to come with?"

"Poland? I'll never go back there." Her eyes close for a few seconds, looking inward, as she often does when Poland is the subject. Then she says, "Kate and you …"

"I think it's over. I fucked up, Rachel. I should have listened to you and told Kate the truth a long time ago."

"Is that what this breakup is about? That you lied to her?'

"And that I can't commit to having a family."

"Wait, what? You really buried the lede there, kiddo."

"Huh?"

"She wants a family, and you don't?"

"I really don't know what I want."

"Yeah, maybe think about that. Not your lies about the fucking book."

**FRANIA**
(age sixteen)

**SRULEK**
(age eighteen)

**SRULEK**
(the photo Frania's parents saw
in a magazine of him as an actor)

**ZVI ZEV RUBINEK,**
(Srulek's Father)

**SARAH (ZAWADZKI) RUBINEK**
(Srulek's mother, who died
just after he was born)

**RABBI MICHAEL ZAWADZKI**
(Srulek's grandfather from Busko Zdroj)

**DAVID MINTZ**
(Frania's grandfather)

# ALL IN THE TELLING   153

**SRULCIE**
(Frania's oldest brother)

**FRANIA AND HER YOUNGEST BROTHER, YOSSELE**
(taken just before the war)

**CHAMEL**
(Frania's middle brother)

**SHLOIME-BARUCH GREENFELD**
(Frania's father)

The square in Pińczów, before the war.

The burned-out remains of the square after the German invasion.

ALL IN THE TELLING 155

THESE PHOTOGRAPHS WERE TAKEN THE DAY THE JEWS OF PIŃCZÓW WERE ROUNDED UP FOR DEPORTATION.

# NINE

ONE WEEK AFTER THE PLAY CLOSES, I'm watching my mom and dad at their kitchen table.

"I want to go back, but I'm scared to go back," my dad says.

My mom says, "To go back there, I don't want to at all."

They're not talking to me. They're talking to a camera. Four other people are in their kitchen—a documentary film unit from the CBC, the Canadian Broadcasting Corporation. My mom and dad are being interviewed by my co-producer, Melanie. It's three weeks before the planned trip to Poland.

My dad: "It will remind me everything. We were nine kids. I was the oldest. The youngest was two years old. I am the only one alive. Now if I'm going back, I'm going to see everything again. It's going to come back to me."

And then my mom says, "The memories are too hard to take, those memories. There's nobody left. Nobody."

My dad takes a deep breath. "Listen, if we change our minds…" He looks at Vic, the guy behind the 16mm camera. "Stop it for a minute."

Vic is a pal. We worked together on a few CBC dramas that I acted in, and he knows my parents from the couple of times they visited the set. He looks at Melanie, who is totally taken by surprise by my dad's "if we change our minds." She turns to look at me for support, but I shrug, waiting to see where this is going. I'm not going to meddle. Not yet.

Melanie, in her mid-forties, is a seasoned documentary producer. She's not used to partnering with a "civilian"—me—but she has no choice. She badly wants to do this doc, it has award possibilities written all over it, and if she's going to do it, she has to work with me.

Melanie turns back to my dad. "Srulek, would you like some time to talk in private?"

"Private? No, I just am thinking loud." He looks at Vic. "You stopped?"

Melanie nods to Vic, and he stops filming. Vic, an award-winning documentary filmmaker, is the one who walked me into the CBC executive's office to sell this idea. It wasn't hard to do. First, it wasn't expensive. I was putting up ten grand and was asking CBC for the same amount. Second, I was becoming known as an actor in Canada because I had played four leading roles on CBC television, so the executive who could green-light this already knew who I was. Third, it was a great idea: I bring my parents back to Poland to have a reunion with the Polish farmers who hid them for two and a half years during the Holocaust. And for me personally, all this is taking my mind off my breakup with Kate.

Recording sound on a portable Uher reel-to-reel tape recorder is Ian, a Scottish Canadian veteran of dozens of documentaries. He nods to his assistant, our "swing," Terry, holding the boom—a four-foot pole with a microphone on the end of it—and Terry pulls the boom back. Terry, in his early twenties, is going to Poland with us as both the sound assistant and the camera assistant, and for that reason, he's called a "swing."

"If now I say it's maybe not such a good idea," my dad says, looking at Melanie, and glancing over to me, "is it too late?" He's a little embarrassed by saying it, I can tell. But if you don't know him—and Melanie doesn't—he seems pretty sure of himself, so the expression on Melanie's face is *Oh, fuck no!*

Just to make sure, Melanie asks, "Not such a good idea to ...?"

"Go to Poland," my dad says, confirming Melanie's worst fear.

"Dad," I say, "you don't have to do anything you don't want to do." Melanie doesn't even bother to look at me. I know she feels betrayed, but I know what I'm doing. Arguing with him would cement him in opposition. My mom comes to the rescue. I knew she would. Well, I hoped she would.

"Wait a minute, Srulek." She turns to look at me. "You are still going to write the book?"

"I am," I say.

"And to get a publisher, like Penguin, it would be a good thing that we are going to Poland to film this documentary?"

"It would," I tell her.

She turns back to my father. "Srulek, listen, they will be together with us there, making a film the whole time." And then to Melanie: "Right?"

Melanie grabs the lifeline with both hands. "Right! Absolutely!"

My father is not that easy. "So?"

My mother knows exactly what to say. She knows what my father is afraid of. "So it's the CBC, the government of Canada is making the film. So nobody will say boo to us."

Nobody, not me, not even my dad, dares to say anything about that. Melanie can't help it. "Say boo?"

My mother looks at Melanie. Blond, blue-eyed, not Jewish Melanie. Of course she doesn't understand.

"Antisemites."

---

Ian, our designated driver, parks our rented van near the Pińczów town square. Easy to do, not many cars taking up parking spots. This is the town where my mother was born. The population today, in August 1986, is about ten thousand. Only three Jews—Mom, Dad, and me.

Ian, Melanie, Terry, and Vic climb out of the van, lugging sound and camera equipment. They pile everything on the sidewalk and then look around, energized, chatting excitedly about the first day's work.

I get out and stretch. It's been a two-and-a-half-hour, hundred-and-fifty-mile ride, almost directly due south from Warsaw, just one day after we flew in nonstop from Toronto on Aeroflot, a Soviet-owned airline.

My mom and dad are still in the van.

"Mom, your house was on the square?"

She answers from inside, "One minute. I'm coming." But I can see she's sitting beside my dad and not moving at all, just staring out the window. He's doing exactly the same thing.

The town looks much like it might have looked at any time in the past hundred years. A horse-drawn wagon full of hay clomps past, the lone farmer holding the reins openly stares at us. He's moving slowly in front of a Fiat, the young woman driver in no hurry to get past him, because she's staring at us too.

This is Communist Poland, and, as we'll find out, on the verge of collapse. But right now, the Ministry of Culture of the Polish People's Republic loves that this documentary is about Polish farmers who hid my parents during the Holocaust. A reunion? Fantastic. Filming permits? No charge. The Ministry even threw in a translator. For free.

A young woman climbs out of the van. This is Agnieszka. She is twenty-four, very serious, thin, glasses too large for her face, no makeup, straight mousy hair. She looks like a student and is, in fact, a University of Warsaw graduate student in media and communications. She's our free translator. Oh, and she's also a spy for the government. No big secret. If I ask her if she's a spy for the government, she'll say, "Of course."

Agnieszka takes a small red hardcover notebook out of her beat-up leather briefcase. She watches our crew for a minute and then uses a ballpoint pen to write something in her little red book.

"Mom? Dad?"

"We'll stay in here till you are ready," from my dad.

"What are you afraid of? I'm getting out," my mom tells him.

My mom carefully steps out of the van and occupies herself with smoothing the wrinkles from her dress. She's waiting for her husband. He reluctantly emerges and stands beside her. She reaches for his hand, and they both stand there, side by side, holding hands, silent, looking for landmarks. Or ghosts.

---

A block-long, block-wide garden defines the Pińczów town square, with three-story row houses on three sides. The fourth side leads to an eighteenth-century Catholic church, St. John the Evangelist. My mother has a story to tell that involves this church. It takes about an hour for Vic to set up the shot. As Ian and Terry test their sound equipment, my mom sits on a canvas chair next to our van. She's holding a hand mirror, checking her makeup and hair. A few curious Pińczów locals stand nearby, watching.

Melanie is not quite sure what she should be doing. Talk to Vic about the shot? He knows what he's doing. Talk to my mom? My mom and Melanie are oil and water, and there's no real reason for it. Melanie just rubs my mom the wrong way, and that's all there is to that. Melanie has already made all the necessary arrangements—permission to shoot in the church courtyard, snacks and coffee for everyone—so she's got nothing to do except pace nervously and think of stuff that might go wrong, the producer's job.

Agnieszka, as usual, stands apart, taking notes in her little red book.

Vic finishes his first setup. My mother and father sit side by side and talk to Melanie, who is sitting just to the side of the lens.

Melanie asks, "Srulek, Frania, would you tell us a little about this town?"

My father should be in his element, performing for the camera, but he's nervous and slightly self-conscious, so he's a bit stiff. He says, "In 1939, here in the town of Pińczów, there were ten thousand people—fifty percent Polish, fifty percent Jewish. We got along. Antisemitism was here, before the war even, but we got along."

He stops talking, not sure what to say next. He looks at my mother. She is not nervous at all and is far more natural on camera. She says, "You see this garden here, this main square? All around was houses and stores. The whole square was Jews, and we had our house there, my parents, right here, in the square."

My father is relaxing a bit. "When the Germans came into Pińczów in 1939," he says, "a German soldier was killed in the church by a sniper. For revenge, the Germans burned the whole square, which was mostly Jewish homes and stores. Frania's parents house was burning with the others. Everyone was forced out. All the Jews on the square. And the Germans chased them all to that church."

Melanie says, "Frania, will you show us what happened next?" Melanie knows this story, of course. We've gone over a dozen stories that we want my parents to tell for the camera while we're here.

My mother gets out of her chair, and Vic follows her with his 16mm camera as she heads into the church courtyard. "They were chasing us here," she tells the camera, "my whole family. They were chasing us right here, to the church. We heard shots, and we saw blood on the road."

Following along, Terry holds a boom mic. Farther away, Ian is recording the sound. Melanie, Agnieszka, my father, and I watch, standing beside a few curious Pińczów residents.

My mother tells the story to the camera: "The minute I came here with my family, we saw here machine guns. We saw one here, every three meters another one, and then on the other side, another one. And so many people were here, my father said, 'That's it. Now they're going to shoot us all. We're all going to be shot.' So then my father said, 'Let's run to the wall. Let's be the first one at the wall.' And we ran. We ran fast here, to this wall."

Vic follows my mother to the door of the church. "We came to the wall here, at this door. And we were standing here with my brothers and my two sisters, all together, and my parents, we were standing right here. And here, people, they're chasing more people here, more people. And then the Germans came. And when they stood at these machine guns, we went right to the floor and in a second, there was a mountain of people here, and they were shooting and shooting and screaming, the screams, I could still hear the screams. And then, after half an hour—a half an hour—they stopped. And when they stopped, and it was quiet, I got up slowly and said, 'My gosh, we are all alive? This was a miracle. So many bodies here, and we're still alive? This is a miracle: We're still alive. We're still alive.'"

That night, my nightmare, its black darkness invaded by white bars that grow into overwhelming whiteness, comes back. My own scream startles me awake.

---

Letters have been going back and forth between my mother and Zofia since we arrived in Canada in 1949. Letters and money. My parents sent whatever they could: five dollars, ten, twenty, and much more once my parents were settled in the 1960s. Every month.

Today is the second day of filming. I can see that the Bania farmhouse is in much better shape than any of the others nearby, and there's a fairly new pickup truck parked outside their neat two-story stucco-and-brick house. On the other side of the house is their barn, freshly painted red. A cow has its head stuck out of an opening. Chickens run around freely, pecking at the ground.

My mom and dad, Agnieszka, Melanie, and I watch Vic set up an establishing shot of the Bania house.

My mom turns to Melanie and asks, "Where is Zofia and Maniek?" Maniek is Zofia's son, fifty now, only seven when my parents were hiding there. Ludwig, Zofia's husband, had died a few years earlier.

"We don't want you and the Banias to see each other until we film the actual reunion," Melanie tells her.

"So when is that going to be?" my mom asks.

"We're working on the schedule, and I'll let you know as soon as I can," Melanie says, and then, to avoid further questions, she says, "Sorry, Frania, I have to talk to Vic about something," and she walks away.

"That woman, I don't know how she got to be producer, she is not very organized," my mom says to me, put out, as usual, by Melanie's abrupt manner.

"The Banias' house looks nice," I say to change the subject.

Agnieszka predictably announces, "Under Communism, farmers do much better than before."

"Communism!?" My dad is instantly ready for an argument. My mom puts a hand on his arm to stop him, but my dad is unstoppable. He lays into Agnieszka with a stream of vehement Polish.

Agnieszka turns to face him, just as ready to argue, but my dad looks like he's way too eager for her to do just that. So she keeps quiet. Seething.

I have no idea what he said in Polish. I turn to my mom, the question on my face.

"He said Communism didn't pay for their house, that we sent money to the Banias for the past thirty-seven years." And then, to Agnieszka, because she's already writing in her little red notebook, my mom adds, "What Srulek said is true. Write that." Then, to lighten the mood, my mom says, "I think Communism forgot to cross the street."

On the other side of the narrow road, a farmhouse looks run down, in need of paint. The barn's roof is caved in on one side, and the truck in front looks rusted and thirty years old. The farmers who live there, a man and wife—probably in their seventies but look older—are standing fifty feet from us, watching the filming from across the road.

"Who are they? Do you know them?" I ask my dad.

"Neighbors. I know who they are," he says and turns away from them.

The old farmer couple mistakenly thinks we turned to look at them. They wave. Politely, I wave back. They take that as an invitation and cross toward us.

"Oy vey," my mother says under her breath.

"What's wrong?" I ask, but too late—the old couple has arrived right beside us. They don't say a word, just stand there, all of us studiously watching the nonevent of Vic filming the Bania house.

Finally, the old man turns to my father and says something in Polish. My father, without looking at him, replies briefly, harshly, in Polish.

The old farmer couple looks like they've been slapped. Agnieszka's mouth is open, astonished.

Later, my mother tells me the old farmer said, "Why didn't you come to us? We would hide you better." My father answered, "If we came to you, we would be dead the next day."

---

My parents and I stay in a small hotel in Pińczów. Almost every night, I go up to their room before bed to talk over the plans for filming the following day.

I tell them, "We want to film the reunion with us and the Banias next week, on the last Sunday we're here. Zofia told Melanie she wants to prepare things for everyone."

"Prepare?" my father asks.

"Sure," my mother says. "I know Zofia. She'll make a lunch for everybody. And the whole family will be there: her grandchildren, Maniek's daughter and her husband, and their children. And the nephews and nieces, everybody. There will be twenty people there, you'll see. I know her, she wants that everything should be perfect."

"How do you feel about seeing them again, Zofia and Maniek?" I ask.

"I'm nervous, that's all," my mother says. "All the memories will come back. The good thing is, we came *here* and they didn't come to us in Ottawa."

"Why?"

"Because if they came to us," she says, "they would think we're rich and we didn't send them enough money. That's why."

"Rich? You still live in the first house you bought twenty-five years ago that you could barely afford. You're far from rich."

"But compared to how they live here? Believe me, it's better we came to them."

My father says, "Not everything we are going to say in this film. Zofia is a good person, no question, but she wanted to save us because she knows the flour mill belongs to Frania's grandfather, and later she's going to get a lot of money out of us. Listen, one day after we got there, she asks, 'How much money do you have?'"

"So what?" My mother is suddenly angry with him. "So what if she asked about money. We all had to survive together. I was eight months pregnant! You are saying if we didn't have money, she would throw me out?"

"No. She was thinking that after the war, she will—"

"She could not think farther than the next day! They didn't have a slice of bread there."

"They had a little—"

"Nothing! *Nothing* is what they had! A mouse in a church is poor? That's the way they were poor. Ludwig didn't even have a horse for the field. One cow, he had. And chickens. Naturally, we gave them right away whatever money we had, and we told them later we're going to be in contact with the rest of our family for more money, but I didn't believe that myself. My sisters went to Warsaw, how should I know where? Where will I write? How could they know that I am hiding on this farm?"

"Wait," my father says. "You have your tape recorder? Maybe you should record, for the book?"

I take the little cassette tape recorder out of the bag I carry everywhere. My father has become invested in the book being published. That and the documentary are things he is now counting on. It's become important to him, and to my mother, that their story goes out into the world. And it's become important to me, too.

I start recording. My mother moves her chair closer to the cassette recorder. "Ludwig said that before he lets us stay in the house, first he wants my baby to be born, and he wants us to be in the hayloft. He was afraid, so afraid. I don't blame him.

"He was such a character, that man. The first night we are in the barn, Ludwig came in. He caught a chicken that was running around, and while he was looking at us, he smiled, and at the same time, he broke the chicken's neck. Such a character he was.

"All I can tell you is he scared me to death. And I could see he wanted me to feel like this. Zofia was a different story. That first night we were there, she came in with a big bowl of hot soup for both of us and a blanket for me. Zofia said to us, 'Ludwig has two sisters, Juzia and Wichta. They are both coming here tomorrow from Warsaw. They come every week to Pińczów to buy things at the market—butter, geese, ham—and smuggle all that back to Warsaw to sell on the black market. Listen, we have to tell them about you because they are going to find out anyway.'"

"The next night," my father says, "they took us into their house to meet Ludwig's sisters."

"House? It was two rooms with a dirt floor. A wood stove, a bed, a table, and four chairs. No running water, even. There was a well with a bucket outside. And the toilet was also outside. Ludwig was already drunk, asleep, and snoring on the bed. Little Maniek was sitting in a corner, shy, afraid to say a word. We sat at the table with Zofia and Ludwig's two sisters, and we told them our story—how we got there—and they listened to us. One of the sisters, the younger one, maybe forty, was Juzia. She was married with a young child, a boy. She had such a kind face. The other one, Wichta, was a nothing—an ugly old maid, a rotten character, with a face like a witch. When we finished our story, Wichta was cold. She didn't show even one drop of sympathy. But I knew if she betrayed us, she would betray also her brother."

"But Juzia," my father says, "she was different. Juzia said to us, 'My husband works in a post office. He doesn't make much money. So on market days, I come here to buy different things hard to get in the city. Some of the money I make by selling in Warsaw, I bring back for Ludwig and Zofia. Still, it's not enough. For any of us.'"

"I told her we gave all we have to Zofia already," my mother says.

"And Juzia said, 'I know. Zofia told me already. My husband and me, to make more money, we decided to rent out a room, so we put up a sign a few weeks ago, and a woman came, a single woman, Zosia Lipinska, and she pays rent every week. Then another woman came—

she said it's her sister, Marisha—to share the room, so they pay a little more now. This Marisha, she looks Jewish. And the other one, Zosia, I am sure is hiding her.'

"I could see that Wichta is surprised by this news, and she said, 'Kick them both out!'

"But Juzia said, 'It's none of your business.'

"Then Juzia said to me, 'I thought one woman is a Jew and the other one is not. Now I think maybe both of them are Jews. What are your sisters' names?'

"I told her, 'Shaindel and Malka.'

"Juzia said, 'Maybe to hide they are Jews they changed their names?'

"I said to Srulek in Yiddish, 'Chamel made new papers for them. What was the name?'

"He answered me, also in Yiddish, 'He told us new papers. Not the name.'

"Then Wichta yelled at us, 'What are you saying?!' and she said to Juzia, 'Whatever they tell you, don't believe a word!'

"Juzia said to me, 'What do your sisters look like?'

"I didn't answer. How do I know if I can trust her?

"So Srulek, he said to Juzia, 'You tell us what they look like.'

"Juzia said, 'The first one is maybe twenty, light hair, blue eyes. Tall. The other one is younger, short, dark.' Oh, I knew right away that this is Shaindel and Malka. And Juzia could see from my face that I knew it. She said to me, 'Nothing bad will happen to them. Not because of me.' I believed her."

"But then I looked at Wichta," my father says. "She had a look on her face of just hate."

"Juzia went back to Warsaw and told her two renters, who were calling themselves Zosia and Marisha, about us, and they said, 'Yes! We are Shaindel and Malka! That's my sister and her husband!' Can you imagine a coincidence like this? So Juzia brought money from Shaindel straight to us every week. She didn't even trust Ludwig—her own brother—and never told him about it."

"If not this, we could never survive, because we didn't have enough money to keep Ludwig from throwing us out," my father says.

"Zofia would stop him, even if we didn't have money from my sister. Zofia would never throw us out," my mother says into the cassette recorder. She turns to my father. "And you know it's true, so you be quiet."

"Her sister Shaindel saved our lives. That's all I want to say. For your book."

"Put this in the book: A Polish woman, a Polish Catholic woman, Zofia Bania, saved our lives," my mother says.

"But most of the Poles were not like this," my father says. "Listen, when Shaindel went to live in Warsaw, she took Malka once for a walk. Two Poles walked right over to her: 'You better give me money because you are hiding here a Jew.' They meant Malka. Shaindel paid. They didn't go home a whole day. They were watching if those two Poles would follow her because if the Poles knew where she lives, they would come every day for money."

"*That's people*," my mother tells him. "People are like this. 'Most of the Poles' you said. So most of the Poles—tell me—you met them?"

"All right. Not most Poles. Some people. Good enough? That's what happened to her brother Chamel. Some people—all right?—*people* squealed on him. The Gestapo caught him and took him to Majdanek concentration camp. But he found a way to—"

"Wait, let me tell it. I don't know how he did it, but Chamel smuggled a letter out of Majdanek to a Polish woman he trusted."

My father says, "We all knew this woman's name and address in Warsaw in case we want to know who is where in the family, or if we need help, this woman would be like a post office."

"My brother's letter was for Shaindel. 'Help me. I am dying. I am starving. Help me.' Before this letter, Shaindel knew Chamel went to Majdanek, so he must be for sure dead. But now? A letter like this? He must be out of his mind with sickness to think she could help him. But she went. You hear me? Together with Polish workers, my sister Shaindel walked straight into the Majdanek concentration camp."

"Shaindel smuggled in food," my father says. "She figured if she found there a guard, a worker, someone who would do it once, maybe for money, they would do it again and again."

"All day she worked, cleaning and doing laundry in the guards' barracks, but she didn't see an opportunity. Then she sneaked into a little building, like an office. And a man was there on his hands and knees cleaning the floor. He was wearing, you know, the prisoner clothes with stripes, and he had two triangles—a red one and a yellow one on top of each other, like a Star of David—on the front to show he is a Jew. Believe it or not, Shaindel knew him right away. He was in the same class as her in Pińczów. Can you imagine? Mendel was his name.

"Shaindel was wearing a big kerchief around her head, all her hair underneath, and she saw that Mendel does not recognize her. So she decided not to trust him right away. She talked to him in Polish, like she would be a shiksa. She told Mendel she is looking for a man called Chamel Greenfeld, that this man's sister paid her to come here because she heard her brother Chamel is starving. She told Mendel she brought with her money and will give it to him if he can find Chamel and bring him food. Mendel said he knows Chamel Greenfeld. Shaindel opened a bundle she had with her. Inside was bread, fruit, eggs, and money. She gave Mendel the money.

"Suddenly, they heard German voices right outside. He said to her, 'If a guard thinks you are here to help Jews, he will kill us both.' He right away gave her back the money and went straight down to the floor to keep cleaning. Shaindel put the food and the money back in her bundle, and she waited, scared to death. But no one came in. So again, she gave Mendel the money, and also the food for Chamel. He said it's already late, the other Polish workers probably left, and she should wait here in the office until it's dark. Then she could sneak out. So she was waiting there with him, and she got scared, the way he was looking at her.

"Listen, he was a young man, he didn't have a woman for who knows how long, and he must have thought to himself, she's a shiksa, who cares? He grabbed her and threw her down on the floor. Shaindel was a virgin. She tried to fight him. He tore off her clothes and started to ... you know. But she stopped him. Because she said to him in Yiddish, 'Mendel, Mendel! Hehr oif! Du kenst mir! Ich bin Shaindel! Mendel, kik oif mir! Ich bin SHAINDEL!' Mendel, Mendel! Stop! You know me! I am Shaindel! Mendel, look at me! I am Shaindel!

"He stopped and looked at her. The kerchief on her head was off, and her hair was out. Then he recognized her. He crawled away in the corner and started to cry. Shaindel put on her clothes and gathered the money and food that fell on the floor. She tried to give it to him, but he couldn't even look at her. She put everything on the floor near him and said to him in Yiddish, 'Zug mein bruder az ich bin du geven.' Tell my brother I was here. She never heard from Chamel again."

# TEN

IT IS AMAZING FOR ME TO BE IN PIŃCZÓW, to see the town I've heard so many stories about. My parents are sometimes as excited as kids on a field trip, and sometimes in a trance—unnaturally quiet and introspective. It is very hard for them to recognize landmarks. Everything has changed, except for the church at the end of the square. The park in the middle of the square has been totally rebuilt. All the houses are different. My father says the town seems five or six times bigger than he remembered. My great-grandfather's flour mill used to be on the outskirts and now is quite central. The house where my father used to live with his grandmother, the house that was attached to the church, has been torn down.

I am in a whirlwind of activity. I can't remember a time in my life when I've been this driven. Every day, I help Melanie and Vic decide which stories to film, and every night, I tape my parents. Agnieszka has found a typewriter I can use, which takes me some time to get used to because of the Polish keyboard. Whenever I have a few hours, I work on the transcripts and type them up.

### FRANIA

One night in December, a week before I gave birth, I walked to Pińczów with Zofia. Imagine—five kilometers by foot and with my stomach—dressed like a farmer woman, walking at night when nobody could recognize me. In Pińczów was a Polish woman who used to be a customer of ours in the store, and I knew that my mother gave away to this woman blankets, pillows, and tablecloths. I figured maybe this woman will give me something back. I remembered my mother gave her a down comforter, I wanted to get that because where we were hiding, it was so freezing cold. She was a very nice woman—I knew she was nice, or I wouldn't go—she gave me a few pillows and also that down comforter. Believe me, this saved my life, it was so cold. Otherwise, with what could you cover yourself in that hayloft? Zofia carried it on her back, and we went like this back to the farm. It was already two o'clock in the morning.

When I had to give birth, it was December the twenty-second, just before Christmas. I came to the farm in November, so I was there already almost six weeks. In the beginning, Ludwig's sisters were coming twice a week for market days. They bought geese, butter, and whatever would be in short supply in Warsaw. The whole month, Shaindel was sending with Juzia absorbent cotton and flashlights. I could have made a store! Why did she send so much? I should have the cotton for the bleeding. And she was sending the flashlights because if I'm going to give birth, it has to be lit up—and Ludwig said never is he going to allow us to put candles there. I don't blame him—the roof on that hayloft was made of pieces of wood and straw on top. We could all go up in fire. And he was worried what to do with the baby.

Right after I gave birth, the baby died from the cold. It must have been thirty below in that stable. Maybe it's for the better my baby died. If a baby was crying in that house for the next two years, would we be alive now? I don't want to talk about it. It's too hard to take, what happened. Listen, there is a tree, there are branches—as you see, I had another child. Anyway, the baby died, and Zofia buried it.

We were in shock, and we didn't even have time to cry about it, because I got very sick. First of all, I was bleeding a lot. All right, I had a lot of absorbent cotton, that was good. But later, you have to bury it somewhere, so Zofia and Srulek went down at night and buried it outside. I was torn so badly when the baby came out, it was burning, terrible. I just couldn't take it. Zofia brewed a herb, like a tea, to make compresses, and she brought it up to the hayloft. Srulek put compresses on all the time, and it healed like this. It was never sewn together. When I came to Canada years after, the doctor in Montreal said he doesn't have to do anything, it's okay.

After a few days, Ludwig said he just came from the village, people are saying the Germans are going to look for Jews again. Srulek said we have to hide under the straw and our down comforter had to be taken downstairs, they shouldn't see anything. It was dark up there, it was at night. Srulek wanted to lie down, and he didn't know that I sat up at the same time. With his elbow, he went hard right into my breast—oh! I was so sick, maybe also from how much blood I lost—who knows why—but I was already dying. Dying. Everything was just stopped, numb. Srulek touched me everywhere: my feet, my fingers, my body. I didn't feel anything—all the body was dead already—my senses, I had, that's all, I could see, I could hear, I couldn't move.

Zofia said, "Srulek, she's dying, you could see she is dying." Srulek was hanging over me, and he was crying. Zofia said, "Srulek, if she's strong, if she's got a strong heart, one thing we could do. Frania told me you have alcohol. Give it to me. I have pepper I'm going to chop up, and together with the alcohol, this is going to burn through her fever. If she is strong enough, she'll sleep two days, but she'll live. She is dying anyway, we have to take that chance."

So they gave it to me to drink, and I didn't feel—to me it was just like I would drink water. I slept three days. Srulek was over me always, listening if I'm breathing. As long as I breathed, he let me alone. After that, when I woke up, I felt already everything, but I was weak. I was past the crisis. Everything burned through, like Zofia said.

Then my breast started to get boils, and the pains were so terrible that I would bite my finger through to blood. I couldn't cry. I couldn't yell. I couldn't scream. You couldn't go to a drugstore to buy something. Zofia said that she has a leaf, if you put this leaf on the boils, it heals. So what did I have to risk? I used the leaf, but it ate away a piece of my skin. It made a hole. I still have a mark there from that leaf. I was in pain for three months. And after that, all these boils burst, and the pus was just running out. After the war, I went to a doctor and when he asked me about my history, I told him about this, and he said it's unbelievable. To have a child born when you don't know what to do, and not to have an infection? And after this infection in my breast, to live? This is unbelievable.

We lived in that barn the whole winter. In the spring, we finally came down into the house.

We wanted a good watchdog, if somebody comes suddenly, we should have a warning. So we gave sixty złotys to Ludwig, and Srulek told him to go into town to Yankel Roit. He had terrific dogs. This was the same Yankel Roit that gave us the room for the dancing—years before, when we first met. Of course, Yankel went with the deportation, but we were sure somebody took over his house and has his dogs. He had such well-trained dogs that you've never seen in your life. Ludwig went into Pińczów, and he bought a black dog. He was beautiful. He had above his eyes two gold-colored dots, so we gave him a name, Kropka, which means *dot* in Polish.

Kropka saved our life many, many times. I'm telling you, it was amazing how this dog was smart. Kropka knew that he has to watch us. He knew that we come out only at night. He knew that in the daytime, Ludwig and Zofia locked the door and went to work in the field. We were left inside. He had outside a doghouse, he was sitting on top, like a prince. I would look at him through the window, and he would look back at me and wag his tail, flirting with me. When it came night—let's say, around eleven—we went out a little bit to have some fresh air, to stretch our legs. So we took Kropka with us on a rope—the rope must have been two, three hundred feet long—and he ran in the field before us because a mile away, he could smell already if somebody was coming. And he would start to bark and come running and pull us back to the house. You've never seen such a smart dog.

All day we stayed in the house. Srulek was sitting at the window, and the dog was outside watching. The first little while we were there, Srulek slept on the floor for a few hours at night, but later, he was sitting at the window to watch because he was afraid the dog could fall asleep. And when he finally slept, he would sleep beside the little boy, Maniek, on a bag of straw.

They had there an oven for wood. There was a little opening where Zofia baked her own bread every two weeks, twice a month. That oven was the whole wall up to the ceiling, and then there was a little opening on top, a yard by a yard. I put a little sack there, filled with straw. That was my bedroom. I never felt so good as when I went there at night, even though I couldn't stretch. Ludwig and Zofia had their bed almost right underneath, so—you know—everything, I saw and everything, I heard. Well, how could you help it? When I stretched my legs, they would stick out, and he would yell at me because it was almost in their bed. But I was afraid that my legs would be so cramped, I wouldn't be able to stretch anymore. After all, we were there twenty-eight months. It's not a day, twenty-eight months.

On the side of the stove, near the floor, was a small door that went to a little cellar. It was exactly as big as where I was sleeping—a yard by a yard. Zofia kept potatoes there. Srulek made two little chairs—we put the potatoes to the side—and the minute we thought somebody's coming, we opened that little door and slid down. My knees were always bleeding, and Srulek's trousers had one patch on top of the other from sliding down to that little cellar. Usually, the little boy, Maniek, or Ludwig had to run fast and close it. But later, Srulek made two handles on the bottom. He pulled it to himself and closed it right away. We could sometimes sit there for hours—because, once in a while, farmers came to visit on a Sunday. If they came suddenly, we had to run to the cellar, but if we knew that they're coming, we went into the barn and up to that little hayloft because there we could be more comfortable than the cellar, where you couldn't even cough. It was very hard to sit there, especially in the cold wintertime, and in the summertime, it was very stuffy—so like this, it wasn't good, and like that, it wasn't good. But what could you do? Sometimes they came, the farmers, they sat for hours with their stories that weren't worth a single cent—but we had to sit there in hiding and listen.

## SRULEK

Ludwig was thirty-six years old when we came to him. Five feet, eight inches tall, thin, a face with no expression at all. Only when he ate, he smiled. He never laughed with his whole heart. When he got up in the morning, right away he started to yell at his wife. I was sitting at the table, still awake from a whole night of watching out the window, and I looked at him with wonder: *What kind of people are in this world?* He started to yell at Zofia to get up right away. And if she didn't, he threw a wooden shoe at her. She got up, and right away, she would take her kerchief and she would cover her mouth—that meant she was mad.

Every morning, Zofia jumped down from bed and made, right away, potatoes with borscht. When Ludwig was eating, he was sitting at the table with a spoon, looking straight into the plate, not taking away his eyes for a second, and sweat came on his face and ran down from his face right into the plate, and he still didn't move until he finished. And then he started to smile. Then he walked over to us—we were looking out like dogs from the hiding place in the cellar—he looked down at us and asked, "Would you like a little potatoes?"

"Yes."

"Would you like a little bit more?"

He was always teasing: "What is a Jew? A Jew is nothing. They're not human. Everybody can kill them. I can't kill a dog, but if I'll kill you, I can always get some money for you. It's nothing." We are nothings.

Ludwig used to come back from working in the fields at six or seven o'clock at night, he would sit down at the table, put his head in his hands, and sit—not moving, not talking, waiting for Zofia to make supper. It was usually noodles, and it had to be the right amount. He always put his spoon into the plate and if the spoon stood up in the noodles and didn't fall, he was happy. He ate the same way as in the morning—when he finished, he smiled.

Later, he used to whittle wood for whatever he needed around the farm, like sticks in the garden for a fence. He used to show off what he made and told me that a Jew cannot make that. So I made a bin you put corn into for the chickens to eat. He didn't want to believe it—he was so mad. He was scared to put it out into the yard because people would wonder when he had the time to do that. Also, he was spitting on the floor, and that was disgusting, so I made a wooden spittoon for him. I hollowed out a piece of wood with four legs, and I put sand in it, and he had it near his bed.

Sometimes he would come from the market with a newspaper. I was anxious to read it, but he kept the paper in his hands, not reading, till he sat down to eat. He hardly could read, and what he read, he didn't understand. After an hour, he just threw it to me, like to a dog. He asked me always, "Now tell me what they're writing." The truth is, I only told him about what they were writing that was good for me: that the Russians were winning, no matter what was happening really. The paper was German controlled and never wrote that the Russians were leading. But my main point was, I wanted him to believe the Russians are always nearer and nearer.

Sundays, the farmers sometimes used to come together at Ludwig's, and they used to say, "Hey, Ludwig, you know the politics the best, tell us." So he used to repeat like a gramophone what I told him. He became for them the smartest in the village. Once, he was telling them about politics, and I heard how the farmers said, "Oh, Churchill says it's a good thing the Germans and the Russians should hit each other, and we will come in the middle, hit them both, and take Poland back." Sometimes what they talked about wasn't so funny. Some of them said the only good thing Hitler did is kill the Jews, that's the first thing. They talked like this: "There was a Jew with a corner grocery store. I liked to buy from him because he always asked me about how my cows are, my chickens, how's my wife. And I brought him some onions, beans. He was a nice Jew. They shouldn't kill him. The other Jews, I wouldn't care they killed, but him, they should leave." Only that Jew they shouldn't kill because he was asking about his cow and his wife. Another farmer said, "Oh, what are you talking? It's the best thing that Hitler kills all the Jews. They killed Jesus Christ. They should all be killed."

---

A few days into the filming, we're on a little hill that overlooks the town of Pińczów. It's a spot my parents used to go to when they were first dating. Seeing the two of them there transforms them in my eyes into the young lovers they once were. I feel privileged, blessed, to see my mom and dad in a way that most children never do. There is a break in the filming, and my parents are sitting, holding hands. I'm about ten yards away, just watching them. They look at me with tenderness and love, quietly talking to each other about how nice I look. They don't know that I can hear them, that the wind is blowing their words my way. I feel a hundred and fifty years old and five years old at the same time. It's a magical place. It has been raining all day, but when we get to the hill to start filming, the sun comes out. They seem to bring miracles on themselves, my mother and father. They're quite a team.

# ELEVEN

I'M ON A MISSION. I want to finish the book, so I do as much taping as my parents will let me—and they are willing to do it, even when they're tired. For them, making the documentary film and talking into the tape recorder, sharing their story, is a way to make meaningful the senseless murder of their family, their friends, an entire generation of their people. For me, it feels somehow redeeming to help them to do that, a relief that what was once a total lie, this imaginary book, is now becoming real.

### FRANIA

Shaindel was sending us letters every week with Juzia, and she sent us newspapers to read and books. And money. Ludwig knew we haven't got all the money with us. That would be dangerous, who knew what he could be capable of doing? All he knew is that the money comes from Warsaw, from my sisters.

### SRULEK

We gave Ludwig money—but slowly. We got scared that if he will know we have money with us, he will kill us. Just the same, I was prepared because I had a hunting knife with me. Ludwig used to buy leaves of tobacco, and I sharpened this knife, very sharp. At night I would cut tobacco from the leaves—for him and for me—for the next day. I was always thinking, maybe Ludwig will want to kill us, but I won't let him, I'll kill him first. I always had my knife with me. We were living from minute to minute.

Once, we heard him talking to his wife: He is sick and tired of the Jews. He has sharp axes. He will cut off our heads and show them to the Germans—and for that, he would get two kilograms of sugar. In the morning, he started to walk around and look for his axes, but the axes were hidden. Every night, Frania hid them in a new place because she got scared that when he comes home at night, he'll cut our heads off. He was cursing, looking for his axes and cursing. He couldn't talk good Polish, so he couldn't even swear with the right pronunciation. Finally he would find them, sometimes under a cushion, or in the stable, just where he wouldn't have it handy. He took the axes, his saw, and went to the woods to work. When he walked out, we could breathe a little bit easier.

I was looking for ways to show him I would not go so easy, that I'm stronger than he thinks I am. The farmers were ordered to cut down trees and bring them to the Germans, but they stole a little bit for themselves too, to have wood for the winter. Ludwig had a lot of those cut-down trees in his yard. One time, Zofia told Ludwig that she heard the man who looks after the forest is going to every farmer to see how many trees were stolen. So we had to hide those trees. A tree has a thin side and a thick side, and he told me to go to the thin side because he was considering himself very strong. I picked up my side, but he couldn't pick up his. I told him that he is not so strong, like I am. I said let him go to the thin side, and I'll go by myself to the thick side. I picked up the thick side better than him. I did it special with all my strength to show him that I'm stronger than him. After that, he looked at me differently.

## FRANIA

Ludwig told us once a story. I don't know if it's true, but Srulek said that he could believe it because Ludwig was so cold-blooded—somebody who could kill and not even give a wink with an eye, such a man he was. Ludwig told us that once he worked in a factory in Warsaw where there were big ovens. There was a man working with them they didn't like, so during the night, they threw him inside that oven and burned him alive. Srulek said he could believe it—such a type he was, Ludwig.

## SRULEK

One time, Ludwig came in the house, busting with laughter—so I knew that something is not right. He said he was at the Pińczów market, and the Germans caught a Jew named Herschkowic. I knew him. Ludwig said the Jew was begging the Germans not to kill him, and they asked him to show where he was hiding his money. After he showed it to them, they killed him anyway. Ludwig thought it was funny: "That stupid Jew! Why did he show where the money is?"

I said, "You know what, Ludwig? If Gestapo comes in here, I'm not going to beg. I will be on top of him with my knife." I grabbed Ludwig with all my power, I nearly squeezed him. I said, "Just like this, I'm going to do it. I'm going to kill right away. Before he takes out his revolver, I'll be on him with my knife."

I wanted him to be not just scared of the Germans, I wanted him also to be scared of me. So I wrote a letter to Shaindel that she should write back to me a letter in Polish, saying that since she knows I am secretly an officer in the Polish underground, I should write down who is doing bad things to the Poles and the Jews, and if I need a revolver, she will send it to me. You see, I wanted that letter to fall into Ludwig's hand. Shaindel wrote me such a letter, and I pretended I forgot it and left it on the table when I went to the cellar. He took the letter and read it. I was afraid he wouldn't understand it. But Shaindel wrote it with very simple words. The next day, when he got up, he told me that he is surprised. He didn't understand why I didn't tell him. I said that it is a secret and he has to shut up about it. He got scared and treated us better.

When Ludwig and his wife were good to each other, it was very bad for us. At the beginning, when they started to fight between themselves, we got scared, and I tried to make peace between them. But it turned out, whenever they fought, each was good to us, each gave us things to eat. She had a babushka over her head, and when she put it over her mouth, we knew that they were mad at each other. And then they both were good to us: when it was time to eat, they gave us the first portion—everything the best. When they were good to each other, they forgot us and didn't give us to eat. They just made us miserable. How? Everything we did wasn't good, and they're afraid that over us, they're going to be killed. And they made us miserable—that's all, period.

## FRANIA

They were fighting over things. It was ridiculous, a comedy. You could make theater out of it. For example, he would say to her that she came with no dowry. You see, for them to have a decent plate, or just a spoon, was a fortune. When I brought there some pillows and that down comforter, this was like getting, I don't know, a treasure.

Ludwig said to Zofia, "You came to me with what? With a bastard and with a naked behind." When he took her in, she already had Maniek.

So she said, "What? You're going to tell me that I came with nothing? I brought here the *cebzik*."

There wasn't a bathroom to wash. Where did you wash? There was a barrel, and this was called a *cebzik*. It was made from wood, and all around it was iron, holding it—thirty inches around, with two handles. And in this, you wash the dishes. In this, you wash yourself. Took me time to get used to it, but listen, I wanted to be clean, I *had to* get used to it. Ludwig washed in that. I washed my body, my hair. Later, we washed the dishes. Everything was in that *cebzik*. All of us, all five of us. When Ludwig went to wash himself, he took his two hands with a little bit of water, threw it on his face, and that's it—washed.

Zofia said, "I came with nothing?! I brought you that *cebzik*. And I brought two spoons! How would you eat if you wouldn't have the two spoons I brought you? And what do you think to who are you praying? To my picture! This picture of the Virgin Maria is my picture!" Honestly, this picture, you couldn't even see if there's a Maria there—it was all faded away. She said, "How could you pray if you didn't have my picture!"

So he didn't know what to answer because she really did bring the *cebzik*, and she brought the picture and the two spoons.

But he said, "I gave you the house! You would have nothing over your head if I didn't have this house. Where would you be?"

That house, the floors weren't made of wood—the richer ones, they had it—but the majority of the farmers around Pińczów, nobody had it. There was just earth. They were bringing in everything from the yard, so I swept with a broom they had. And the broom wasn't a broom like you have here, but it was made by themselves. I swept a little bit that earth because always it was filthy. I took some yellow sand—they were buying it or getting it, I don't know from where—and I spread it around a little bit so it looked a little nice.

## SRULEK

Zofia was a very small woman, very hardworking. And she was a woman of good nature. If we wanted something, we always asked her when Ludwig wasn't there. She suffered a lot, Ludwig treated her very badly. We always had pity for her. Ludwig hit her once in the mouth—with his foot. She was passing him down the hay, and she didn't do it right, he didn't catch it. So he came up to her and hit her with a foot to the mouth and made a swollen mouth. He was a sadist. He told me once that he got a dog and put a rope to his neck, put him down in the well, and he was pulling him up and down in the well till he was dead. Such a sadist was he.

He was cruel to Maniek. He wasn't really his son, so he used to kick him around. At nighttime, I was the one who taught Maniek how to read and how to write. The boy liked me very much—and Ludwig treated him always very rough. Maniek was very sweet and very good and very understanding. He was told by his mother that if somebody asked him anything, not to say a word, because if he will say something, Mr. and Mrs. Rubinek will get killed. He didn't want that, so he kept his mouth shut and never opened it for anybody, not even his friends. He was very smart and reliable.

## FRANIA

One day, Ludwig and Zofia were away in town. Srulek wanted to have a little sleep, so he said to the boy, "Maniek, you're going out to play, but if you'll see somebody's coming, wake me up because now I need to sleep a little bit. Frania is going to do the washing, so she is going to be busy." He said all right.

All of a sudden, I go to the window just to give a look, and I see Maniek waves with his hand, he was only seven years old—and he kept his hand low. I didn't know what he meant, so I woke up Srulek. I said, "Something is wrong—Maniek is making a sign."

Srulek said, "I think if Maniek is not running, it's probably nothing, but I don't know. Let's go first to the cellar."

We ran into that little cellar, and sure enough, a woman came, she was looking for somebody.

Later, when she left, Maniek said, "You see, I am not stupid. I saw her coming. I know she is coming to visit my parents. If I would run, she will think right away *Oh, Maniek is running? Somebody is there, hidden.*"

We ate only black bread without butter, with nothing, because every piece of butter Zofia made, she ran to Pińczów to sell it. They went out in the field, and every day, Srulek was watching at the window, and I did everything in the house: the ironing and washing. The only thing I couldn't do is cook, because the neighbors would see smoke come out of the chimney. Ludwig and Zofia are working in the field—so who's inside? I wrote to Shaindel that maybe she'll speak to Juzia: if she could only buy something for us when she goes to the market. I was just very weak. We needed some butter, some fat. We ate dry bread, two weeks old. Milk, we didn't have much either, because they had to give it away for the contribution the Germans demanded. Potatoes, we had a bit.

Ludwig was raising chickens and rabbits. When the little chicks came out of the eggs, me and Srulek, we were helping them go out of the shells. And Ludwig—I told you, he was such a man that you could write a book about him—when he killed the chickens, if I wouldn't have seen him do it, I would eat. But, you know, I raised those chickens from little chicks. You know how he killed them? The chickens were running outside in the yard, and he took a piece of wood, and with such a sadism, he said, "Which chicken would you like to have for Sunday?" And he threw that piece of wood into the chicken so hard, he killed it, just like that. We couldn't eat it. We never ate chicken there because we raised them. The rabbits, the same thing. The way he killed a rabbit once, I thought I'd die. We couldn't eat any meat there.

So we had to have something. We went to the fields at night, and we took some carrots, beets—but this was only in the summertime. In the wintertime, we had nothing, just the dry bread. Zofia cooked potatoes and a white borscht—that's all. We gave them money, so she bought some flour, and she made noodles. But she made it with ham fat, and we couldn't eat this. So I had to have a little butter with a little onion to fry with the potatoes or something. So that's why we wrote a letter to Shaindel: maybe she'll speak to Juzia to buy us some butter, a little cheese. You know, the farmers made such a beautiful cottage cheese there, not like here.

Anyway, Shaindel spoke to Juzia and she said yes. Imagine, she was buying for us, and she threw it down for us in that little cellar so that Ludwig shouldn't see. Her own brother. She knew he is not eating much himself, but she said that he's got the fresh air and is eating some meat, he's all right. So she brought cheese, and she brought us sugar and a lot of butter, and she was even buying for us eggs.

Srulek said, "What do we need the eggs for? How are you going to cook them? The smoke will go out the chimney, and they will know."

I said, "Don't worry." You know, when you are in trouble, you think faster. I made scrambled eggs like you never ate in your life. What did I do? They didn't have any electricity, so when I had to do the ironing, I took the hot coals left over from the fire and put it all into the iron, and the iron got hot. Well, when we were alone in the house, I didn't even have the coals, because in the summertime, when Zofia went to the field, she put some water there to put it out. So I took a little bit of the charcoal that was left and put on just a drop of kerosene we used for the little lamp that we have at night, and I started to make the fire. I took that iron—I was shaking a little bit, blowing, blowing the charcoal till it got all good and red—then I took a tiny little pot and put it right on the iron. And I made scrambled eggs with fried onions and the black bread Zofia baked, with so much butter and cheese. I'm telling you, a feast.

Maniek always ate with us. Whatever we had, we shared with him because he was so thin, so pale. He was so afraid of Ludwig's shadow—he was right away in a corner. He didn't know, but he felt that this is not his father. So I knew that I could trust him. He knew everything that is going on, but he didn't tell his mother. I never saw such a smart child in my life. I told Maniek when we would be eating, so when Ludwig and Zofia went to the field, Maniek went with them to help, but he would say he has to go back to the toilet. Zofia said, "What do you mean, you're going to the toilet? You have the field here—that's your toilet." We didn't even have a toilet—you went outside in a corner, where Ludwig threw out all the things from the stable, there you went, that's it. So Maniek always had an excuse, he wants to go home—because he knew that we are going to eat. He hardly even ate with them. Zofia would say, "What's the matter with you—you're not eating?"

"I'm not hungry." He knew if he is going to fill his stomach with potatoes, he won't be able later to eat his scrambled eggs that I gave him, with the butter, with so much cheese.

I said once, "Maniek, you've got to eat a little bit because your mother will suspect something." He wasn't Ludwig's child, so he was very close to us. Maniek felt that for us, he would give away his life. He saved our lives once.

### SRULEK

Just once?

### FRANIA

All right, but this time was a miracle. It was one month before the war ended. We were eating, and suddenly the dog started to bark. Maniek went right away to put his ear at the door. "You better hide," he said. "Fast." And we went into that little cellar. In a split of a second we were there.

### SRULEK

And when I closed the cellar door, they opened the front door. Then we heard German talking, and we thought, *This is the end now.* We were frozen, both of us.

### FRANIA

We heard the voices of two German soldiers talking to the Banias, who didn't understand what they were saying in German at all. We understood right away: they said they're going to sleep here tonight. *That's it*, I thought. We survived two years, and this is the end now.

Then we heard Zofia take some straw and right away put it down by our little cellar door for Maniek to sleep there. Because she was afraid that if a soldier will lie there to sleep, he's going to hear us breathing. It's impossible he should not hear, that little door, it was almost open all around the edges. So she put Maniek there. And on the other side of him, she put some straw for the two soldiers.

### SRULEK

It was hard for me. You see, I had a cough, from smoking. I put my fist in my mouth to stop myself, and then I told Frania, "If I'll faint sitting like this because I can't breathe, just you be quiet."

### FRANIA

They lay down to sleep. It must have been eight o'clock. And Maniek started to cry, to cough. Every ten minutes, that boy was crying and coughing. And the Germans, they were so mad. What are they going to do? Shoot him?

### SRULEK

Zofia was going to him, "Maniek, what's the matter? Be quiet. Go to sleep." She didn't understand what he's doing.

### FRANIA

And we did?

### SRULEK

In the morning, the soldiers left. Maniek said, "You don't understand a thing. I did it so you could cough there, in the cellar. To save your life."

### FRANIA

You're going to tell me this is not a miracle? This is a miracle of miracles.

# TWELVE

WE'VE BEEN FILMING FOR A WEEK. As Vic sets up a shot, my mom and dad and I decide to wait in the van, the air conditioner on. It's a particularly hot August afternoon. I have not yet told them that Kate and I are most likely finished. They have not asked about her—not once. The subject of Kate hasn't come up at all since the night they came backstage after the play.

My dad is holding a large hardcover book that has a beautiful front cover drawing of the medieval walled city of Pińczów. Its title is *Ilustrowana Historia Pińczowa*—which means Illustrated History of Pińczów. He's got two slips of paper, and after he inserts them as markers into two sections of the book, he gets out of the van and with a determined look on his face, heads toward Agnieszka, standing a little way off, as usual, writing in her little red book.

I hurry to follow him out of the van and reach to put my hand on his shoulder. "Let me do it."

He shrugs off my hand. "No, no, no. This is my problem and my solution. Don't worry—I will not start a new cold war."

"You might. Please let me do it."

My mom has been watching us. She calls to him, "Loz im"—Yiddish for "let him"—which is all it takes for my dad to hand over the book.

"Fine," he says. "Take. But tell her—"

"I will," I say, interrupting him, convinced—wrongly, it turns out—that I know exactly how to handle this.

I walk over to Agnieszka and stand in front of her, waiting for her to look up from writing in her book. She doesn't.

"Agnieszka."

"One moment," she says, finishing what she's writing before looking up at me. "Yes?"

"My parents got this as a gift from the provincial governor. His office, anyway. Please return it." I hold out the book. She takes it.

"What is the problem?"

"My father wanted to hand it back to the governor personally, but I'm trying to avoid an international incident." I chuckle at my own wit, but she doesn't join in, taking me seriously, as she does most everything. She glances over toward my father, who is now studiously looking in another direction.

"*Ilustrowana Historia Pińczowa*. History of town of Pińczów with pictures. I do not understand why—"

"My father read it. He's sure the governor didn't read it, or he wouldn't have given it as a gift."

Agnieszka turns a few pages of the book. "Why not? It is beautiful."

"My father marked two passages. The reasons will be very clear. Just ... please return it."

She studies me for a moment. We've had a few discussions, and we've enjoyed them. "You do not wish to talk about?"

I've been waiting for this question. I'm ready for her. In fact, I'm way ready.

"Agnieszka, you report every conversation to the Ministry, and I don't want to be taken out of context. You know what I'm talking about."

"No." But I know she does.

"You would report what I say without including the larger subject of why I said it."

"I would not do this." She does not sound sure of herself.

I pounce. "Oh, you already did it. You listened to a private conversation my father had with our crew. I was there. About empty shelves and long lineups at the Pewex state store. My father said it's because so much stuff is sent to Russia. What you reported to the Ministry of Culture..."—I take a letter out of my pocket—"persuaded them to send an official letter, this one, to our documentary TV executives in Toronto, who pretty much told us to shut the fuck up about Russian Polish politics because you said my father described Russia's relationship with Poland by using the word *rape*."

She's quick and suddenly quite sure of herself. "I was not only Polish citizen who heard your father say this word. He was not quiet."

I was not expecting her to be this aggressive. "I don't—"

She interrupts me. "There was witness, so I must report. Three years ago, we have here martial law. You know about this?"

"Yes, I—"

Interrupting me again and gaining ground, she says, "To suppress opposition to government, to stop Solidarity movement. My father was mathematics professor. Not anymore. Four years ago, he participate in demonstration to free political prisoners and to support Solidarity. Many arrested, some killed. My father arrested, and he lose his job."

"I'm sorry your—"

Third interruption, and very sure of herself now: "If your father is critical of the Polish People's Republic, if other Polish citizens hear it also, it is my job to report to Ministry. If not, I lose my job, and today I am only support for my family. The only support. You understand?"

Yeah, I understand. I'm properly rebuked. I regroup. "Agnieszka, do you know about the history of the Jews here?"

She's thrown by this new angle. "Jews in Poland? Maybe two, three hundred years? My degree is in media and communications, not history."

"It's a thousand years," I tell her offhandedly, as if it's a known fact. "But I mean here, in Pińczów."

She has no idea where this is headed. Good. "Oh. Pińczów?" She looks around, stupidly, as if she can locate the answer somewhere nearby. "No. I don't know this hist—"

My turn to interrupt: "Since the fifteenth century, half the population here in Pińczów were Jews, until October first 1942, the day the Nazis began roundups for extermination."

"A tragedy. I am first aware of—"

I interrupt a second time: "In this 'History of Pińczów' book, my father says there are only two references to the Jews, who lived here for four hundred years." I take the book out of her hands and open it to a place my father marked with a slip of paper. "Here, this paragraph talks about an onion-smelling, unhealthy segment of the population, Jews, who lived secretively and apart, often cheated local Christians, and caused the spread of disease in the community. And ..." I open to the second place my father marked. "This sentence. Here." I thrust the book back at her.

Agnieszka, a bit nervous now, hesitantly reads the Polish: "*Jesienią czterdziestego drugiego roku wszyscy Żydzi w Pińczowie zniknęli z niewiadomych przyczyn.*" She takes a moment as she digests this, then translates: "In autumn 1942, all Jews in Pińczów disappear ... for unknown reason."

She looks at me blandly, like ... so? Which lights a fire under me.

"Unknown reason. *Unknown?!*"

"Ah," she says, trying to have a reasonable discussion. "You are saying reason is, in fact, known."

"*Genocide* is the reason! Everybody on the planet knows the reason! The reason is, they were taken to concentration camps and murdered!"

Agnieszka, a little frightened by my vehemence, moves a step back away from me. She glances toward my father, who is now openly watching us.

"I see," she says, trying for composure. "Of course." She looks down at the book, frowning. "I don't know what makes possible this mistake."

"Mistake!? They're *lies*! Plain and simple!"

She takes a moment. She keeps her voice even. "During this short time with your family, I see how complicated is our history, yours and mine. Not plain. Not simple. Be careful making your film. You are here two weeks only. Be careful your opinion about our story is not like chicken who looks out through crack in barn door and says to other chickens, 'The universe is a field with a cow.'"

She's taken me off my stride. I regroup. "Lemme ask you something. Antisemitism. You think that's like from a dark period of Polish history?"

She wants to agree with anything I say now. "Dark, yes. A dark and terrible time in Poland's past."

"Past? Oh, so fear and hatred of Jews, you say is what—a phenomenon of pre-Socialist Poland? Is that it?"

She still tries for some kind of restraint, as if we're two academics discussing a paper. "I believe that before Socialist Republic, Catholic Church influence was very strong, definitely, and—"

My third interruption is loud: "Take a good look at who published that book! And the date!"

She is stunned by my rage and takes a further step away from me. She glances at my father, who is now hurrying toward us.

Agnieszka looks quickly through the book and finds what I want her to find. "I see," she says. "University of Kraków, 1985."

"This book was published *last year*! In your fucking Polish People's Republic!"

My father arrives, a bit out of breath. "Everybody relax. No reason for yelling." He puts his hand on my shoulder. "Agnieszka didn't give us the book, she didn't write the book, and she'll take the book back to the governor and tell him why. Correct, Agnieszka?"

Agnieszka nods, too nervous to say anything aloud. My father takes me by the arm and walks me away from her.

I'm humiliated, embarrassed. "Sorry," I mumble to him and then turn back to Agnieszka. "*Przepraszam!*" One of the few things I know how to say in Polish: I'm sorry. I know how to swear in Polish too, but that doesn't seem appropriate at the moment. Agnieszka just watches my father lead me away.

"I don't know what happened to me."

He's got his arm around me now. "Poland. Poland happened to you."

# THIRTEEN

WE ARE ONLY TWO DAYS AWAY FROM THE REUNION. After that, we are going back to Canada. I spend every spare moment working on the transcripts. I feel I have to complete a first draft by the time I go home. I worry that once I'm back, because of work distractions and the fact that my parents live two hundred miles away, I may not finish it. I decided to call the book So Many Miracles, the phrase my mother always used to describe their survival.

### SRULEK

We had to worry about the Germans coming, but even more, we were worried that a Polish neighbor will find out we are hiding there and betray us. Half a mile away, lived a very nosy woman, Dzubinska, a typical peasant woman: big and fat and walked fast. And always, when she was talking, she kept her hands under her apron, with her thumbs under her fingers so that way nobody could give her the evil eye. Superstitious. Always, she came in suddenly. She wanted to see what Ludwig and Zofia are eating. No matter how suddenly she came, I always saw her before. We had to hide everything right away when she came in—the meat, the noodles—because none of the farmers around could afford those things.

When Ludwig and Zofia went Sunday to church, neighbors used to come near the windows to look in. I saw them coming, the dog used to warn me. I always was watching, not to miss one single minute. It happened sometimes, sitting at the table and eating, you missed with your eyes to look out, or the dog fell asleep. And suddenly you hear the door opening and the dog gave out with a sudden bark. We had two seconds to jump into the hiding place, but we did it.

Not far from us was living a Polish widow. She was also hiding a Jew. When Zofia went to borrow something from her, she saw him and she came back and told us. That widow was such a Cossack, she wasn't scared of anybody. She was so fierce that she could kill even a policeman. Zofia knew he was a Jew when she saw him because she recognized him: his grandfather had a grocery store that they used to go to. The widow knew that Zofia wouldn't talk because she assumed that Ludwig also has somebody hidden. People didn't know for sure, but they talked vaguely. The widow did it for money, and she thought the Jew was going to marry her. He was living quite a while with her after the war. But he couldn't marry her, he just couldn't. After the war, he went away with her, and they opened a store near the German border. But he left her later with the store and the money, and he went to Israel.

## FRANIA

In the village, people were already talking that maybe Ludwig and Zofia are hiding somebody. They saw that Ludwig and Zofia dressed a little better. If they were eating noodles, that was a luxury, so if somebody was coming, everything was right away thrown in the oven, those things could give us away. We were watching out for this, but it's hard, you know. It's hard. We reminded them that before we came, they didn't have even a piece of bread, so if they show the neighbors that they are better off, they'll suspect. But the farmers around, they smelled it: something is different. They were talking that Ludwig is better off than he was before, you know, they're suspecting already. Well, that's why one farmer gave away the other. Jealousy.

## SRULEK

One farmer came into the house in the middle of the week and saw that Ludwig ate meat. He said, "Oh, Ludwig, did you get rich? In the middle of the week, you're eating meat? We're eating meat only on Sunday. Oh, something is going on here." They were suspicious, but they weren't sure.

## FRANIA

One night, Ludwig came home and said they're talking in the village that tonight the Germans are going to come to farms around here to look for Jews. The Germans would find the little cellar right away. We didn't have anything else prepared. Where could we hide? Srulek said, "You know what, we're going to go into the oven." Listen, what can you do? You survive. Srulek went in easily, but my hips, you know I have trouble with my hips. I couldn't get in, I was too wide. Srulek said, "If you cannot get in, it's no use. I'll go watch outside with the dog, and if he will start to bark, I will know the Germans are coming on the other side of the hill, and we'll still have enough time to run into the woods on the other side of the field. They're not going to look there, they're going to look just if there's a hiding place inside the house." Right away, Ludwig crossed himself, he was so scared.

It was in the wintertime, and it must have been thirty below outside. Srulek didn't let me go outside with him because I had so much migraine, and I was so sick all the time. He wanted me to go up to my place over the oven, where I could relax a little bit. Srulek went out, but he came back in every fifteen minutes to warm up a little bit. Ludwig and Zofia went to sleep. Then I didn't see him, I didn't see him. I was so worried, I woke up Zofia. "Srulek didn't come back. He wasn't here for an hour already." She went out and she saw that he is all frozen—but he was already waking up, coming to his senses. He fell asleep from the cold, and the dog—he was so smart, this dog—saw that he's already almost dead, so he started to rub him and lick him and warm him. And he woke him up, the dog. And if not the dog, he would have frozen to death outside. Imagine.

Anyway, that night, the Germans didn't even come. Srulek said we have to make something so we can quickly hide if the dog is barking and we know that Germans are coming. You know what he made? The Germans came and they could never know that we're there. He made a hole, a bunker, under the cow. There is a stable, yes? And there was the cow, and you know what she's doing? She's making all the time, it's always full of manure. Srulek cleaned this away, and he made a hole right under the cow, and he made again that same kind of cover he made for the bunker in Pińczów. The cow was doing her business on this place, but we knew how to find it: exactly where the cow had the tail, we took off the cover, and we could slide down. But the smell, you could die. I'm telling you, if I would have to sit there two hours, I would die. It's a good thing we didn't sit more than half an hour. One time, we went down there, and standing on top of us was a Gestapo with a dog. But under all the manure, even the dog didn't know we were there.

## SRULEK

We never thought what's going to be later, right now was everything. I want to be alive today. I was exact like a fly on the table when I touch with my finger and the fly runs away and stands somewhere else—the fly doesn't think what's going to be later. Events came so fast, one after another, you found yourself thinking the opposite to what you were thinking yesterday.

I kept a diary, but Ludwig told me, if I'm going to keep writing, he will throw me out because if something happens, the Germans will grab it and see how long I was there. I had to throw it away. But I remember everything. What did I do every day? I thought. I absorbed how it happens people can become animals. It always bothered me that in Jewish law, it is not allowed when you get up in the morning to right away go and eat. When you're taking your feet down from the bed, right away you have to prepare yourself with a little bit of water to wash your fingers and your eyes, and you have to say a prayer right away. After that, you can sit down at the table to eat breakfast. That stuck with me, and I couldn't understand why you have to do all that. If you're hungry, why can't you eat before?

You see, Ludwig, five o'clock in the morning when he opened his eyes and sat up, right away he yelled at his wife, "Eat! I want to eat! I want to eat!" And she had to jump down right away. If not, he was so mad, he would hit her. At that time, the thought came to me about the difference between an animal and a human being. The Jewish law says that when you get up in the morning, you're like any animal, no different. An animal runs right away to eat, but a human being has to learn how to keep himself back, not say, "I want it now, and I have to get it right now." On account of that, I understood, when I saw Ludwig, if he would wash himself, make a prayer—doesn't matter, he doesn't have to make a prayer, just wash himself—he would come back to the stage of being a human being, he wouldn't be like an animal. When I was at Ludwig's hidden, I understood for the first time why the ancient people made that law: to turn them into human beings.

I also understood that even a fly wants to live. I can tell you, in the summertime, when Ludwig and Zofia went to church and closed the door—it was made from a few boards put together, it wasn't an elegant door—and the sun shined in between the cracks, I stood there, and I saw flies coming in and out, in and out, freely. You know what that means, that word *free?* I was talking to myself: "Imagine. That fly doesn't know anything, but it can go out and in, nobody looks at it, nobody bothers it, it has a right to live." And I was jealous. Why can't I be a fly and also walk back and forth on the free world and be able to see the sun, like any animal? I was jealous of the chickens outside, running around picking from the earth freely, nobody bothered them. Only me, a human being, I couldn't go out and breathe, free.

# FOURTEEN

VIC FILMS MY MOTHER AND FATHER as they sit side by side under a monument on the little hill overlooking Pińczów.

"Things happened in such a way," my mother says, "that we were meant to survive. Not because we were special, or we're smarter or better, or because God looked down on us, but for reasons you could never imagine. It was just luck, whoever survived. Plain luck."

"Luck?" my father says. "Who knows. I am the only one who lived in the family. Eight brothers and sisters, parents, grandparents."

They're silent. Nobody knows what to do or say next. Melanie looks at me, something she's gotten into the habit of doing during the filming, asking me silently if maybe I have an idea how to keep the thing going.

"Dad," I say, "going through all that, it must change who you are?"

"I haven't changed," he says. "My character didn't change. My *thought* changed." He is quiet for a moment. "I don't believe in people anymore. People are looking only for themselves, don't care for anybody, as long as they have what they want. After I went through so much, I saw that people are just animals. Don't care for each other at all, just for the nearest people to them. Not everybody, but *nearly* everybody. I haven't changed. I just now look skeptical on the whole world."

"You talk like this," my mother says, "but you are not like this. You have a very positive attitude to life—or where would we be, you and me? How would we live if we are thinking everybody is a selfish animal who will turn on us? Yes, it happened to us, and God knows, it happened to other people too—to people everywhere, terrible things for terrible reasons. Who can say why. But to live like this, thinking everybody is underneath terrible, no—impossible. And no matter what you say, I know who you are. You can say what you want, but you still expect good in people. You were like this as a boy when I met you, and even after everything that happened, you are like this now."

"I tell you this," my father says, "I don't know if there is a God or not, but I will take him to court."

---

That night in their hotel room, I can tell the day's shooting has exhausted them.

"Listen, Mom, Dad, we don't have to do any taping tonight. It can wait."

"No, no," my father says, "we have to finish the story of how it was there with Ludwig and Zofia."

"Take out your tape recorder," my mother says.

## FRANIA

My sisters moved out of Juzia's place because it was too small, but Shaindel still gave her the money and letters for us. They rented from another woman, a widow. Nobody knew they were Jews. Malka always stayed indoors because of that blackmailing incident. Shaindel told the widow that Malka is a sick girl, that she has to take so many pills, that she's got a blood disease. Shaindel was buying pills and throwing them in the toilet. She was afraid to let Malka go to work, but Shaindel herself went to work because she didn't want the widow to be suspicious. The money she made—I think in a variety-type store—she didn't need because she had all the gold from Chamel. There was an old bachelor, a Jew from Pińczów—his name was Felix—he was hidden by Poles in Warsaw. He had no money at all. Before the war, he was such a rich man. He had to keep changing places to hide every few weeks. Shaindel always met Felix on the street alone and gave him the money she made from her job.

I told you Ludwig had two sisters, Juzia and Wichta. Juzia was the nice one, and then there was Wichta: an antisemite, a born one. She was terrible. You looked at her, you could see how bad she was. I know you're not supposed to say a human being is ugly, but she was the ugliest thing I ever saw. I'm telling you, she looked like a witch, and Juzia looked like an angel.

Every Tuesday and every Friday, the two sisters came to the Pińczów market to buy food and then smuggle it back to Warsaw. That's the way they survived. Whenever they came, they visited Ludwig, and when that Wichta would look at us, her mouth turned down in the corners, and her eyes would get narrow. Pure hate. She wanted Ludwig to throw us out. Each time she came, she gave him a lecture about it: "Why are you keeping them? Why do you need the trouble? Somebody will squeal on you, and you are going to be killed. You throw them out, or you are going to lose your family and your life." Every single time she came, she was getting hotter and hotter about it, and we were afraid maybe she'll talk him into it. So we thought of a plan. I think it was Juzia's idea, but anyway, the next Thursday night, when Juzia and Wichta came, Srulek and me hid in that little cellar.

Ludwig, when he was alone with Wichta, said, "I listened to you. I threw them out. They went three days ago. I told them I can't do it anymore. I'm sick and tired, and I'm afraid."

Wichta said, "That's good! Now I'm going to go after Frania's two sisters in Warsaw. First, I'll take all the money away from them. Later, I'll give them to the Gestapo."

We were sitting in that cellar and heard everything. Can you imagine how we felt? Who could think that was what she would do? We just thought, if she thinks we're gone, she'll stop bugging Ludwig. But now? Oh, she was like a witch. What could we do, run out and kill her? With bare hands? While her brother, Ludwig, is sitting there?

"I'm going to get those two Jewish sisters," she said.

Juzia and Wichta slept over that night, and then on Friday morning, they went to the market. From there, they would go back to Warsaw. I figured, when Juzia got back, she would for sure warn my sisters, but you know what happened? That same day, two o'clock in the afternoon, we saw Juzia is walking into Ludwig's yard to the house. Alone. I said, "Where's Wichta?" Juzia said, "We were at the market, and the Germans started to grab Polish people to go work in the factories in Germany. They grabbed Wichta, right at the market, and put her in a truck."

They didn't have any Jews anymore, so they took the Poles. They needed them probably for the ammunition factories. I said, "You see? We are meant to survive this war." One day after Wichta said she is going to turn in my sisters, the Germans made a roundup, and they took her.

Shaindel wrote once in a letter: "We have to accept that something terrible could happen—it's a war—and maybe we're not going to have a way to send you money. Ludwig could throw you out. We have to think about it, that it could happen." She sent us a book, and between the pages, she put some money. Nobody knew we had it. We kept it for insurance. And she was right: something did happen—the same thing that happened to Wichta. In 1944, the Germans rounded up young Polish men and women and took them to work in ammunition factories in Berlin, and they rounded up Shaindel and Malka, as Poles. They didn't have much gold left, but they took it with them. Shaindel told us they bought flowerpots and all the gold was hidden there, in the soil. Whenever there was an alarm—they were bombarding Warsaw—they used to go to the public bunker, and they had to grab out that gold because they never knew what's going to happen. And what happened was, they were rounded up and taken right away to work in Germany. We didn't know. Juzia didn't know. All we knew was that the money stopped coming. And you know what? Ludwig was better to us in the last six months, without money, than he was when we gave him the money. He wanted to show us that he is a sport, that he could be so nice to us without money, better than with money. He was such a strange man. You could never reach this man—what kind of a character he was.

## SRULEK

Once, in the middle of the night, the dog started to bark. I wasn't sleeping. I hardly slept there for two and a half years, I was always looking out the window to see if somebody is coming. The dog started to bark, so I looked out, and I saw someone, just a silhouette. Outside was a boy calling, "Srulek! Srulek! Help me! Help me! I know you are there. I haven't got where to go."

I recognized the voice, he was my cousin. But the relation is not important, even if it would be a stranger, I would take him in—but I couldn't. Ludwig stood up and said, "If you're going to tell him you are here, I'll kick you all out. You just sit and keep your mouth closed."

It was just heartbreaking. He was just sixteen years old. He started to yell, "Srulek! Srulek! Help me! Help me!" He stood calling to me, that boy, for probably half an hour. We cried, and we begged Ludwig, but nothing helped.

Later on, we heard that some farmers took him in for a little while but soon threw him out. He went to another city and became a servant to the Germans. You know what he did? When the Germans were hunting, they used him, instead of a dog, to retrieve the dead rabbits. He was blond, and the Germans didn't know he's Jewish. We saw him after the war, and he told us he wasn't sure at that time we were at the farm, somebody told him that probably Rubinek and the Greenfeld girl are hidden there. He had nothing against us, he understood perfectly why we had to do what we did. He lives now in Israel and has two sons in the Israeli Air Force.

Before the ending of the war, the Germans were fighting the Russians right near our farm, the front was right near us. At that time, German soldiers hardly had what to eat, so they were stealing whatever they could from the Polish farmers. In the middle of the night, maybe two o'clock in the morning, I saw six, seven Germans are coming to take away the cow. And they were hiding, sneaking. So I was thinking fast: *Why they are hiding? Because they think maybe an officer is sleeping here.* The officers used to sleep over in the farmers' houses, and the regular soldiers had to sleep outside. Ludwig woke up, and he saw them too. I was scared he would get mad—he had only one cow—and he would yell at them, and they would find us. So I didn't hesitate at all. I opened the door and started to yell at the soldiers in German: *"Was ist hier los?!"* What is happening here?! Those German soldiers thought that I am an officer of the German army, and they ran away. Ludwig looked at me like I am a hero. For saving his cow.

## FRANIA

Not long after that, I think right at the end of 1944, German soldiers came into the house. We were hiding in the cellar, and we heard them say they're going to make some exercises in the field. Our roof was straw, it could catch fire. So the Banias had to go out of the house.

You should see Maniek, how he cried. "What's going to happen to Srulek and Frania?"

So Ludwig said, "What's going to happen? They can't go out. If they're going to burn, they'll burn, that's all."

We had to be left in the house. Que será, será. Where will we go? He didn't want to leave us, Maniek. They dragged him. They took the cow, and they took the dog. And you should see the dog howl. He did not want to go. They pulled him, but he didn't want to move because he knew that we were still in the house. Well, our life was just meant to be. Nothing happened.

At the beginning of January 1945, because the front was coming so close, the Russians and Germans fighting, we had to have somewhere to hide. The whole house could be destroyed in a second. The Banias could go to neighbors in the village, but we, where will we go? We knew that it's already the end, the end of the war is coming. The Germans could come any day to take everybody out of the house and level the ground there. So we had to be out. If they came, we were so pale, they would see right away that we're Jews.

## SRULEK

Just before the end of 1944, a farmer told Ludwig that the Russians are four miles away, near the flour mill. But they stopped their advance. We didn't see any Russian soldiers yet. So it was a question whether to go to them or stay and wait for them. I said to Ludwig, "If the Russians came so far, they will come a little bit further. I'll go out when the Germans surrender or if the Russians surround the whole area." I was thinking, *Why did the Russians only go so far and then stop?* It happened that the front was always moving. I wanted to be sure. I decided I'm not going anywhere, and sure enough, the Russians pulled back, probably a hundred miles back.

Every night we went out and we put our ears to the earth to hear if bombs are falling. When I put down my ear and heard an echo from the bombs—it could be a hundred miles away, but we heard the echo—it was just like the greatest, nicest music.

Two weeks later, the Russians advanced again and started to bombard the Germans. One night, we noticed there was fire not far from us, and we were thinking that all the houses could be burned. I went out with Ludwig in the field behind the house, and we dug a hole. It took us two nights to dig it, and I dug it exactly like you make a grave but big enough for two people. Very deep so we could stand up. I covered it flat with wood, and on top of that, I put hay. Then I took a stick and made a hole in the hay for air. I made the hole not straight up to heaven but a little bit on a slant so that I should be able to look out in the morning and see what's happening. We went into the hole just before the daybreak, Frania and me. It was cold, but when we heard the shooting between the Germans and Russians, it made us hot enough—believe me.

## FRANIA

There was no air there at all. Even the little lamp we brought didn't want to stay burning. And the worms, I'll never forget it. The worms were biting me, my body was all bleeding, alive, they were eating me up, white worms, flat ones, they were sucking from me blood, I was covered in blood. I don't know why they didn't touch Srulek, just me. What do you say to that? And I had to go out of that hole, I just couldn't be there. Que será, será.

## SRULEK

Frania had to go back into the house, the worms were eating her. I stayed another two, three hours, and when it was light, I looked out. I saw a German soldier walking crazy, I didn't know what's wrong with him, he was walking back and forth like he was lost. And suddenly, he ran away. Then from far away, I heard Ludwig yelling with his whole soul, "Srulek! Srulek! Come out! The Russians are here!"

We were liberated on the thirteenth of January 1945. During the fighting, the Russians shot probably forty German soldiers, and they put them together in one pile, maybe thirty yards in front of Ludwig's house, in the field. The farmers started to come out of their houses, and I'll never forget, they just walked around and around those bodies. "I recognize this one," one farmer would say. And he swore at the body. All the farmers were walking slowly around the dead Germans in a circle, talking out loud about how the Germans made them suffer, talking to no one in particular, telling about how they recognized this one or that one. One by one, they started to grab the boots, the shirts, the uniforms. Everything they grabbed from them. In a few minutes, there was nothing but naked bodies.

A high-ranking Russian officer came into Ludwig's place. He looked at Frania and me. We were pale, white like the walls. We told him that we are Polish Jews. We saw right away from his eyes that we were still in trouble. More officers came in. They sat down and asked, "Who speaks Russian? Or German?" I said I can understand and speak a little bit. They wanted to know where the Germans are. I knew every corner of the area, and I made them a sketch of the village and where possibly the Germans were. I also showed them where there was a German tank—around three miles from us, on a high hill in the forest. One officer gave the orders to blow up that tank, and they did it. They gathered together what was left of the Germans, and they brought them out of the woods, one by one, hands in the air.

The Russian soldiers came with tanks and with trucks, but mostly on foot. I was shocked when I saw them. So hungry, ripped in pieces, like beggars. But they were happy and singing. I went out to the yard and looked in the soldiers' faces—maybe I'll see a Jewish face. And I saw one. So I asked him in Hebrew, "Amchu?"—which means *One of us?* He did not answer, he just pushed me away and went into the house. There was sitting an officer smoking a cigarette.

The soldier said to the officer, "Hey, *tovarisch*, give me a cigarette."

The officer looked at him and said, "Shut your Jewish mouth!"

The soldier answered, "I'm not a Jew, I'm Gypsy." That was a shock to me. And Ludwig was standing there with his mouth open because he didn't know that the Russians didn't like Jews either. I used to tell Ludwig that Stalin would put him into the Golden Book for saving two Jews.

I was always looking for ways and means to make Ludwig be good. I told him that he is so smart, that he should be the leader of the village, that I don't believe he could kill a fly on the wall. And I talked him into being human. When he did something brutal, I said, "That is not Ludwig." So I made him believe in himself, that he should do better things. He was anxious to know what will happen after the war. He knew that we have a flour mill, and I told him we will try to help him have a better life.

Later, even with all of us still there, the Russians made their headquarters in Ludwig's house. And they cursed the Germans and the Poles. And the Jews.

## FRANIA

The Russians, when they came in, one of them saw right away that I am Jewish. He picked me up in the air, "Hurrah! *Evreiskaia Devushka!*"—that means a Jewish girl. "Hurrah! *Evreiskaia Devushka!*"

You know, when the Russian soldiers came, Srulek was always close to me. The Russians were starving for a woman. If they see that I have somebody, they wouldn't dare touch me. So Srulek never went away for a second. Not for a second.

We were at Ludwig's farm for eight days after the Russians came. We wanted to be sure, before we left, that the Russians wouldn't be pushed back again. The soldiers were coming like mushrooms, we didn't see from where, the fields were full of them.

Again a miracle happened to save our lives. We were cooking big pots of potato soup for the soldiers. And hot water to wash, they were so black from dust and dirt and who knows what. I was cooking all day. When night came, I was so tired, I could hardly go on top of the stove, to my place where I slept. The soldiers slept in the house, and they slept in the stable, they slept everywhere, and how big was the whole house? From cooking so much, all the smoke from that wood went to the top, where I was trying to sleep. I thought I'm going to choke. It was terrible for that eight days. I was liberated, but I worked like a horse. Every morning, Zofia was getting up at six o'clock—it was still pitch-dark—and she made the fire. All the smoke was coming right on top to me. This was going on already for four or five days, and I knew I had to clean the ashes out of that stove so there wouldn't be so much smoke. That day, it was just meant for us to be alive.

That morning, Ludwig started to wake Zofia. *Matka*, he called her. *Matka* means *mama*. "Matka, get up! You have to make the coffee for the soldiers."

So I thought to myself, Oh my God, I can't take the smoke anymore. It's already six days she didn't clean that stove down there. What the hell, I said to myself, I'm going down, I'll do it. So I told her, "Zofia, I'm going to make the coffee."

She said, "No, no, I'm going."

I said, "No, you stay in bed. I'm going to make it today." I went down, and I cleaned out that piece of iron there—all the holes—cleaned the ashes. And I see something metal in there. I said to Srulek, "What is this?" I saw a little box. "Oh my God," he said. He took it right away out to the field. It was a grenade.

One soldier, a Ukrainian, went away the night before, and I knew he was the one who put the grenade in the stove. I didn't like him. He had such terrible eyes, that man. He was such an antisemite, I could see it when I looked at him, the hate in his eyes. Before he left that night, he knew we're going to make the fire in the morning. The grenade will explode, and the whole house would go, just like that. Can you imagine what kind of an antisemite this was? And that day, I said to Zofia, "I'm going to make the fire." She never cleaned. We would have all gone with the fire. The whole house was mostly straw. So what do you say to this coincidence? A miracle.

## SRULEK

The Russians caught a German army officer, but they couldn't talk to him so they brought me to be the translator. They were keeping him in another farmer's place, not far away. I walked over there with two Russian soldiers and sat down in front of the German. He was just a plain soldier—an officer, but young and very scared. He was shaking. I didn't want to have pity on him, believe me, but I couldn't help it. A Russian officer started asking questions: "Were you at the front in Stalingrad?"

The German looked at me, he looked at the Russian, he didn't know what answer to give to stay alive. He said, "No."

They knew it was a lie because they already found papers on him that said he was in Stalingrad. They asked him all kind of questions. He was lying all the time. On his chest, he had the Iron Cross from Hitler. The Russian officer took out his gun and gave it to me.

"Shoot him."

I couldn't believe he asked me to do it. But he meant it. The Russian was yelling at me, swearing, "Shoot him, goddamn you! After everything they did to you! Kill him!" I couldn't. They took him out later to the back of the house. As I was walking away, I heard the shot.

Finally, the Russians advanced further west. Some farmers from the village came to Ludwig's, and they wanted to kill me because they thought I'm going to squeal that farmers were killing Jews. I spent two hours persuading them that I am not going to do anything. I said, "I don't know anything anyway, you're squealing on yourselves." I said, "I'm glad I'm alive, and I'm going to look for my family, that's all."

I walked with Frania into Pińczów. Two and a half years since we were there. For us, it was like a fog, it wasn't real. Everybody we knew was gone.

We walked into the town, and Poles that recognized us said, "Oh, you're still alive?" Not with warmth, you understand, they were just curious, surprised. The stomach turned.

"That's right," we told them. "We're still alive."

Jews came to Pińczów who we didn't know. They came and went, came and went, every single one of them, looking for family. And so did we. We couldn't find anybody. From a population of nine thousand people, maybe ten, twelve

Jews we knew from Pińczów came back. One came with the Russian army. One came from hiding. One from the woods. Everybody was wondering who is left alive. "Maybe you saw ...?" And they kept walking. "Where are you going?"

"We don't know, we just want to look, maybe some family's left over." It was so chaotic that you couldn't think straight.

We couldn't go back to Frania's house because Poles were living there, so we went to the flour mill that used to belong to Frania's grandfather. A Russian soldier came to the mill, he said he heard that some Jews were staying here. I looked at his face, and I asked him if he's Jewish. He was. We told him that we're Jewish too, and he fell on us and kissed us and cried his head off. He said that the Germans killed his bride two days before the wedding in Odessa, and he swears to God and to the whole humanity: "It is a thousand miles to Berlin, but if I live, and I get to Berlin, whatever German I'll meet, I'll kill."

The Russians were moving west, to the front, so he couldn't stay very long. We told him that our house used to be in the town square. He said, "Don't worry. Come with me, and we will do something." So we went with him, and he asked the Poles very politely to give us back one room. They moved down, and we moved up.

We were going to the flour mill and working every day. At first, we did it by ourselves for a few days. Later, the Russians came in, asked our names, and said that we have no right to do anything there, it belongs to the city. They put a commissar over me. I was taking in grain and giving out flour, and he was standing over my head all the time, this commissar.

I sold a few hundred pounds of flour, and I bought a wagon and horse for Ludwig. And he never went away without two big sacks of flour. Later on, all the farmers came: "Why didn't you come to me to hide? Why didn't you come to me?" After everything, they were all smart.

### FRANIA

You know, at that time, we used to go from Pińczów to visit the Banias. The minute we got to the little hill—it was still half a mile to the house—that dog smelled us already, and he came running. He was so excited, he didn't know what to do. He came running! And Maniek, when he saw that we were free, he was very happy.

### SRULEK

We used to go visit them at that time, and when we left, I saw with my eyes that the dog knew and went crazy. I actually saw the dog with tears in his eyes when he felt we are going away.

### FRANIA

Later, we found out what happened to my Uncle Itchele from Działoszyce—the one who found the farmer with a wagon to take us to Zofia. He went with his son, Leibick, to a farmer he knew so well—he used to buy grain from him—and that farmer hid them. Six months before the war finished, the farmer killed them. Imagine.

### SRULEK

There was no shortage of cruelty. How about her Uncle Meyer, what he did to us?

### FRANIA

Why do I have to talk about that? Why mix in such terrible things?

### SRULEK

Because it's true.

#### FRANIA

So it's true, so what? A lot of families, you see that they're selfish.

#### SRULEK

No, this is a story that is cruel.

#### FRANIA

So it's cruel, what can you do?

#### SRULEK

Her family—

#### FRANIA

You know what? Listen, I am going to tell you something: you keep your family on that side, and I'll keep mine on this.

#### SRULEK

All right.

#### FRANIA

This Uncle Meyer, he was a brother to my mother. Before the war, he married a girl from Miechów. They had a little boy, two years old, and his wife—oh! She was a beauty. In the first roundup, the Germans took the Jews from Miechów. Meyer paid so much money to find out where they took his wife and child. Nobody could find out.

### SRULEK

Meyer survived. He was hidden at a farmer's. He was hidden not far from Pińczów, at the house of the leader of the antisemites.

That man was the head of the Polish nationalists partisans, the *Armia Krajowa*. They fought the Germans, but if they found Jews hidden somewhere, that man gave orders to kill them all. But he was hiding Meyer. Meyer was so rich, he promised if he will survive, he will give him everything and sign it over to him.

### FRANIA

He gave him plenty, don't worry.

### SRULEK

So he hid Meyer in a drawer. You opened the door to a big wardrobe, and there were drawers, big ones. Meyer was a tall man. But he lived in a drawer. He couldn't do nothing, just eat and sleep. It took him a half a year to shave. He picked with his hand every hair from his face.

### FRANIA

You know, he had such a habit later that I always slapped his hand because he always was picking hairs off his face.

### SRULEK

And he couldn't straighten his legs after laying like that so long, almost three years.

### FRANIA

After we were already a few days free, a Pole came in and said, "Your uncle is alive." When we went out, we saw Meyer coming down the hill, crawling, he couldn't walk. Well, I don't have to tell you, we took him in, and I washed him. And what I didn't do for this man, you just can't imagine, for months, to put him back on his feet. And I really cared. After all, how many uncles did I have left? I didn't know yet about my two sisters. I didn't know that I have anybody left over. But Meyer couldn't swallow it, that I am alive with my husband. Listen, he was young too, you know, and jealousy was just eating him up alive. I have Srulek, and what does he have? Nobody. Nothing. Meyer was jealous that Srulek is alive. He wished that Srulek was dead so he could marry me.

### SRULEK

He wasn't like that before the war.

### FRANIA

Maybe he was, and we didn't know it.

### SRULEK

I have to tell you about what I am now certain: A human being is basically an animal. The environment keeps him back to be normal, just the environment. Sometimes the society. Sometimes parents, family. When they lose their family, they have no shame, the whole badness from the animal comes out free because he's not scared, nobody will tell him off.

And that was a hundred percent that Uncle Meyer. We took him in, took care of him, and he could still say "You are alive!? You are alive!? You shouldn't be. My wife should be alive, not you." Just plain said that to me. I was crying my head off, and

I told Frania, "He's cruel." After everything, after helping him, after carrying him on my hands from bed to the toilet.

## FRANIA

Then another miracle: Shaindel and Malka came back alive.

## SRULEK

They were taken from Warsaw to work in a factory in Germany—and there, Shaindel met Jean, a Frenchman, a Catholic. They fell in love. Jean was with them when they came back to Pińczów.

## FRANIA

Naturally, they came to Pińczów. Where else would they go? They wanted to see if someone's alive. We fell on each other and cried.

Meyer was saying always, "I don't need anything. I don't live for myself. I only live for the children." Only for the children, that meant us. You know talk is cheap. He only wanted to marry Malka. He saw that Shaindel, he cannot have. And by the way, he wanted to talk her out of Jean, but she told him to go to hell. And I had Srulek. So he wanted Malka, and he went after her.

He said, "If you're not going to marry me, I'm going to take my life."

She said, "I'm sorry—I can't help it. I like you as my uncle, but I'm not going to marry you, forget it."

She was only eighteen years old. So I guess from bitterness—who knows from what, anyway—he didn't give us anything. Later, he sold the flour mill and the houses, and whatever he sold, you know how much money he had?

### SRULEK

I said to my dear wife, "Your uncle wouldn't give you a cent, he's so egotistical. I'm working my head off at the mill for nothing because if I give the money to him, I tell you, he won't give us a cent. Frania, I'll give you our money, and you hide it."

### FRANIA

I said, "Hide the money? My uncle is going to cheat me? No. He lives only for us. I'm not going to hide the money."

### SRULEK

Meyer went to the girls—Shaindel, Malka, and Frania—and he said, "Children, I live only for you. But you wouldn't be able to sell all those houses that belong to you, to all of us. Give me a blank signature, and I'll be able to sell." They gave him the blank signature. He sold everything. Not less than a quarter of a million dollars.

### FRANIA

Oh, we were then fools.

### SRULEK

Wait. He sold everything and bought gold. The gold, he hid in a bread, a round bread, twenty inches in diameter. I'll never forget it. He's still alive. In Israel. He took all the money.

### FRANIA

We didn't get even one cent.

### SRULEK

He was so cruel. I'd spit him right now in the face, if I could.

### FRANIA

Ah, what good is revenge?

### SRULEK

My cousin Moishe Finkelstein arrived in Pińczów. He was looking for family too, he didn't know who was alive or not. Whenever Jews came into the town, the Poles told them that a Jewish family is alive and stays in the flour mill. Everybody who came, came to us. Moishe lived in Łódź, and he was taken from there to a concentration camp. He knew what happened to my family in the Łódź ghetto. I was afraid to ask.

### FRANIA

You didn't ask, but he told you anyway.

### SRULEK

Moishe told me right away.

### FRANIA

He told him, "Everybody's dead."

### SRULEK

He told me that one of my brothers, Chaim-David, went to the wires that surrounded the ghetto and got electrocuted—on purpose. And the rest of the kids died from starvation. Moishe told me my father buried them all. I asked about my father. He said the Germans wanted him to squeal on somebody about some possessions they were hiding. He did not want to squeal, so they broke him—the hands and the legs, piece by piece—so he should talk. He did not tell them. They physically destroyed him, and he did not say a word.

### FRANIA

First, the father buried all his children, and then Moishe buried the father.

### SRULEK

Anybody who is alive feels guilt. "Why not me? Why them?" Maybe if I would be there, maybe I could help.

### FRANIA

How can it help, this thinking?

### SRULEK

Because I was the most capable. No one else could go without an armband, and when I was there, I used to bring bread. If I would be with them, maybe it would be different.

### FRANIA

It does not help, this thinking. You were young, and you were in love, and you wanted to come to me. So what's the use of talking? If I wouldn't be pregnant, I wouldn't be sitting here. I would have gone to Lublin, then to Majdanek, and I would be the first one in the ovens. I knew already that my parents and my brother Chamel were dead in Majdanek. We heard this already from the letters we got from Shaindel while we were still hiding. Now here we were, alive, in Pińczów, with Shaindel and Malka. And the stories started. Those stories, they go on till today.

# FIFTEEN

WHEN THE DOCUMENTARY UNIT interviews Zofia and Maniek Bania, my parents and I are not present. We don't want to meet them until the actual filming of the reunion. The crew is in the Bania house—Melanie as interviewer, Agnieszka translating.

Zofia, now in her early eighties, is still active around the farm. Her letter to my parents six months ago said she wanted to see them again because she didn't know how long she had to live. It turns out not to be because of cancer or a disease that will claim her life. It's simply because she's in her eighties and doesn't know how much time she has left.

Zofia speaks to the camera. Agnieszka later provides the translation.

"Forty years have gone by since I have seen the Rubineks. After so many years, I wanted to talk to them face-to-face, to talk over how we lived through everything, the hard times. In the war, I felt so much pity for them. It was impossible to betray them. I especially liked Frania, Mrs. Rubinek, very much. I loved her as if she was my own sister. Even though she was Jewish. Sometimes I didn't have money, and when I went to their store, Frania would give me a little food and other things on credit. Frania and I, we got to know each other, and she liked me very much. Later, I was thinking she and her husband could be hidden in my place. I didn't know if I should take them in or not. My son, Maniek, was only six years old. We hardly had enough to eat. I wanted to live through the war somehow. But I did it. I took them in. After some time, my husband wanted to throw them out, but I told him no, we couldn't. We have to keep them. It would be on my conscience for all of my life if they met their death because of us. When I told him that, he hit me. He beat me a lot when we fought over this."

Maniek is lean, weathered from farmwork, and fifty years old now as he sits in the living room of his mother Zofia's house, waiting to be filmed by Vic and the crew. He's married with three children. He's a grandfather too. He and his wife live with Zofia, and they work on the farm there.

He's nervous in front of the camera—stiff and a little formal.

"Even though I was very young, I was quite aware too. I felt I had an obligation, a human duty. I felt that responsibility to the last moment the Rubineks were with us. I was afraid of death the whole time. I could not tell our neighbors that we were hiding Jews. After the war, they were angry that we did not trust them. If one word slipped out—even *one* word—it could have been my death. You know, my father was a hero. His life, and mine, and my mother's were in danger for two and a half years. We were all put in the situation, and we had to live it. This is the way the cards were dealt. So that's how it was."

---

Tonight my parents tell me they want me to know something about Maniek before I meet him for the first time.

"First of all," my mother says to me, "I don't know if Zofia even told Maniek the truth."

I have no idea what she's talking about. "The truth about what?"

"Maniek is not Ludwig's son," my father says. "Zofia was a servant in a place where the landowner had a relationship with her."

"Just say it," my mother says, irritated with him. "Why don't you say it plain? That Polish landowner where Zofia was a servant, he raped her. He raped Zofia, and when he saw she's pregnant, he threw her out. Zofia gave birth to Maniek on a field—she told me—by herself. And Ludwig later took her in, her and the baby."

"Should we say that in the film?" I ask them.

They look at me, shocked, and both speak at the same time: "No! Are you crazy?!"

"Listen," my father says, "Maniek was only six years old when we came there. He said to me once, 'I was at my friend's house, and I saw him playing with his father. My father never wants to play with me, never.' I said, 'What do you care, Maniek? I'll play with you.' Right away, he came running, and he grabbed me around, and he kissed me. I said, 'Maniek, would you like to learn how to write and to read?' Many, many hours I spent with him. And also that helped me to stop worrying what is going to happen to us. They had Catholic prayer books there, so I also taught Maniek the ..." He turns to my mother for help.

"The catechism," she tells him.

"The catechism. I would ask questions, and he would answer."

I'm amazed to hear this. "You taught Maniek the Catholic catechism?"

"For children. What is a good angel? What is a bad one? Questions like that. Listen, Ludwig wouldn't do it. And he couldn't read very well, anyway. He was cruel, Ludwig. He used to kick Maniek around. He was never ... how to say it?" He turns again to my mother for help.

"Affectionate," she says. "Never affectionate with Maniek, never. I don't know what happened between them later—if before Ludwig died, Maniek found out the truth."

"Or if even now he knows," my father adds.

"When we were hiding there, with me, Maniek was a very sweet boy. But with your father? With your father, he was like a son."

**Frania's sisters Malkale** (Left) **and Shaindele** (Right)
(While living in Warsaw as Gentiles. They are carrying Bibles and are on their way to church. The men in the background are German soldiers.)

**Frania, Srulek, Shaindele, Malkale, Jean**
(Lodz, Poland, 1946)

# SIXTEEN

MY PARENTS AND I HAVE ANOTHER DAY OFF from filming as the documentary crew interviews Zofia and Maniek, so we have a full day for taping. Tomorrow is the reunion, so I barely sleep as I work on the transcripts through the night, trying to finish.

### SRULEK

We stayed in Pińczów till May of 1945, and then we had to run to Łódź. The Polish antisemites—the partisans, the AK—came to the flour mill to kill us. It was lucky: When the Germans were operating the mill during the war, they were scared of the partisans too, so they made iron doors. When the partisans came, they couldn't get in.

A day later, we took a bus to Kielce. We didn't stay in Kielce, we felt it wasn't safe for us in small towns. We heard that a year later, in 1946, the Poles made a pogrom in Kielce and killed over a hundred Jews.

We took the train to Łódź, but on the way, we had to pretend to be Poles because the Poles were still killing the Jews. The Russians didn't mix in to stop it.

In all the little towns from all over the area, whoever survived, came back. It took a few months, but they came. From towns with populations of thousands came back two, three. And then they couldn't stay in their own towns—no parents, nobody. So where did they go? To a point, where more Jews are. Everybody was running to Łódź. Warsaw mostly was burned.

We came to Łódź, and we stayed with my cousin Moishe. I didn't have any money, so I started to look for work. Frania and I wanted to have our own place. I found a job working in a factory with knitting machines, like before the war. An apartment, I found too. It belonged to a Gestapo. He probably took it during the war from a Jewish family, and now it was deserted. We moved in, just like that. It was wide open. When we went into the house, everything was intact, even a fork and a knife, pots and pans, everything.

I used papers that identified me as a Pole—Josef Lewitski. Why? I'll give you an example. Before the war, there was on that one street alone probably ten thousand Jews. After the war, was five Jewish people. From ten thousand, five.

When we were sitting there in our apartment, came in a neighbor. He was a Communist—he didn't know I'm a Jew—and he said to me, "Comrade Lewitski, the whole street is again with Jews."

So I said, "How many?"

"I don't know, I see them everywhere."

Altogether was maybe five Jews. That was the personality of my neighbor, the Communist.

He said, "Something is wrong. Your wife looks Jewish."

So I said to him, "She is a convert."

That was in 1945, when the Russians were already there. After two weeks, the radio said that two Jews were living on another street. Those Jews were found, and killed. After liberation. After coming back from concentration camps.

I went out at that time, in 1945, walking in the street, you could see people with pale faces, the hair cut off from the camps—you could recognize right away who is Jewish and who not. Later on, I found a Jewish community center. Really, it was just an office, and whoever came in wrote his name down in case somebody wants to know if you're still alive. Everybody who came in was looking for family. Everybody wanted to know how did you survive. Hundreds and hundreds of people used to come every day, looking at lists, at faces.

## FRANIA

We wrote a letter to Ludwig, and he came to visit us in Łódź. That was the summer of 1945. I went out with him to the market to buy a chicken. I'll never forget. You know, they were selling there live chickens, and I'm telling you, it was so funny! He was so proud of himself, the way he took that chicken to see if it was fat enough, like a professional. I made dinners for him, and we treated him like a king.

## SRULEK

We gave Ludwig more love than he understood even. He was proud of himself that he saved us.

## FRANIA

He stayed a week. Later, when he was going home, I had to buy two valises for all the things we gave him. He could hardly carry everything.

## SRULEK

After he left, something amazing happened with Shaindel and Malka on the street.

## FRANIA

Let me tell it. First, you know that during the war, Malka and Shaindel lived in Warsaw on false papers as Poles. Their apartment building was not far from the Jewish ghetto. When the Germans were bombing the ghetto after the resistance, they could see the ghetto burning from their window. For days, it was burning. You can imagine their hearts.

Suddenly, a man—a neighbor—knocked on their door. He had a bottle of wine, and he said to them, "Hey, girls! I cannot see the Jewish ghetto burning from my window. Let me come in to watch how the Jews are frying there like chickens! Let's celebrate! Let's drink to it!" He laughed his head off, and they had to laugh too. And drink with him. If not—the Poles were such antisemites—if you wouldn't laugh, they would accuse you that you are Jewish. So my sisters had to celebrate the burning of the ghetto. They could not forget that incident.

Well, the war ended, we were all walking in the street in Łódź after the war, suddenly, the girls—Malka and Shaindel—stopped. They couldn't believe their eyes. They saw that man, the same neighbor who came in to celebrate when the ghetto was burning. And he saw them. They both stopped.

He ran over and yelled at them, "You goddamn Poles! I fooled the Germans, and I fooled you too! I am a Jew!"

Shaindel didn't say anything for a second. "You better sit down, mister, I've got something to tell you. We're all fools. That day we drank wine and watched the ghetto burn, all three of us in that room were Jews."

## SRULEK

After that, Shaindel and Jean went away to Paris on false papers. They wanted to get married. Malka stayed with us.

## FRANIA

Srulek's cousin Moishe had staying with him two Russian officers, both Jewish. One was a young man, the other one was Major Zorin, who was in his sixties. What a nice man he was. The young one was such a handsome man, and he was crazy about Malka. The older one, Major Zorin, said to me, "Look, he's my friend, but you have to make sure your sister does not go with him. He cannot remain here. What will he do, desert the Russian army? Is she going to go to Russia with him? You know what life there will be like for her?" He closed the windows, he closed the doors, he whispered to us, "Children, run away because it's coming very bad times here. Run! And fast! You lived through such a war. Run, I don't care where, just run out of Poland!"

## SRULEK

At the Jewish community center, I met some people that I knew before the war, and they told me there is a possibility I can get out of Poland. I should go to Zawadzka Street, number sixteen. There, I will find people to make the arrangements for me.

It's a story that I'll never forget. I came there, I knocked on the door. "Come in." I opened the door, and it was altogether dark, you couldn't see a thing. Suddenly a light came up, like a spotlight right on my face, so bright I couldn't see who was behind the light. "Srulek, we know you. We know who you are." They knew everything about me: what school I went to, my father's name, everything. And they tested me to prove I am me. "We cannot tell you who we are. The Communists are now in Łódź, and we don't trust them." They told me they have sixty Jews that want to go out of Poland.

I said, "Where are they?"

They said, "That, we will tell you later. But you will be the leader. You'll get a sign, a code number. You must go to Krakow. At the train station will come to you a man. He will tell you the code number, and he will show you the sixty people. You must tell these people not to speak to anyone. If anyone asks them questions, they should send them to you. That's all that I have to tell you. On a certain day, I'll tell you when you're going to go to Krakow."

I left. A few days went by, and a man walks to me in the street, takes me to the side, and says I should be prepared to go to Krakow right away.

## FRANIA

At that time, my Uncle Chaim came back alive from Russia. My mother had three brothers who survived: Meyer—you know what kind of character he had. Leon—he survived. In fact, he already had a factory in Lublin. And the last brother, the best one, was Chaim. He ran to Russia when the war broke out. Now he didn't want to stay with his brothers Meyer or Leon, just with us. Well, when Srulek told me we had to go right away to Krakow, we went with Chaim and also with Malka. But we left in such a hurry that the few pieces of jewelry that I had left from my mother, I forgot them on the bed.

## SRULEK

We came to the Krakow station, a man came up to me and told me the code number. He showed me the sixty people, they were there, at the station—children, elderly people, young people, all kinds of people. From all over, from Hungary, Lithuania, Poland—all Jews, all refugees. The man said that me and Frania's Uncle Chaim and another man, Chaskel Rosenblatt, would be the trustees, the leaders. We have to go with everybody to another town, Katowice. It wasn't far. He gave me an address, and he told me I should knock three times on the door, and a man with a very big moustache will open the door. I should tell that man with the moustache that I have sixty sacks of flour and he will ask me how much is a sack, and I should say a hundred złotys a sack.

We went. Nobody recognized that there's something special about us, or that we were even a group. In Katowice, it happened just like the man said. The man with the moustache gave me sixty Greek passports. He taught me also a few Greek words: *kalinikta, kalispera*—good night and good evening, or something like that. Also he told me to go out and buy for everyone berets. I went out in Katowice and bought sixty berets. He told us to go to Bratislava in Czechoslovakia, and he gave us an address.

At the Polish border, a Polish official stopped us, took us out from the train, and didn't let us go further. I told our people to remember if somebody speaks to them in Polish, just answer them with some Hebrew prayers, for example, say Kaddish to them, and the Poles will think it's Greek. The Polish border official talked to us in Polish, and we pretended not to understand. We were supposed to be coming from concentration camps, so we had to be able to talk at least a few words in German. We said only "*Nichts verstehen.*" We don't understand.

He said, "Passports."

So we gave them our Greek passports. We had hidden money—a little bit, not much—in soup cans, and we put in stones so that they would have the right weight. All of us had our money hidden this way because we knew that the Poles would search us. The Polish official made us put out everything on the table. We had bread. We had salami.

## FRANIA

He took away from us the salami and a few cans—the real soup cans, not the ones with the money. Just lucky. I had with me a carpet, a small one, but beautiful. He said that is smuggling and took it away.

## SRULEK

I don't know what the Poles did with other people, but they put us in jail for the night. That night, the guards were walking, sneaking around to see if we're Polish Jews. Maybe they'll hear us talk between ourselves Yiddish or Polish. But they couldn't find out. A funny thing was that Frania was wearing high boots, and the Poles right away "recognized" that these were boots from Greece—but really, those boots were made in Poland. They started to talk between themselves: "They are Greek people. We have to let them go. We don't want to start up with Greece." Of course, we understood every single word. They didn't let Polish Jews out of Poland. Why, I don't know. In fact, I don't think they let any Poles out. People were smuggling out anyway, by foot and by bicycle and by train. Not only Jews. Poles left too, anti-Communists ran out because they were scared of what the Russians will do to Poland. But we were "Greeks"—so the next day, they let us go.

We went on the train to Czechoslovakia, and we came to the station in Bratislava. They stopped us: "Where are you going?" So everybody pointed at me, and the station master came to me. I told him, in German, that we are Greeks who were in the camps in Poland and now we want to go home. The station master said to me very politely that since we are going to Greece, he has a Greek refugee here at the station and he should go with us. Can you imagine the kind of situation I was in? He brought over that Greek man, and he embraced me and kissed me and started to talk Greek to me. And what did I do? I answered him in Hebrew. He looked at me like I'm a crazy person. So I had to make up my mind right away: I could not take him with me. I told the station master in German, "I don't know who this man is, but one thing I can tell you for sure: he is not a Greek. I just spoke Greek to him, and he doesn't understand a word." The Greek man didn't understand the German I was speaking to the station master. They took him away—where and what, I don't know. It bothered me very much, but what could I do? He was one man and we were sixty.

We went further. In Bratislava, already we saw a lot of Jews from all over Europe—from Russia, Hungary, Romania, Germany, Poland. I have to mention that the Czechoslovakian people were so kind and so nice to us. I have no words to thank them. You know how they were taking revenge on the Germans? During the war, the Czechs were not allowed to walk on the sidewalk, where the Germans were walking. Only on the street. So now they reversed it: the Germans were walking only on the street.

I went with Chaim and Chaskel to the address that we had, and I found out the organization helping us was the Bricha, specially sent from Israel to help the Jews from the Holocaust get out of Communist hands. We stayed at the community center just a few days. One night, a man from the Bricha came and he said that tonight, now, we are going to cross the border. We went to a bridge that crosses from Czechoslovakia to Austria. On that bridge were standing Russian soldiers. The Bricha man went to them, bribed them with vodka, and he drank with them. "Cross," he said to us. "Now." We walked across the bridge, and the Russians soldiers made like they don't even see us. And we went through to Austria.

In the middle of the night, we got on a train and arrived in Vienna. The Bricha led us to the Rothschild Hospital. To that big hospital came all the Jews that ran away from the Communist countries, from all over Eastern Europe. There were hundreds and hundreds of people. A family got one bed, not more. There were children, grown-ups, old people, all categories of characters—doctors, lawyers, intellectuals—all kinds of people. They gave us a little bit to eat, but the worst part of it was that we didn't have any hot water. I took two spoons, and I put a piece of wood in the middle, connected two wires to the spoons, connected it to the electricity, and put it into a glass of water. After a few seconds, the water was boiling. I was the talk of the town in that Rothschild Hospital. Everybody came to me for a little bit of warm water. They told me that I made a miracle.

Later, there came some dignitaries from England from a committee for refugees, and they started to ask everybody "Where do you want to go?"

All of us said we wanted to go to Israel.

They started to laugh. They asked, "How can you go? Palestine is forbidden to take refugees. You are in Vienna, how can you go to Palestine? By train? By water?"

We said to them, "It was forbidden to walk the streets in Poland. We walked. It was forbidden to stay alive. We lived. It was forbidden to leave Poland. We are here. Don't you worry—by hook or by crook, we will be in Israel."

By this time, we knew we had to get to Munich, a city that was in the American sector. There was the biggest center for refugees in that part of Europe. From there, who knows?

The Bricha later changed our Greek passports for Austrian ones. These new papers said that we are Jews from Innsbruck. On the train to Munich were two American officers, and they started to talk to us in English, we couldn't understand a word. But we had in our group a girl from

Lithuania, highly intelligent, she spoke Polish, Russian, Lithuanian, German, English, French. The officer asked her from where we are coming and where we are going. She told him that we are Innsbruck Jews, returning home. They wrote down everything, the Americans. That worried us. Sometime later, they got off the train. A jeep was waiting for them.

On the way to Munich, the train stopped in Innsbruck. At the station was waiting for us those two American officers. And standing on the platform with them? The mayor of the city and a whole orchestra to greet the Jews back to their "hometown," Innsbruck. Can you imagine how we felt? The mayor even gave a speech. And none of us were from Innsbruck. We had to stay, at least for a few days. The train left without us. We thanked everybody and asked where is the Jewish community center. I went in to the president of the center and told him who we are really, and he said for us to wait here and he'll help us. We waited, we stayed there a few days. That's when the group of sixty split up. Some went to Italy and from there to Israel. Some went other places.

I heard there was a place for refugees nearby, in Gnadenwald, in the hills. During the war, it was used as a health spa for high Nazi officers, for skiing, beautiful dry air. I heard that there's place for over a hundred and twenty people, and only fifty were staying there. We wanted to have a little bit rest, we were so tired from wandering.

I went to the president of the community center, and I spoke to him very politely. I said, "There's only fifteen of us left in our group, and we would like to go to Gnadenwald."

"Impossible," he said. "There's no room."

I went out and talked to Chaim and to Chaskel. "We are going back in there, and I'm going to do something about it, but don't laugh, no matter what I say."

I went in, Chaskel on one side of me and Chaim on the other. I told the president: "I am not anymore the same man that I was an hour before. I have a knife with me. The Germans killed my parents. They killed my brothers, my sisters. I'm not scared of anything. Now I want to have a place where to sleep and to eat. And if you're not going to give it to us, I'll put my knife right into you. I am giving you five minutes to get a bus here to take us to Gnadenwald. If not, you will be a head shorter. Not more than five minutes!" And then I looked at my watch.

He turned white. Right away he called for a bus, and it took us to Gnadenwald. When we came there, I was walking like a leader. I ordered: I want this, and I want that. We really had a hell of a time. Everybody was scared of me, and I couldn't even kill a fly on the wall.

## FRANIA

We stayed in that beautiful resort for a couple of weeks. It was like a dream. The weather was gorgeous, and we met such nice people. I'll never forget, we met there a man—I don't remember now his name—but I can picture him: young, maybe twenty-eight. This man got so warmed up to Srulek and me.

It's funny, you know, that the whole life we went through, me and Srulek, we had so much luck with people. People liked us so much! The minute we met somebody, they didn't let go. Maybe because we had a sense of humor. We had friends all our life.

This man in Gnadenwald, I'll never forget him. He said, "You two are married?"

I said, "Yes."

"I hope you'll have children."

I said, "I hope so. But my husband doesn't want to think about it. We lost a child in the war."

He said, "I was in a camp, and a doctor there used me as his experiment. I can never have any children." And he started to cry so much that I'll never, never forget it.

### SRULEK

After two weeks, we got already tired sitting. We left and went to Munich. It was a city full of refugees from all over. We were thinking only to get out of Europe.

### FRANIA

To go to Israel. We weren't thinking about America at all. In Munich, we went first to the community center. They gave us an address, and they said, "Germans are living at this house, but here is a paper which will allow you to move in." We went—Srulek, me, Malka, my Uncle Chaim, and Chaskel Rosenblatt. A German was living there with his wife and a daughter.

### SRULEK

We found out later that man was a Nazi.

### FRANIA

Not just a Nazi. An SS officer. He treated us royally. He fell down so low, that big Nazi, that he took our shoes to shine. Every night we put our shoes by the door, and he took them and shined them.

### SRULEK

Every other minute he asked us if we need something. He was scared of us. He knew we were survivors. In 1945, all the Germans were scared. In his library we found albums with pictures of him in his Nazi uniform. He told us, "I had to do everything the Führer said. But I didn't know about any killings. I don't know about any concentration camps."

## FRANIA

Nobody knew anything. It was a big secret. A big secret kept by millions of people.

## SRULEK

We were there with these German people only a few days because we wanted to be together with other Jews. We went back to the center in Munich, and they gave us papers to go to the displaced persons camp called Föhrenwald. You remember?

## FRANIA

I remember even the date: November 5, 1945.

## SRULEK

You know what Föhrenwald was? The Germans used to have an ammunition factory there, where they used slave labor. Now it was a refugee camp with maybe fifteen hundred families.

We knocked in the middle of the night on the door of the leader of the Föhrenwald camp. He told us there's no place for anybody. I got mad. "We are here, and we are going to stay here," I said. In the middle of the camp was a big lecture hall, like an empty theater. I said to the leader of the camp, "I want mattresses for all our people. If not, you're not going to sleep tonight." I learned already that with politeness, I'm not going to get anywhere. I told him off and said if he's not going to do it, I'll take all the twelve people that were with me, we will go into his house, and he wouldn't be able to do anything about it. He brought the mattresses. There were kids with us, and they needed something to eat. I made him bring milk for the kids. We were there all night. In the morning, we went to the camp office for a place to live. They gave us an address in the camp to go to.

All the streets in the camp were named after American states: Pennsylvania Street, Missouri Avenue, Tennessee Avenue.

Every block of houses had a boss, the block leader. We were sent to Illinois Street, where the block leader was a Hungarian. He told us that in his block, there was no place. We went to look, we saw there's some places there, and we figured out that he probably was saving it for his friends, but they didn't come yet.

He said, "No, I'm keeping space for my family."

I said, "We are here. Your family is still in Hungary." I told him that we had from the office an order to live there. He said he doesn't believe it. I said, "If you don't believe it, go to the office and ask them." A lie? Sure, it was a lie.

He said, "I'm going to ask." He went, and in the meantime, we moved into the houses. We went back to that empty theater, took some chairs and mattresses, and moved in. When he came back, I said to him, "Mister, as you can see, we live here now. When your family will come from Hungary, we will think again." He couldn't do anything about it. Nine of us were already in there. After a few weeks, the office put a Hungarian couple in with us. You remember?

## FRANIA

They were fighting like cat and mouse. She threw him out, he always slept in the hallway. We were in one big room, everybody had their separate corner.

## SRULEK

The camp was like a small city, with all the facilities. There were already around five thousand survivors there. As the survivors from all over Europe left their birthplaces, they came to the transit camps. There were lots of these camps in Germany. Most of us were hoping to go to Israel as fast as possible. In the meantime, people started slowly to live a little bit of a normal life. Everybody started to do something positive. The so-called government of Föhrenwald had a mayor, its own police force, a jail. There was a cultural office and all kinds of schools, from kindergarten to professional training. It was only a transit camp, but they tried to make it in such a way that everything should be just right. The whole thing was operated by the United Nations Relief and Rehabilitation Administration—UNRRA.

## FRANIA

You know how many children were born there in that time? I heard later that these camps had the highest birth rate in Europe after the war. Every day, we went to a central kitchen for our provisions. We didn't like to go stand in line there, and besides, the kitchen was terrible. We bought our own things, and I cooked myself. We had a little oven, and I used to make big pots of soup for everybody.

Later on, we traveled to Munich quite a few times—to an opera, to the theater, movies. Near us was the town of Wolfratshausen. It was only two miles, you could walk it. Oh, the stores—it was wonderful! I found there a dressmaker. I chose materials, and a German lady was making me clothes because the dresses that the camp gave me didn't fit. We still had a little money, but you could get things practically for nothing. But the best was coffee. If you had some coffee ... for coffee, they gave you everything, the Germans.

## SRULEK

The first few months, we were just walking around and looking, looking, maybe we will find somebody from our family. Every day, survivors came from all over Europe. People started to look for some entertainment, so the camp administration created a special culture committee to look after theaters and concerts. The schools put on some children's theater, there were choir concerts, music concerts—the camp had a lot of good musicians. There was a teacher who started a theater there, and he did it with some enthusiasm. He encouraged those who were professionals before the war. I remember an older man named Wisokodworski came forward, he said that he was a professional actor in Lithuania before the war, and he took over that theater that the schoolteacher created. At the same time, a man called Jacob Sandler set up another acting troupe, called Maapilim, that put on very nice, good plays. Our refugee camp also had a weekly newspaper called *Bamidbar*, which means "In the Desert," and they wrote very intelligent reviews. I saw all the plays in Föhrenwald, all the concerts. That empty theater, they made into something just gorgeous, with six or seven hundred seats, with all the facilities.

In 1946, a man approached me and gave me to read a story that he wrote about his own family. The name of the book was *The Heroic Family*. He asked me if it was possible to turn the book into a play for the stage. I read it a few times. I liked it very much, and I said I'll try my best. I worked for a few weeks with actors—both amateurs and professionals—

and when we put it on, it was very well received. *Bamidbar* wrote a very good review about it. I was so encouraged, I started looking for something else to put on, and I found a beauty: a comedy by Sholem Aleichem called 200,000, about a man who wins the lottery.

## FRANIA

I was going with Srulek to all the rehearsals. Just from sitting and listening, I knew everybody's part, that was the funniest thing! When 200,000 opening night came, one of the actresses got sick with a hundred and three temperature. Srulek came running home, and he said, "Rivka is sick, and the opening night is tonight! You have to go to play the part!"

I said, "Me?"

He said, "You! You know all the lines."

What could I do? I had to go play it. They said I was terrific, but I don't know. I did it only for Srulek. Oh, it was such a terrific success in that time, wonderful!

## SRULEK

Later on, the culture committee called a meeting with all three directors in Föhrenwald: Wisokodworski, Sandler, and me. Wisokodworski wanted to go separate, but me and Sandler came together and made from our two troupes, one troupe. We called it Negev. We were two directors, and we both were acting, but Sandler did most of the directing. We got along beautifully. We put on a play called *The Gold Diggers*, also written by Sholem Aleichem, and we had a big success. Everybody came to see it from all over Munich and the other camps, it was just marvelous. We were traveling with the plays around the camps in Germany. In that time, when we weren't performing, we went to Munich to see German theater. The truth is, they made excellent theater. Later on, in 1948, Sandler and I went to a German drama school run by a very learned man, a theater director named Heinz Galetzki, a professor of drama. We both received diplomas.

## FRANIA

When Srulek started in the theater, he didn't get paid with money, but with products. We had so much coffee, and you know, coffee could buy anything. Srulek bought himself a motorcycle. He brought it up to that big room, and he was driving around the table. When you're young, you know how it is. I said, "If you're not going to get rid of that motorcycle, honest to God, I'm leaving." I couldn't take it. In the house, in the room, he was driving around the motorcycle. I said, "After the whole war, I have to get killed by a motorcycle?" I don't know what he did with it, but he got rid of it.

## SRULEK

I bought a car, a beautiful BMW that was driven around in the war by a Gestapo. You know, when you're an actor, you have to go in style. In 1948, I wanted to go to Israel already. I went to Munich, to the Histadrut, the Zionist organization, to inform them that I'm ready to go.

"How are you going to make a living there?" they asked me.

"I'm not a beggar," I said to them. "Money, I haven't got. But I have a beautiful BMW, and I want to take it with me. I could drive taxi."

They said, "How can you take a big car? You'll travel by ship, it's not allowed."

I said, "I'm a good mechanic. I'll take it apart, in pieces. I'll show you." I came prepared. I took from my pocket papers with my drawings of how the car could be taken apart and packed. "You see? I'll put the car in boxes, and when I'll be in Israel, I'll put it back together."

They said, "We will take fifty-one percent of what you make from that car."

I got so mad, I said, "What? I'm going to work, and the car is mine, and you're going to take away *more than half?*"

They said to me, "Take it or leave it." So I left. The hell with Socialism! I went away with a broken heart.

## FRANIA

We would be in Israel if this incident wouldn't happen.

## SRULEK

I know one single thing: that people went to Australia, to Canada, to United States, all over, and didn't go to Israel on account of that.

## FRANIA

We moved after a year from Illinois Street to Tennessee Avenue. Every house was the same, but now we had a little more privacy. Chaskel Rosenblatt and Malka fell in love and left for France, where his sister was living. Shaindel and Jean were already living near Paris. So it was left only me and Srulek and my Uncle Chaim, who married a wonderful woman, Eva. The four of us shared the new place. Downstairs there were two rooms, and upstairs was one large room. Srulek bought some boards, and he made us beds. Oh, there I had a palace. Eva and I were good housekeepers, so when Srulek got some parcels every week, we took out some coffee and gave it to the Germans. We bought paint, and we painted the whole house, me and Eva. We got good mattresses, and we hired a man to build a stove. And we got everything from trading coffee. Our house was always full of people, it was like a center, you know? And the friends we made there, we still have them. What can I tell you, in the middle of all the chaos of the war just finished and not knowing what's going to happen with our future, it was probably one of the happiest times of our lives there, in that displaced persons camp.

## SRULEK

We started looking for some good plays, something classical. We found *The Golem*, written in the 1920s by H. Leivick, one of the greatest Yiddish writers. That play originated with a legend from sixteenth-century Prague, Czechoslovakia. There lived a very learned rabbi called the Maharal, respected by all the Jews in the world and even by non-Jews. That was a time of many pogroms—killing of the Jews. The legend was that a Christian boy was found murdered, and a priest accused the Jews of killing the child ritually for his blood. The priest said the Jews had to use Christian blood to make matzo, the unleavened bread for Passover.

That particular lie is old like the hills. Even recently, in Russia, Jews were accused of this. In the legend, the Maharal, to protect the Jewish population, creates a man from clay, a kind of Frankenstein monster, a golem, by using the rituals of Kabbala, mysticism. This golem was about nine feet tall and very powerful. The Maharal is forced later to destroy that golem because he starts to kill his own people. One message of the play is that you cannot use murder to fight murder because it destroys you in the end. I played the part of the golem—on stilts. I was very much known in the camp, and nobody could believe that it's me. We had a big success with *The Golem*, mostly because of the vision Jacob Sandler had as director. All over, they were talking about it: how beautiful it was made, how beautiful we played it. When the curtains opened, we heard from the audience,

"Ah!" It became so quiet, that you could hear drop a pin.

One night, an American army general from Munich came to see the play. He didn't understand Yiddish, but he came back after, grabbed me, he said he saw a lot of plays in the United States, but this was an amazing experience. To prepare that production, we were reading *The Golem* for quite a few weeks. And the more we were reading, the more we saw that nothing has changed. From the Inquisition in Spain, through the Holocaust, to now—nothing has changed. In that time, Frania was pregnant with you, Saul. One night, during the first act, a friend of mine came backstage, he was standing at the side, and he practically yelled at me, "Srulek! Srulek! Mazel tov! You have a son!" I cried for happiness, and I nearly fell off my stilts. But I had to play, the show has to go on. What can I tell you? I played the second act like never before.

## FRANIA

Srulek was playing in the theater, and I was making a coffee cake for after the play. Suddenly, the labor pains started so bad, I went right down to the floor. A neighbor took me to the camp hospital, two minutes away. I tell you, they didn't have time to do anything, I went on the table, my water broke, and you swam out. You know, I was in a corner room, so there were windows on two sides. When you were born, a little bird flew to one window, knocked three times with his mouth, and then flew to the other window and knocked again. The nurse who was there said, "You're going to be lucky, your family."

## SRULEK

We made a big celebration, but the champagne we had prepared was stolen by some Romanian Jews. Soon we had to think to go somewhere out of Europe. I wouldn't stay in

Europe for no money. Chaim and Eva had papers to go to America already, so we wanted to go too. At that time, there was a Jewish organization, HIAS, that was helping Jewish refugees to come to America. I went to them in Munich and put in my name. A man gave me an interview.

He said, "You are Srulek Rubinek, the grandson of the rabbi from Busko-Zdrój?"

I said, "Yes, how do you know about me?"

He answered, "Never mind. You are not going to America. You will go to Israel."

I didn't understand why he said this and who he was and how he knew about me. Till this day, I never found out. And I could not get papers to go to the United States.

## FRANIA

My Uncle Leon made arrangements, through his wife's relatives, to immigrate to Canada. They were already in Montreal. My Uncle Chaim wrote to his brother Leon and said that Leon should sponsor us to come to Canada. Canada let you come in at that time, but you had to have a close relative to sponsor you. So Chaim said to Leon, "Don't worry. I'll pay for it," because he knew his brother Leon wouldn't give away a cent.

## SRULEK

In May of 1949, we went on a ship, the *Scythia*, to Canada. You were nine months old.

## FRANIA

That was a ship? It was meant for cattle, not people. The whole boat was refugees. I was so sick on that trip, other people had to look after you. There was a sailor, I remember, he took pity on me, and he was bringing me oranges to make me well.

## SRULEK

I traded that sailor a beautiful cigarette lighter for an egg so you could have something healthy to eat. I remember, there was a Christian missionary on that ship. He came to me and wanted me to believe in Jesus.

I said to him, "I don't know if there's a God or not, but I'm *sure* he didn't have a son."

We arrived at the port in Québec City. People from the Jewish Congress welcomed us and also a delegation from the Canadian government. I came down from the ship, and I cried. That's it. I'm alive. I'm here.

## FRANIA

A French-Canadian man came over to Srulek, put his arm around him, and said, "Don't you worry. Don't cry. You're in a good country." And then he gave us a loaf of white sliced bread and ten dollars.

## SRULEK

In Montreal, we stayed for a few days with her Uncle Leon and his wife. They made us feel very low. She would say to me, "You know, I can't even think in Yiddish anymore. Only in English." That burned me up. She was a greenhorn, an immigrant, just like me. And she would tell me not to eat like this, not to walk like that, do this, do that. Just like servants, she was treating us.

We lived in a little room, no windows, in the daytime, it was nighttime. And I was sitting there with you on my lap and thinking that before, in the camp, I was a somebody, and now I am nothing. I got a job in a fur factory, sixty hours a week for thirty-six dollars.

## FRANIA

We saved money from Germany, five hundred dollars, but we had to use it for "key money" to get an apartment. So for two dollars, we bought a table, and for another four dollars, we had two chairs. And we slept on the floor.

## SRULEK

And then I began to understand my new country. A man came in and said we could fill the whole apartment with furniture. Not to pay him now, just to give five dollars a week. I said to him, "You don't know me. How can you trust me to pay?"

He said, "Welcome to the new land."

## FRANIA

Then Srulek got a job in a factory as a presser. That was considered the lowest job for immigrants. But he was working only forty hours a week and making a hundred twenty dollars. People that knew us from Föhrenwald came to me and said, "What happened to your husband? He was a director, an actor. How can you let him go so low? A presser?"

I said, "Look. We have a child. We're starting a new life. We take charity from nobody. He's the same man he always was. Yes, he goes into the factory as a presser. But when he comes out, for me, he's the prime minister."

# SEVENTEEN

THE REUNION WITH THE BANIAS is on Sunday, August 10. My mother has terrible stomach cramps this morning—but, thank God, she doesn't have one of her migraines.

She says, "Well, listen, I can't cry anymore, so all my feelings go to my stomach and twist it in a knot."

Vic, Melanie, and the crew are already at the Bania farm, filming them, waiting for our arrival. I drive my parents from Pińczów through the little village of Włochy, and then I take the little road that leads to the Bania farm, all three of us nervous.

When I drive through the gate that leads to the farmhouse, I see that sitting on chairs are grandchildren, sons-in-law, daughters—I didn't know who was who—and in the middle of it, on a bench, is a tiny old lady in a babushka: Zofia.

My father and mother barely wait for me to stop the car before they jump out and run to Zofia. I see a man who must be Maniek, because my father runs to him and kisses him like a long-lost son. Maniek looks nothing like I expected, I guess because in all my parents' stories, Maniek is a little boy. Now he looks as old as my father. My mother hugs Zofia, and then they trade: my mother embraces Maniek while my father hugs and kisses Zofia. My mother's stomach pains completely disappear. They all keep trading hugs and kisses and touching each other as if they can't believe it's real. I just stand there and watch, tears running down my face, speechless.

My father takes me by the hand and brings me to Zofia. "This is my son," he tells her in Polish. I take her hand and kiss it, and then hug her. It's like meeting a grandmother I never knew.

Zofia is the only person who doesn't cry that day. She looks very happy and smiles and laughs all day, and she is clearly full of joy about my parents being here with her. But not one tear.

At one point, I see Zofia whisper something into my father's ear. Later, my father told me she said, "I know you brought money, don't give it to Maniek, he'll drink it. We need a new tractor."

Through it all, Vic films everything. Stories are told, memories are shared—all of it in Polish. I don't ask Agnieszka to interpret. What I'm experiencing needs no translation.

# ALL IN THE TELLING 261

**FRANIA AND SRULEK**
(at their home in Ottawa, after their return from Poland)

**FRANIA AND SRULEK**
(Föhrenwald DP camp 1947)

**IN THE DISPLACED PERSONS CAMP**
(Föhrenwald DP camp 1947)

**SRULEK PERFORMING IN GOLD DIGGERS**
(by Sholom Aleichem, in Föhrenwald)

**SRULEK PERFORMS THE TITLE ROLE** (on stilts), **OF THE GOLEM**
(by H. Leivick in Föhrenwald)

**SRULEK AND JACOB SANDLER**
(co-directors of the theatre company in Föhrenwald)

**LUDWIG AND FRANIA IN LODZ**
(circa 1945)

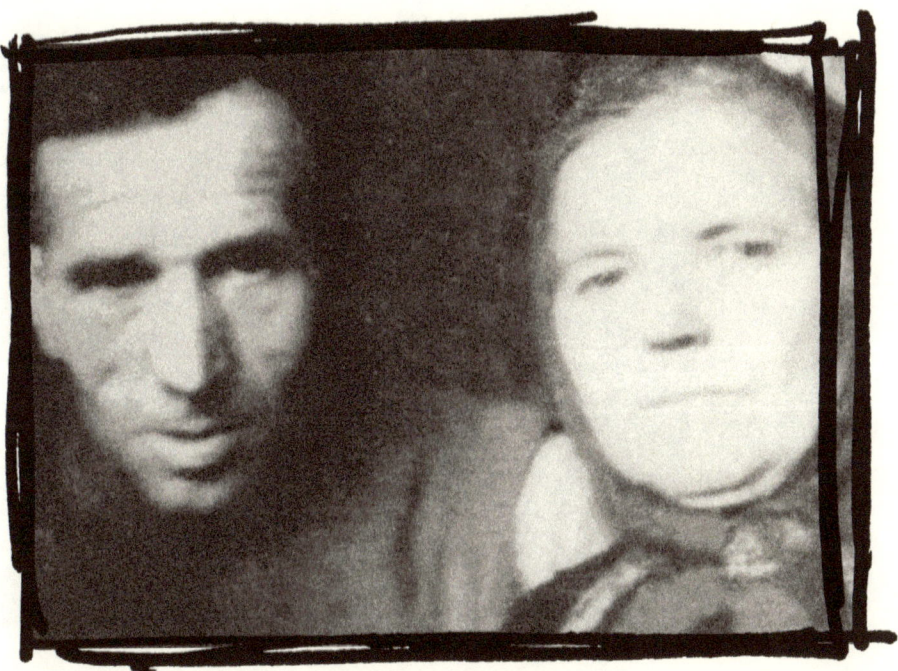

**ZOFIA AND LUDWIG BANIA**
(after the war, circa 1950)

**SRULEK'S ARRIVAL TO CANADA**
(Immigration card)

Srulek looking around inside the old farmhouse.

Maniek and Srulek during the reunion.

## ALL IN THE TELLING 265

**SRULEK AND MANIEK**
(during the reunion in Poland 1986)

**LUDWIG AND ZOFIA'S OLD FARMHOUSE**
(that hid the Rubineks 1942-1945)

**ZOFIA BANIA IN 1986**
(the day of the reunion)

ALL IN THE TELLING 267

**ZOFIA, SRULEK, AND FRANIA**
(outside the new house in which Zofia and Maniek now live)

**SRULEK IN LODZ**
(standing by the wall where people were lined up and shot for breaking curfew)

THE RUINS OF FRANIA'S FAMILY HOME ON THE SQUARE IN PIŃCZÓW.

SRULEK AT THE ENTRANCE OF HIS APARTMENT HOUSE IN LODZ
(where he saw his father for the last time)

**SAUL WITH HIS MOTHER AND FATHER IN PIŃCZÓW.**
(Israel and Frania used to rendevous here when they were young.)

**Saul and Srulek**
(in Föhrenwald DP camp 1949)

**Frania and Saul**
(in Montreal, 1950)

**The Rubinek Family**
(in Montreal, 1952)

# EIGHTEEN

BY THE TIME I GET BACK FROM POLAND, Kate has moved out of the apartment. I can't say I am surprised.

We meet a few times to talk things over, and she tells me she has forgiven me for lying to her, she's over it now. She seems genuinely eager to know how the Poland trip went, and she's pleased that I've continued to work on the book. She says she would love to read it when I'm done. Then she tells me she's started seeing someone else.

I feel sad, but I have to admit, I'm also relieved. I've had the whole time in Poland to get used to the idea that our relationship has run its course. We were good for each other for a time, until we weren't. She's the one who had the courage to end it, not me, but I now know she was right.

Soon after my return from Poland, my nightmare comes back again. I'm panicked it will keep coming again and again, as it did until I was eighteen and found out the cause of it, and thought I'd killed it forever. But knowing what caused it doesn't stop it. It took almost fifteen years, but it came back when I was living with Kate, when I started telling lies to her and to my parents. And it came back again the first night in Poland. And again now. I sit up in bed, too frightened to sleep, and wonder: *What triggers this fucking thing? Lies? What kind of lies? Whose lies? I've told Kate the truth, and I told my parents the truth. So why?*

Six months later, I finish writing the book, called So Many Miracles, the same title as the documentary film.

I find a publisher. By complete coincidence, the publisher is Penguin.

Penguin decides to release the book the same month as the documentary has its world premiere at the Toronto Film Festival, in the fall of 1987, a year after we shot it.

It's an amazing thing for me to have my parents there, in the audience, seeing the film and experiencing the audience's emotional reaction to it. When the film is over, people spontaneously stand and turn to my parents—sitting in the middle of the theater—and applaud them.

Later, when I'm alone, Rachel comes to see me.

"It's good, the film—really good. Mom and Dad were really happy with it. It's a great thing you did, going back there with them and telling their story."

"I wish you'd been there. In Poland."

She is silent for a moment. "You know why I can't go back."

I do know why, but it's something we have promised each other we will never talk about.

Before we both get too gloomy, she changes the subject. "What else is happening?"

"I met someone, Rachel."

"Wow. Who?"

"Her name is Elinor. She's a literary agent, handling playwrights and screenwriters. We've been seeing each other for a couple of months now."

"Elinor? Elinor what? Jewish?"

"Are you planning to dump ashes on your head?"

"No," she laughs, "but I might rend my garments."

"Elinor's last name is Reid. Her background is all Scotland and England."

"You seem to have a type."

"Not Jewish? Maybe. Or maybe my type is Celtic. Anyway, Elinor told me there's an Irish great-grandmother who the family always said had her 'ways,' her strange 'wee ways.' Apparently those 'ways' included lighting candles on Friday nights and keeping dairy dishes separate from meat."

"So Elinor is, like, one-sixteenth Jewish?"

"I don't know. But she's a redhead, and so is most of her family, so maybe she's more Viking than Jewish."

"You two serious?" Rachel asks me.

"I think so."

"Have you told Mom and Dad?"

"They've already met her."

"And?"

"They think she's too good for me."

---

After the Toronto Film Festival, the So Many Miracles documentary screens on television all over the world.

But not in Poland.

Nine months after its premiere in Toronto, the film is being vetted by the Censorship Committee of the Polish People's Republic.

I've been getting letters from Agnieszka, our film unit's translator/spy. We've become colleagues, and through shared experience, even friends. She has a lot to tell me.

---

Agnieszka is instructed to present the documentary to what they call *Główny Urząd Kontroli Prasy, Publikacji i Widowisk*, or the Main Office for the Control of the Press, Publications, and Public Performances.

It's tough times in Poland for the Communist regime's bureaucracy. Over the past eighteen months, the government has arrested one committee member and fired three. Two men are left.

As these two leftover committee members take their seats, they are startled by a loud electronic blast of static. The culprit is a speaker set up on the boardroom table. Actually, the real culprit is Agnieszka, nervous to begin with, who has mistakenly turned on the television while attaching a wire from a VHS machine to the wrong input.

Józef Radzik almost falls over when the noise hits him. He looks like it wouldn't take much to push him off balance. Radzik, in his mid-forties, is thin—too thin for his six-foot-two frame—and anyway, he's got about four ounces of vodka in him. He's saved from a sprawl by a strong hand that grabs his arm. The hand, which has thick, blunt fingers, belongs to Aleks Kosevich, who is in his mid-fifties and built like a fire hydrant—short, stocky, bald head like a pink bullet, cursed with a permanent scowl even when he smiles, a rare event.

Oddly, Radzik laughs at his near fall, which earns a suspicious glance from Kosevich.

"Przepraszam," Agnieszka says in a shaky voice. I'm sorry. She's embarrassed, and even worse, she can feel she's blushing. She does not want to be here, but she was assigned this Censorship Committee position by the Ministry of Culture—a job she's never done before—and not only that, she was given explicit instructions to present the film in a specific way. She is sure this will not go over well.

"My name is Agnieszka Kadinski. My report today—Sunday, May 1, 1988—to the committee is for approval to broadcast a documentary film made in the summer of 1986, in the Polish People's Republic. The documentary unit came—"

Kosevich interrupts her with the irritated, gruff bark of a lifelong smoker: "No, no, no. We don't approve or disapprove. I am Aleksander

Kosevich, committee chairman. Miss Kadinski, I don't want any misunderstandings, especially in the press. I don't know how they get the minutes of these meetings, but they—"

"Because we're being recorded," Radzik declares, looking up at the ceiling as if he knows exactly where there's an "eye" watching them. "Recordings get leaked."

Kosevich nervously looks up. So does Agnieszka. There's nothing on the ceiling except a few ugly brown stains from water leaks over the years.

"For the record," says Kosevich to one of the suspicious stains that could be concealing the eye, "that was committee member Józef Radzik. Personally, I don't believe there was a leak."

"If there was no leak, then why were there six on this committee, now two?" Radzik asks, his tone more wry than confrontational.

Kosevich is thrown off balance for a moment. "These are sensitive times. And the point—"

"Fucking horrible times," Radzik persists.

"My point is, this committee makes recommendations only. The Ministry of Culture makes the final decision." He sits back, his stiff posture indicating the discussion is over.

But Radzik isn't done. "Unless the decision is unpopular. Then they'll say it was *our* decision. At which point, there will be zero members of the Censorship Committee," he says with a laugh, "which will *definitely* be popular."

"Enough! Józef, what the hell is the matter with you today?"

"Well, for one thing, I've been drinking ... in honor of May Day. I have more, if you want?" He pulls a flask from his briefcase.

A noise from outside makes them all turn to the sound. The windows on the second floor at 5 Mysia Street in Warsaw are cheap, thin glass. Street noise is constant, but this is not normal. This sounds like a crowd of people not very far away—a rumbling, with shouts mixed into it.

"May Day protest," Radzik says, smiling.

Kosevich's scowl deepens. "It's under control."

A police siren speeds past.

"Is it?" Radzik asks. Then another siren blasts by. And one more. He lifts his flask in a toast: "Happy International Workers' Day!" He drinks.

Kosevich swears under his breath and looks up at Agnieszka, who stands at one end of the table, beside the television. "Please continue your report," Kosevich tells her.

Agnieszka checks her notes and does her best to be professional. "The documentary unit came to film a reunion, after forty-one years, with the Rubineks and the farmers: Zofia Bania, age eighty-four, and her son, Maniek, age fifty. Ludwig Bania, the husband of Zofia, was not present for the reunion because ..." She searches her notes for the reason. "Because ..."

"Because he was probably drunk," Radzik jokes, laughing.

Agnieszka finds the reason for the farmer's absence in her notes. "Ah. Because in 1972, Ludwig Bania fell from the roof of his barn—"

"Because he was drunk!" Radzik says too loudly, still laughing.

"And he ..." She turns a page in her notebook. "...died."

This stops Radzik's laughter, more from surprise than respect for the dead.

"I am required to inform you," Agnieszka says, reading from her notes matter-of-factly, "there has been an accusation of murder that may have occurred while the Jewish couple was hidden at the Bania farm."

Radzik is first to respond: "Murder! Now I can stay awake!"

Kosevich isn't sure he heard what he just heard. "What? Murder? I was not told anything about—"

"The Ministry has a concern," Agnieszka says, raising her voice to make sure she's heard, "that if the film is broadcast, there may be public controversy. The Ministry asks this committee to form an opinion about—"

"Will there be controversy?" Radzik interrupts, astounded by the question. "A public accusation of a murder that took place while the Banias were hiding Jews, and the Ministry wonders if there will be controversy? Let me think for a quarter of a second." He looks up at the invisible eye on the ceiling. "Is the pope Catholic?"

Kosevich hurries to restore order. He speaks directly to where he imagines the eye is watching. "No, no, there is only a *possibility* of controversy if we decide to recommend broadcast, and then, only if the Ministry—"

"Well, of course, only if it's broadcast, Aleks! Or the only controversy will be here, in this room!"

Kosevich pinches the bridge of his nose. "I'm getting one of my migraines." He begins searching through his briefcase. "I'm sure I brought my pills."

Radzik holds out his flask to Kosevich, who glances up at the eye and pretends he doesn't notice the offer.

Kosevich turns to Agnieszka. "May I ask, please," he says, trying for calm, but his voice is stretched thin, "who is doing the accusing, and who was murdered?"

Agnieszka, expecting this, reads her reply from her notes: "Thank you for your question. It has been determined that you should see the film before any explanations—"

"Wait!" Radzik interrupts. "Of course! This murder has something to do with the farmer falling off the roof!"

Kosevich stops his search for pills. "What? No, no, no. She said it happened while the Rubineks were hiding there."

"So while they were hiding there, maybe the farmer did something to them, and the Rubineks killed him in revenge."

"Thirty years later, the Rubineks hired an assassin to push him off the roof of his barn?"

"Well," says Radzik, "when you put it like that ..."

Kosevich has emptied the contents of his entire briefcase onto the table. "I don't have my pills." This time, when Radzik holds out the flask, Kosevich grabs it and takes a long drink. "Show us the fucking film," Kosevich says, eyes closed, hoping the vodka will do something about the pounding in his head. He suspects the film might make it worse.

The documentary plays on the Censorship Committee room's television. It's the same version that was screened a few months ago at the Toronto Film Festival, and also on Canadian television. The same version I will play sixteen years later for my daughter Hannah's eighth-grade class.

Several times throughout the screening, Agnieszka pauses the video to make comments, as she has been instructed to do by the Ministry of Culture.

Early in the film, the narrator says a German soldier was killed in the Pińczów church by a sniper. Agnieszka pauses the film and says, "According to the University of Kraków's Department of Contemporary History, the assassinated German was not a soldier, he was a Gestapo officer. The shooting did not take place in the church, but rather, in the street. And not by a sniper. He was shot face-to-face by a member of the Polish resistance. I was instructed by the Ministry to tell you this as an example of ..." She reads from her notes: "As an example that not everything in the documentary is factual."

"Oh, really?" from Radzik, sitting back in his chair, amused. "How about the statement 'Not everything is factual.' Is that factual?"

Agnieszka has no answer for this. She takes a breath and restarts the video.

Kosevich's migraine has him leaning all the way back in his chair, a cool, damp cloth over his eyes. Radzik takes occasional pulls of vodka from his flask.

After a few minutes, Agnieszka pauses the video again. "I am instructed to inform you that the next section of the documentary contains photographs taken on a Pińczów street by an anonymous photographer. They have been verified as authentic and correspond with the October 1942 date of a German order to relocate the Jewish population of this area. However—"

"*Relocate?!*" Radzik interrupts her, suddenly furious. "When they replace the oxygen in your lungs with poison gas, it is not to relocate your breath!"

Kosevich, leaning back in his chair, eyes still covered, says, "She didn't write the words, Jósef. She's just reporting them."

Agnieszka says, "*Relocate* is better than *for unknown reasons.*" She says this without thinking, remembering the argument she had with me about the Pińczów illustrated history book.

Kosevich takes the cloth off his eyes. "What are you talking about?"

"Nothing. I will continue showing you the—"

"Wait a minute," Kosevich says, sitting up. "Let me ask you: You heard or you were told about the Polish attitude about the killing of their Jewish neighbors, yes?"

"Me? I don't—"

Radzik gets involved: "Aleks, leave her alone, this has nothing to do with her."

"It has *everything* to do with her. She is the future of Poland."

Radzik lifts his hands in surrender. "You're absolutely right.

Which reminds me." He holds up his flask, offering it to Agnieszka. "Vodka?" She shakes her head. "Well," he says, "when you change your mind—and you *will*—let me know."

Kosevich continues: "Let me ask you, Miss Kadinski, do you think maybe it was a natural reaction for the ordinary Polish citizen at that time to say the fate of the Jews was not entirely undeserved? That maybe Jews are not completely blameless, or why have they been so often punished by history?"

Agnieszka is taken aback. "'Not completely blameless'?"

"Not said by me!" Kosevich raises his voice. "Ordinary Polish citizens said it! Felt it. After living for centuries under the Catholic Church."

Radzik, energized now, says, "You mean before Socialism saved us all?" Then, to Agnieszka: "Would you like that drink now?"

Kosevich turns angrily toward Radzik. "You are asking to be replaced or arrested, I hope you realize that."

"I know—you think they're going to take me out and shoot me." Radzik looks up at the ceiling's eye that may or may not be there. "Have you considered that after this regime falls, Aleks, the new regime will see this tape and declare me a hero? Maybe I'm being very clever."

"Your mouth is your worst enemy."

"Me? Your 'Jews are not completely blameless' statement is on the record. And personally, I find it offensive, if you want the truth."

Kosevich is surprised by this. "'Personally'?"

"My father was a Jew. Still is, as far as I know."

That stops everything for a moment.

"You're a Jew?"

"Well, on my father's side, so not according to Orthodox rabbis, but it would have been plenty good enough for Hitler." He studies Kosevich's face. "Are you all right, Aleks? Are you going to faint?"

Kosevich shrugs, leaning back in his chair. "So you are half a Jew. So what? I'm not impressed. I only wonder why you kept it a secret for ... how many years?"

"From you? Well, when did we meet? Ten years ago? Since then. But don't take it personally. I don't tell anybody."

"Why? You could have told me. I'm your friend."

Radzik suddenly whirls on Kosevich. "Why? You want to know why? Twenty years ago, my father was a captain in the army. After Israel blew away Egypt, Syria, and Jordan in a war that lasted less than a week, our brilliant Polish leadership realized that Poland and Israel were now in two opposite blocs, and in the case of armed conflict, there could be a loyalty conflict for officers who are Jews. My father sells used furniture now. He was never a Zionist. Now, he's thinking about it."

"You are understandably oversensitive in this area, Józef, you're a Jew."

"Well, Aleks, your 'oversensitive' remark is also on the record."

"I think ..." Agnieszka hesitates. Radzik and Kosevich are both surprised, since neither of them expected her to join in the discussion.

"I think," she continues, "that even under enormous pressure—religious, social—Poles risked their lives—and, as this documentary shows—they saved this Jewish couple."

"And," adds Kosevich, "and under the threat of death. Did you know, did they teach you in school, that during the Nazi occupation, a death sentence was automatically imposed on Poles who helped Jews? Poland was the only occupied country, the only one, where this was done. Did you know that?"

"No," Agnieszka says, "I was not—"

"No," Kosevich says, "they don't teach you that in media and communications. Your parents, your grandparents—they told you about it?"

"They don't talk about it."

"Of course not. They were living in hell themselves, forced to watch it day after day. What could they do about it?"

"What you are saying, Aleks," Radzik says, "is people are human in human conditions, and it is cruel nonsense for the world to judge things people do in *in*-human conditions."

Kosevich, surprised to be agreeing with Radzik, says, "That's … right."

"As if water could be measured by air, or air by fire."

"Exactly."

"Or deeds done in hell measured by the rules of heaven." Radzik drinks more vodka. He looks at Agnieszka and Kosevich. They're both staring at him. "What? Only half of me is a Jew. The other half drinks."

Near the end of the documentary, Agnieszka pauses the video one more time.

"This next section contains the facts around the central problem of the accusation of murder. The Ministry asks that you—"

She is interrupted by a ringing telephone.

Kosevich picks up the receiver. "Aleks Kosevich speaking." He listens. "Krysia, not now, I am in the middle of—" He listens, his expression grim. "What? They are searching his room right now? Where is Tomek?" He listens. "Call the university and find out." He listens. "Calm down. Put whoever is in charge on the phone." He waits, then says stiffly, "I am Aleksander Kosevich, Tomek's father. I am chairman of the Committee for Control of the Press, Publications, and Public Performances. What is the problem?" He listens, anger growing. "If he was there—and I doubt it—then Tomek certainly was not there as a protest leader. He is only eighteen years old, the idea is ridiculous. What is your name and rank?" He listens. "Hello? … Hello?"

Clearly, the person on the other end of the line has ended the call.

Kosevich, shaken, hangs up. "Please excuse the interruption. Nothing serious," he says.

"Sounded serious," Radzik says, concerned.

"A bureaucratic error, nothing more."

"A bureaucratic error," Radzik replies, "is the exact opposite of 'nothing more.' Aleks, you have to go. They will arrest him."

Kosevich grabs his coat and quickly walks out.

Radzik turns to Agnieszka. "Like I said, fucking horrible times. Well, this is Poland, when has it *not* been horrible times?"

Agnieszka opens her briefcase, takes out a copy of *Ilustrowana Historia Pińczowa*, the history of Pińczów book that I asked her to return to the governor. "Mister Radzik? I have this book. I was hoping a member of the committee could ... The Ministry of Culture should be aware of ..." She peters out, uncertain of how to continue.

"Aware of what?" he asks her, curious.

Agnieszka hesitates. "You mentioned earlier, you are Jewish?"

"Yes. Is there a problem?" he says, his tone suddenly wary.

"No, no. Of course not."

Radzik looks at her for a long moment, then puts his coat on and starts to go.

Agnieszka stops him. "Mister Radzik, you said if I changed my mind ... ?"

Radzik turns to her. "About?" And then he realizes and smiles broadly. "Ah! Of course!" He takes the flask out of his pocket and hands it to her. She looks around for a cup, then—fuck it—she drinks straight from the flask. She hands it back, and he drinks too. Feeling more comfortable with her now, Radzik says, "You graduated from ...?"

"University of Warsaw."

"My mother was once a University of Warsaw professor of literature."

"Not anymore?"

"Did you know that by 1940, the Germans had closed all the institutions of higher learning here?"

"All?" She's surprised by the information.

"All. Education in Polish was banned. Punishable by death."

Surprised has turned into astounded. "By *death*?"

"Why educate Poles if their fate is to become serfs of the master race? But there was resistance. My mother helped organize what they called the Secret University of Warsaw. One of my mother's students was a Jew. She saved his life. They … they became involved. I was born during the war, during the time she was protecting him. The Germans found out. Not that she was hiding a Jew, but that she was teaching Polish literature in secret. And they hanged her for it. My father raised me by himself. I never knew about any of it. Not about my mother, not that he's a Jew. Nothing. Until twenty years ago, when the Polish army threw him out for being a Jew. That's when he told me about who he is. And about my mother."

"I can understand," Agnieszka says carefully, "why your father didn't tell you he is a Jew. Why not tell you about your mother? She was a hero."

Radzik takes a moment before he says, "My father could never forgive himself that she saved him, but he couldn't save her." He takes another pull of vodka from the flask. "You said this last part of the film is about the murder accusation?"

"Yes."

"Play it."

Agnieszka starts the video. On film, an actress hired to play young Frania is in labor, in a lot of pain. An actress playing young Zofia and an actor playing young Srulek do what they can to help Frania as she gives birth.

Frania's voice in the documentary: "It's so hard to talk about it, really hard to talk about it. You see, it was so cold. It must have been at that time twenty below. She said, 'Twenty? It was thirty below.' And I was dressed in my coat, a winter coat, and I had boots right to my knees. So cold it was, such a wind, it's no wonder that the child couldn't survive. How could a child survive? When I gave birth, my husband, when he saw the little head, he wanted to pull. This is the irony of it: my husband now, if somebody will cut his finger, he could faint, he's flat on the floor, and here when you have to do things—to survive, I mean—you do the most difficult things what you can imagine. But she's right, Zofia, it's meant to be like this. Maybe I would still look for my daughter somewhere. I have a friend in New York, she's still looking for her daughter. She'll never find her, she'll never have her."

Agnieszka stops the video.

"I don't understand," Radzik says. "There is no accusation of murder."

"During the filming," Agnieszka tells him, "I was a witness to a Rubinek family argument. They had just finished filming the scene you just saw. The actors went to have lunch. I stayed there with the Rubineks. My job was to report on their conversations. By now, after two weeks together, they forgot about me, or they didn't care that I was there."

---

My mother says, "She was very believable, this girl playing me. Where is she? I should tell her how good she did it."

"They're getting something to eat," I tell her. "Is there anything we should be filming to make it more accurate?"

My father says, "We didn't even know how to cut the cord."

"Zofia knew. She knew how to do it. Then she took the baby away. A baby girl. And then she came back. Alone."

Then my father says, "She probably killed it."

My mother turns to him, her voice sharp, "Srulek, what's the matter with you?"

"He knows this already," he replies.

She looks at me. "Does he? I don't remember what we told him and what we did not."

I'm in shock. "What? Told me what? What are you saying? Zofia ... she told you she killed ... ?"

"No! She did not tell us anything. Nothing," my father says. "Just, she said the baby died. That's all. And we did not ask."

"You didn't ... you didn't say anything?"

"What was there to say?" my mother asks, getting upset by my questions. "We understood right away. She was thinking: *If a neighbor hears a baby crying in that house, we are all dead.*"

"But, Ma, I thought she died of the cold, or ... But you, you let it happen? To save all your lives?"

My father is getting upset with me too. "No, no, no! That's not what we did! It was dark. It was freezing cold. It was chaos. We did not know what Zofia was going to do."

"Listen. We had a plan. We set up, secretly, that a few days after the birth, Juzia, Ludwig's sister, will take the baby to Warsaw and give it there to my sister Shaindel. And Shaindel will give the baby to the nuns. The point is, we did not tell Ludwig or Zofia the plan. Juzia told us to keep it a secret until the last second. She didn't trust her own brother not to betray us, and to tell you the truth, it's our fault too because we didn't yet know if we could trust Zofia."

"We didn't think," my father says quietly, "we didn't know what was right, who to trust."

My mother is getting more distraught. "And if she lived? If we sent her to a convent? People who did that are still looking for the children today. You read the stories—I don't know if you did—but I read plenty of stories. How many children they don't even know who they are?"

"We have to change what we're filming," I tell them. "We have to put this in the documentary."

"No!" they both shout at the same time.

"You are not going to do that!" My mother's voice is more vehement than I've ever heard it before. "We are not going to accuse Zofia of something that if she did it, it's our fault too! If not for Zofia, we wouldn't be sitting here, of that, you could be sure!"

"We have an obligation to tell the truth," I say.

"This is our story! Not yours!" My father's voice is no less harsh. "We will decide what truth to tell!"

"Well," I say, "the truth is out now. Agnieszka is standing right over there, listening to every word we say."

"So what?" my father says. "You think Agnieszka will give a press conference to say Zofia killed our baby?"

"But Mom, Dad, if we say this in the documentary, we'll show it was a tragedy, not a murder," I plead.

My mother puts an end to the argument: "Zofia will be alive to see it! And Maniek! And their whole family! In the documentary, my daughter died at birth from the cold, or we stop the whole thing this minute!"

---

Agnieszka tells Radzik what happened, the gist of it. He says to her, "The Ministry of Culture is worried an accusation of murder—that Zofia Bania deliberately killed the infant—could come out in the press, especially from the Rubineks' son, Saul. Right?"

"I think so," Agnieszka says.

"You spent time with him. Would he do that?"

"Not while his mother and father are alive. Not while Zofia and Maniek are alive. But if he did, he wouldn't call it murder."

"Well," Radzik says, "in any case, these committee proceedings are over, so the Ministry will have to do without our recommendation." He looks up to the eye.

Agnieszka says, "You think we are being ...?"

"Really, I have no idea." Radzik walks toward the door, then looks at Agnieszka one last time. He smiles, places his flask on the table near her, and leaves.

Agnieszka looks up at the eye. She picks up the flask and takes a long drink for courage. Then she holds up the *Ilustrowana Historia Pińczowa* book and shows it to the eye.

She's nervous but resolute. She knows she's about to speak to someone who could have her arrested. Or she could be about to speak to absolutely no one.

"This book, *Ilustrowana Historia Pińczowa*, is about the history of the town of Pińczów. It was a gift from the governor of the province to the Rubinek family. The Rubineks asked me to return it. They said it is unacceptable. This book, a four-hundred-year history of Pińczów, does not mention the murder of three thousand Pińczów Jews. Half the population of the city. I returned the book to the governor's office, but you can still find a copy of this book in many bookstores all over Poland. I did. It is also, right now, in the University of Kraków library. The university published it three years ago. Today, the chairman of this committee asked me what I was taught in school. I was *not* taught that three million Polish Jews were murdered during the Nazi occupation. I *was* taught that six million Polish citizens were killed. Three million Polish Jews, now that they were dead, became full Polish citizens, taking the total number of Polish victims to six million. This is, I would say, an extraordinary feat of accountancy that makes invisible what happened here to the Jewish people. Six million cancels out three million. In this book are two specific passages about Jews. Only two. One passage is on page eighty-one, and the other is on page one hundred forty. For anyone listening, or watching—I assume I am speaking to the Ministry of Culture—when you read the lies on those pages, you may find those lies to be of cultural significance."

Agnieszka starts to leave but looks around one last time, as if the people monitoring the recording devices might suddenly reveal themselves.

---

When I was seven years old, I overheard my parents talking about their daughter, who had died. Died the day she was born. My parents never named her. So I named her.

Rachel.

When I have no one else to talk to about my parents, about anything, all my life, I have Rachel. She is my guardian angel.

# NINETEEN

THE IDEA OF BEING A FATHER, of having to put a child's welfare ahead of my own, scares me. I have never felt adult enough, unselfish enough, to commit to that. I've been on my own since I left home when I was eighteen, and I never had to think about anyone else when I made choices. I never asked my parents for money, and so I never felt obligated to check in with them about the important decisions in my life. The first time I did that as an adult, my father dumped ashes on his head and my mother wept.

The next time the subject was made real to me was when Kate said that maybe I was writing the book for children I might someday have.

But now, after being with Elinor for a year, I realize that I am no longer terrified to be a father. Something about being with her takes all my fear away. Well, most of my fear.

Elinor and I have been living together for a couple of months or so, and my parents have invited us to come to Florida for Passover. It won't be the first time they meet, but it'll be the first time since they know we're living together.

We decide to drive to Florida. The whole trip, Elinor reads about the Passover ceremony. She even studies a Haggadah she brought with her, the guidebook we use during the seder, the Passover ceremonial meal.

We arrive in Hollywood, Florida, in my little Honda Civic in the early afternoon, and after checking into a hotel, we drive to my parents' condo. My mother opens the front door with a big, genuine smile. Behind her, standing a little in the shadows, my father seems shy.

Elinor has a bouquet of flowers, which she hands to my mother. "These are for you."

"Beautiful!" my mother says. "Come in! Come in!"

There's an awkward silence as we take off our coats and hang them up in the front hall. We all follow my mother into the living room. I see she has removed the plastic from the living room couch. Yes, she does that in Florida too. Tea and cookies are waiting for us on the coffee table.

"We will have an early dinner," my mother says, "but a few cookies and tea wouldn't hurt."

Tea is poured. Cookies are nibbled. "These are wonderful," Elinor says.

"*Mandelbroit*," my mother says. "Almond bread. But made without the usual flour because that's not allowed on Passover."

"So," my father says, "your first Passover, right?"

"It is. Thank you so much for inviting me."

"Well, listen," my mother says, "what can I tell you. I hear you're already living together, so we figured we have to know you better, right?"

"Right," Elinor says, not quite sure how to react. She already knows the whole story about the ashes on the head and the prayer for the dead in response to Kate.

"All right," my mother says, "Elinor, you make yourself at home. You," she says, taking my hand, "come with me."

I follow my mom into the kitchen.

My father is now alone with Elinor. After a brief and uncomfortable silence, he takes a newspaper clipping out of his pocket. "This is for you." He hands her the clipping. The headline is "Nazi Doctors in Death Camps." "Read," he says. "Later, we will discuss."

Elinor stares at the clipping and immediately starts to read it. She's afraid that later there might be a pop quiz.

In the kitchen, my mother puts the flowers into a vase. "She's very nice," she says. "But when I first met her, I knew that already. So. You are together now for...?"

"Over a year."

"And how long living together?"

"A little over two months."

My mother sits at the kitchen table beside me. "You're going to get married?"

"Do I need to pretend to write another book?"

She doesn't find that funny. "So, yes?"

"Okay. Don't go crazy, Ma. Elinor and I plan to get married. We want to have children."

My mother does not go crazy. In fact, she doesn't seem at all upset. She takes a deep breath. "All right. Go help your father with the table." She calls into the other room: "Elinor!"

"No, Ma! What are you going to do?"

"Me? Nothing. Go. Elinor! Come help me in the kitchen!"

Elinor passes me in the hall outside the kitchen. She raises her eyebrows in a question. I shrug, *No idea*.

Elinor looks around the kitchen. There's absolutely nothing to do to help. It's spotless, all the prep dishes are cleaned, and dinner is under tinfoil, ready to be served.

"Sit," my mother says. "Let's talk. How is the hotel?"

"It's fine," Elinor says, taking a seat opposite my mother at the kitchen table.

"Call me Frania. You know, you could have stayed here. I'm not so old-fashioned like he probably told you. Your parents, they met Saul already?"

"Yes, Frania, a few times. We were all together for …um …"

"For what?"

"For … the winter holidays."

"You could say Christmas, I'm not going to faint. You have a big family?"

"I have two sisters."

"I have two sisters also. I used to have brothers. We were a big family. My husband also. So. You and my son. How are you doing?"

"We're good."

"You're talking about marriage, he told me."

"Frania, I understand that you might be afraid of having a daughter-in-law who shares nothing with your own history, with your culture, music, cooking, stories. I understand because that frightens me too—that I don't share those things about you. One thing made it a little less scary for me. We have one thing in common, one thing that could bring us together."

"My son? You're too good for him. But do me a favor, marry him. Listen, I already know you're going to do it, or you wouldn't be here." Elinor smiles, telling my mother she's right. "You probably know my husband recently survived lung cancer?"

Elinor has no idea where this is headed. "I'm … I'm so happy he's better."

"One lung, they took out already."

"I know. But he looks very strong."

"Oh, he has a very positive attitude to life, my husband."

"That's important."

"He says 'I used to have two horses to go up the hill. Now I have one, but I go to the top anyway, just a little more slowly.'"

"That's great."

"Listen, you know that stress and health are related?"

"Yes, of course."

"If my husband has non-Jewish grandchildren, it will kill him."

Silence. Elinor is speechless, flabbergasted. Frania gets up from the table and calls: "All right! Are we having a Passover seder or not? What are we waiting for, the Messiah?"

The dinner table is laid out with my mother's best dishes. My father explains the significance of all the ritual dishes on the table. He's in his element as rabbinical explainer-in-chief.

My mother lights the candles and gives the blessing. Everyone says, "Amen."

My father says, "You see the candlesticks on the table here?"

"They're beautiful," Elinor says. She looks at the two brass candlesticks on the table, their candles lit—old brass, not particularly ornate, and slightly mismatched.

"When we went back to Poland," my father tells her, "they let us go into the house where Frania lived with her family. The government gave us permission to film wherever we wanted."

"The people that were living there, oy vey," my mother says, "you should see their faces. They right away thought we're coming to take the house back. The Poles, they stole everything when the Jews were taken away."

"That day when the Germans took the Jews, in October 1942, that was the first night of Rosh Hashanah, the Jewish New Year. And that day, those candlesticks were on Frania's parents' table."

"When I went in my house," my mother says, "after so many years, in the dining room upstairs, sitting there, those two candlesticks. I right away grabbed them. Oh yes, it was ours. I tell you, I almost fainted."

"The Polish people living there, they got scared when they saw her pick up those candlesticks, so they gave them to us right away. The government person who was there with us, he said the candlesticks have to stay in Poland, they are very old, from the eighteenth century, and they are historical ... what do you call it?"

"Artifacts," my mother tells him.

"Those artifacts, they went straight into our suitcase."

After dinner, Elinor is in the kitchen, helping my mother put food away. I'm in the dining room with my father, clearing dishes. "Dad. The newspaper article. 'Nazi Doctors in Death Camps.' Really?"

"It's for knowledge! Something is wrong with learning about what happened to our people? That's why we have Passover!"

I call into the kitchen: "Ma! Elinor told me about the stress-related, cancer-causing non-Jewish-children thing!"

Elinor is mortified by the directness of this remark. It's not at all what she's used to in her own family dynamic.

My mother calls back to me: "What did I do? I'm not interfering! She's a wonderful girl! You should only be so lucky to marry her! But if you do, I'm only planting a seed so maybe she'll convert!"

---

Later, Elinor explains to my mother that she feels converting would be disrespectful to Judaism, since she's never been religious, and neither have I. It would be like using the conversion cynically, just for people to be comfortable with the marriage. My mother says off-handedly, "Ah, doesn't matter, do it anyway."

Elinor asks if it matters to me whether or not she converts to Judaism. I say that not only does it not matter to me, it makes no sense. It would make as much sense for me to convert to being a Celt. She says this is different.

"On one level," she says, "appearances matter to both your parents, but on a deeper level, the truth is that both your parents feel that if I'm not Jewish then our children won't be either."

Elinor does not convert to Judaism. When we marry, she doesn't even change her name. The marriage ceremony is presided over by a rabbi who is willing to marry interfaith couples. My parents decide that Elinor's decision not to convert to Judaism is not a reason to stay away from the wedding. They not only come, they are joyous. And Elinor's family are all there, too. Our families get along well, and there's a lot of laughter and happy tears. Our wedding has live music from both a klezmer band and bagpipes.

The next summer, Elinor gives birth to our daughter, Hannah. My parents take one look at their first grandchild, and all the crazy stuff—let me be honest: *most* of the crazy stuff—goes away.

Three years later, our son, Sam, is born, in our bedroom in Toronto. It's a home birth supervised by a midwife. That day, when we introduce three-year-old Hannah to her new little brother for the first time, I leave Elinor and the kids for a few minutes to get some water down in the kitchen.

Rachel is there, waiting for me.

"My son, Sam, will have Hannah. He gets to have an older sister."

Rachel's smile is unforgettable.

---

My parents never expected to have a grandchild, and now there are two. They've lived in their Ottawa house for thirty-three years, but now, in a whirlwind of activity that my father can barely keep up with, my mother sells the place in just five weeks. They move to Toronto to be close to their grandchildren.

My dad gets to spend a year with Sam and Hannah before his lung cancer returns and he passes. Five years later, my mom's heart gives out, and she joins my dad, forever together.

# TWENTY

IT'S THE FALL OF 2016, and my cousin, Gérard, who lives in France, gets in touch with me via Skype.

We haven't spoken or written to each other in over twenty years, we live so far away from each other, and we've never had a close relationship. No one told him I wrote a book about our family and made a documentary film. He has only recently seen the film and read my book. That's why he wanted to get in touch.

We talk about our lives and our parents. His mother died a few years ago. He tells me how much he regrets not having had the opportunity to confront his mother about why she lied about who she was and where she came from.

"Why didn't you ask your mother about it when she was alive? You had plenty of time. I told you all about it fifty years ago."

He tells me, much to my amazement, that he has absolutely no memory of my telling him that his mother, my mother's sister, was Jewish.

I'm shocked. "Gérard, when you were seventeen, I told you—in direct opposition to my own mother's wishes—that you're the son of a Jewish mother. That you're half-Jewish, and that your own mother wanted that kept hidden from you."

"I do not remember that at all," he says. "Probably all I hear that day is you tell me you are half-Jewish, which I already knew."

"That I was half-Jewish?"

"My mother, she tell me when I am young that she and her sisters are Polish Catholic, and that your mother, Frania, and her other sister, Marisha, they marry Jewish guys, but my mother, she marry my father, a French Catholic."

"How did you find out the truth?"

"Only three months ago, I receive email from a Jewish man who say he make a detailed genealogy chart. He wants input from my side *de famille*, specifically my mother's side. I look at this chart and see my mother's side is *désigné* Jewish, *nom de famille* Greenfeld. I email him back that he must have her family confused with someone else because my mother was born Zosia Lewitski, a Polish Catholic."

"Then what happened?"

"The genealogy guy email me back and says he is very sure of his facts. So I call my Aunt Marisha, who is eighty-six years old, living in Tel Aviv. I ask her what was her *nom de famille*. I ask her if she is Jewish. She shout into the telephone, Saul. She shout, 'GREENFELD! WE ARE JEWS!' My Aunt Marisha, I think, is waiting for fifty years to say these words. Then she tell me about your film and your book. You see, what I was told all my life—and my Aunt Marisha was under strict order all my life to say it to me too—that all three sisters are born Polish Catholics. And my Aunt Marisha, she feel *obligée* to say this lie to me because my mother save her life in the war. My mother always say their *nom de famille* is Lewitski. She even show me her Polish papers in that name."

"You saw forged papers my father had made for them after the war, under the Polish name Lewitski, in order to protect the family from antisemitic violence."

"I was told lies, I suppose to keep me from feeling different. Because my mother, for good reason, she mistrust the world."

"And you never questioned her version of the past?"

"*Jamais.* And now I see your film and read your book, and I find out my mother—whose name is really Shaindel—she pretend to be Zosia, a Polish Catholic during the war, in order to hide her sister—whose name is not Marisha, but Malka—in order to distribute the family money to help her family survive. I find out my mother, she was a hero who walk alone into extermination camp Majdanek to bring to her brother food, to keep him alive. None of which she tell me. None of which I knew. Until now."

"There's another thing, Gérard, that you may not know: Our mothers had three brothers. The youngest brother, Yossel, was murdered very early in the war. The middle brother, Chamel, was murdered in Majdanek. But the older brother, Srulcie, disappeared. He ran away to Russia and was never heard from again. Let me show you a photograph of him."

I hold up a photo of Srulcie when he was in his twenties.

The expression on Gérard's face is one of wonder, shock, and sadness as he looks at the photograph of his uncle—a man he never even knew existed, who looks unmistakably like Gérard did when he was young, and who disappeared, much like Gérard's own history.

Gérard, a retired school principal, is now a luthier, he builds and repairs stringed instruments.

I tell him Srulcie played the violin.

YOUNG GERARD

SRULCIE
(Frania's oldest brother)

# TWENTY-ONE

AS FAR BACK AS I CAN REMEMBER, I knew the word *Nazi*. It was, to my childish mind, a scary creature that, for some mysterious reason, hunted my mother and my father, wanted them dead. My little-boy brain tried to find some kind of logic, some meaning in half-overheard stories of terror and murder. I came up with this: My father had been an actor in Yiddish theater in a country called Poland. A man called Hitler was the king of a different country called Germany, and he somehow turned everyone in that country into "Nazi" monsters who got orders to stop my father from acting in Yiddish theater. Hitler had maybe seen him in a bad play? Who knows. When I was very young, I thought maybe the way to save myself was to avoid acting in Yiddish theater, no matter what.

I was introduced to the Holocaust far, far too early in my life—not my parents' fault. I was born in a refugee camp in Germany only three years after World War II ended. How could my parents help what I heard, starting in very early childhood, from every acted-out tale of miraculous escape, every song that grieved the loss of a loved one, every sigh of relief or anguish because of a story finally shared?

Elinor and I struggled with a problem: When is the right time—is there a right time?—to introduce our children to the dark side of their Jewish family history, the side that includes the Second World War and the murder of their great-grandparents, the systematic liquidation of most of their Polish-Jewish family. There is a complex, tragic, and wonderful history from Elinor's side of the family, but nothing so immediately unsettling and potentially devastating to children as the concept of genocide.

In almost all Jewish families, Elinor and I knew, children are told very early about the Holocaust, certainly years before their bar or bat mitzvah. We thought we should wait until they were older.

Hannah and Sam were "lifers"—kindergarten through twelfth grade—in Waldorf education, based on the early twentieth-century educational philosophy of Rudolf Steiner. Steiner was German, and at first, sending our children to a school system founded by a German didn't seem to me like a great idea. But then I found out Steiner's schools were banned by the Nazis. And since there were no statues of Steiner at the school, I figured it probably wasn't a cult, and was, in fact, a humanistic approach to pedagogy—a system of education widely practiced in North America and Western Europe.

I mention it here because the way Hannah and Sam were educated played an important role in all our lives. According to Steiner philosophy, music, theater, writing, and literature aren't simply subjects to be studied, absorbed, and tested. They are to be actively experienced.

When our daughter, Hannah, is nine, Elinor and I show *So Many Miracles*, my documentary film, to the Waldorf school's main administrator (Waldorf schools don't have principals). Her name is Moira, and she's a wise, kind woman in her forties, who we've known since Hannah first started going to this school when she was three. We meet with Moira in her office.

"I think you're right not to tell Hannah about the Holocaust now," Moira says to us.

"When should we tell her?" asks Elinor.

"Well, that's a good question. Around eighth grade, children begin to relate events in history, and the consequences of those events, to their own experiences. I think eighth grade would be a good time to introduce Hannah to both the documentary film and your book."

"Eighth grade," Elinor says. "Hannah will be thirteen. That seems right."

Moira turns to me. "How old were you when you were told about the Holocaust?"

"I can't remember a time when I didn't know about it. This is me, six years old, in the schoolyard: 'Do you have grandparents? Not me! Mine were murdered!' I wanted to be special, I was a child. It wasn't until I had my first sleepover at a friend's house when I was eight that I realized his parents didn't have nightmares, like mine, and that my friend didn't have to go into their bedroom to see if they're okay. That was ... maybe that was just *my* house?"

"When you show Hannah the documentary film, would you consider sharing it with Hannah's whole class?" Moira asks.

I hesitate. "I'm not sure about that."

"Why?"

"When I came back from Poland after doing the documentary," I tell her, "I was playing poker with some of my actor friends. One of them, Gary, was Indigenous, from the Cayuga Nation of the Iroquois Confederacy, a Native American tribe. Gary knew I had just come back from making a documentary with my parents in Poland, and he asked me what it was like. I told him it was an intense experience. Gary asked me if all my people were from Poland. I said, 'I don't really know. In the town where my mom was born, I went to the Jewish cemetery: totally destroyed. They used the gravestones to make the fucking sidewalks. I couldn't find where my ancestors were buried.'

"Gary looked at me and said, 'Yeah, tell me about it.'

"I'll never forget that moment, as I connected to Gary's history for the first time. When I told him about Poland, I was so tone deaf, I had never considered *his* ancestry, the struggle of *his* people. So, to tell you the truth, I don't want to share our story with Hannah's class."

"I'm not sure I understand," Moira says.

"Teaching young people about the genocide of the Jews," I say, "is a problem. At least for me. I'm not sure I would know how to do that without being exclusionary. Exclusionary of tragedies and genocides that happened to other people, other cultures. As if the genocide on one people is somehow more profound than the genocide that happened to other people. I won't do it."

Nobody says anything for a moment. Then Moira asks, "What if you say that to the students?"

"No! No, saying that, just *saying* it, that won't mean a damn thing to them, compared to having just experienced the film."

Elinor comes up with a solution. "What if this: What if showing the film is an opportunity to inspire the class to investigate their own personal history?"

"We could do that," Moira says.

"Wait," I say. "Do what, exactly?"

Moira says, "The students could be encouraged to find, I don't know, photographs, or do an interview with someone in their family, or find a song, or a family story about how they came to this country, whatever, and share that with the rest of the class."

I'm still reluctant.

Then Moira says to me, "How about this: Right after you show your film, the school commits to a Personal-History Week? Would that work?"

"That would work," I say.

Sam is five when Hannah is nine, so we decide, as Moira suggests, to wait four more years. We hope that what might work for Hannah will be okay for Sam when the time comes. We are going to be careful about what Hannah reads and sees and hears, not wanting to create an early cynicism in her by exposing her to things that are too dark to process. Elinor and I don't want to become media police, but some of that kind of control is normal parental behavior anyway, and Hannah will expect it. What will make the whole thing a little easier, we figure, is that the Waldorf school is a relatively small, close-knit community, with a policy of limited media, so the other students in Hannah's class will be unlikely to be exposed to stuff at a faster rate than she'll be.

We are blindsided.

One of Hannah's best friends at school, Charlotte, is almost a year older than her but in the same fourth-grade class. We are not close friends of Charlotte's mom and dad, Lilli and Jim, but we like them a lot and have the kind of easygoing acquaintanceship you develop with parents of your children's school friends. One California late-autumn weekend, we are invited to Lilli's home for dinner. Jim is away on a job. Lilli has a son around Sam's age, and eventually, all the kids are watching *Harry Potter* in another room, while Lilli, Elinor, and I are left drinking wine in the living room. One laugh leads to another, and soon enough, we are sharing stories about how we were raised.

"My grandmother is a Scot," Elinor says. "She did not approve of my parents' marriage. She called my dad a Sassenach. Call anyone English a Sassenach, and you might as well call them bastards and murderers."

"My dad's parents," Lilli says, "did not want him to marry my mom. They're all from Texas, and she sure wasn't."

Elinor asks, "What was the problem?"

"Oh, see, my dad was in the United States Army, stationed in Germany, and he fell for a local girl."

"German girl?" Elinor asks.

"Yep. My dad's parents were not thrilled about that, but he married her anyway, and they settled in Texas. Now his parents like her better'n they like him."

We all laugh. I pour us all a bit more wine. "My mom's parents didn't want her to go out with my dad," I tell Lilli, "because he was an actor."

"And my mom," Lilli says, "wasn't thrilled I wanted to marry a musician. Till she heard him play the trumpet. Then *she* wanted to marry him!" She looks at her watch. "Marry a musician, you gotta get used to how late they get home."

"Saul's parents were not happy about me at first. Because I'm not Jewish."

"But you charmed 'em?"

"No," Elinor laughs, "I had children."

"Grandchildren! Cures everythin'. I was raised by my grandfather. Spoiled me somethin' fierce."

"In Texas?" Elinor asks.

"Nuremberg. Till I was ten."

Elinor and I share a look. "Germany?" I ask.

"Uh-huh," Lilli says.

"So you speak German?" I ask her.

"*Ja, ich spreche fließend Deutsch.* That means—"

"I understood you."

"*Sprechen Sie Deutsch?*"

"Yiddish. It's basically German from around a thousand years ago."

"Didn't know that. Yeah, my mom's dad raised me. He was great."

"And your grandmother, his wife?" Elinor asks.

"Never knew her. Died young, 'fore I was born."

Elinor asks, "So why were you raised by—"

"My grandpa? My mom had to be in Texas with my dad—some citizenship, green card thing. It was complicated. I mean, I saw them a few times a year. And summers. Then when I was ten: hello, Texas for good. Gotta say, I sure miss my grandpa. Passed away seven years ago now."

I ask, "How old was he?"

"Eighty-one. Born in 1912. He was in the war. Drafted."

I take a second, nervous about the answer, before I ask, "Wehrmacht, regular German army?"

"Yep. Your dad was in the war too?"

"He wasn't ... in the army."

"Too young?"

"He was in Poland, born in Poland. Polish Jew. Holocaust survivor. He and my mom."

"I didn't know that, I'm sorry." She looks genuinely upset. "Sorry I brought that up. Specially with my grandpa in the German army in the war."

"No," I say, "listen, please don't feel ... I've met people over the years whose parents or they, themselves, were in the regular German army, the Wehrmacht, during the war. It's not necessarily a big thing."

That seems to make Lilli feel better. She pours us all more wine. "Sometimes grandpa would take out his old uniform. Showed me his captain's hat. It had a skull and crossbones, like the flag on a pirate ship. *Totenkopf.* That's what he called it. Means *death's head.* And he had a tattoo of his blood type under his arm. Army macho stuff."

Elinor looks at me and subtly shakes her head: *No, do not get into this.* But me being me, I say, "Lilli, your grandfather was not drafted."

"He said he was."

"You know what I'm talking about, right?"

"No, I sure don't."

Elinor interrupts. "Maybe we should talk about this another time."

I ignore that. I say to Lilli, "If his uniform had a Totenkopf insignia, skull and crossbones, and he was tattooed like that, he was in the SS. And if you were in the SS, you weren't there because you were drafted."

Lilli looks blank. "The S … what?"

Elinor and I don't know how to react to that. Then Elinor says, "It's late. It's a school night. We should get the kids home."

Lilli quickly says, "I'll get 'em."

After she leaves the room, I say, "Total denial. Everybody's heard of the SS. What are we going to do?"

"Nothing," Elinor says. "None of our business."

"Of course it's our business! Because now we know! I can't show the documentary to the class! To do what!? Have them all participate in Personal-History Week? Inspire Charlotte to find out her great-grandfather was in the fucking SS?"

"Relax. Four years from now, Charlotte might not even be at the school. Unless her mother brings this subject up, we have to let it go. Lilli will either decide this is something she wants to deal with or she won't. We don't have to get involved—not until Hannah is thirteen."

---

Four years later, Charlotte is in Hannah's eighth-grade class.

We tell Hannah about the documentary and the book. We don't say much, we tell her it's up to her whether to read the book first or watch the film. She chooses to read the book, which she does in one sitting. And then, being Hannah, she immediately reads it again.

And then we talk. She asks a million questions, and I try to answer. There's no cassette tape recorder between us, but I can feel the shadow of those early conversations in my parents' kitchen, and I can see how passing on my parents' story is affecting her. Maybe the reason to write the book is happening right in front of me.

Then she watches the documentary, and we watch it with her.

Hannah asks, "Is she still alive? Zofia?"

"No, honey," Elinor tells her. "That film was made sixteen years ago."

"But when it first came out," I say, "Zofia and her son, Maniek, saw it. It was on Polish TV."

Nine-year-old Sam wanders in and sees us all sitting there in silence. The TV is still on. "You watched something on TV? How come you didn't tell me?" he asks.

"You're not old enough," Hannah tells him.

"For what? I am so!"

Elinor says, "We're talking with Hannah about something right now, honey. It's something private." She gets up and takes Sam by the hand to lead him out of the room. He is stubborn and lets go of her hand. He stands there facing everyone. "What are you talking about?"

"We'll tell you all about it," Elinor says to him. "Just not right now."

Sam thinks about this. He got into some trouble this morning for waking Hannah up with a tambourine. "Is this about me?"

This is a hard one to answer.

"Dad wrote a book about your *bubbie* and *zayde*," Elinor says. "We think Hannah is old enough now to read it. And there's also a film about the book. When you get to be thirteen, we want you to see it too, and read the book."

"Why can't I see the film now?"

"You'll understand it better when you get older, Sam," I say.

Sam turns to the authority on major decisions. "Mom?"

"Honey, you will definitely get to see it when you're thirteen. But not now. Okay?"

Sam thinks, then nods, "Okay." Reluctantly, he leaves the room.

Hannah says to us, "Why did you wait so long to tell me about all this? I could have talked to Bubbie about it."

Elinor says gently, "Hannah, you just told Sam he's not old enough. You were right."

I say, "You were Sam's age, nine, when Bubbie died. Too young to talk to her about this."

Hannah thinks about it. Accepts it. She opens the *So Many Miracles* book to the inside front cover. "You dedicated the book to Rachel. Who's that?"

Elinor and I share a moment. Then I say, "My parents' baby, my sister. She died the day she was born, at the farmhouse. My parents never named her, so I named her Rachel."

"Oh," Hannah says. "In the book, it says she died because it was so cold when Bubbie gave birth."

Elinor and I look at each other. One more lie. "That's right," I say to Hannah. I wonder if my nightmare will come back tonight.

"Dad, you want to show the film to my class?"

"We're not sure about that," I say. "If we show the film, the school will encourage the rest of your class to bring in stories about their own families."

"That sounds great," Hannah says. "Why aren't you sure about that?"

"Because," Elinor says, "we're not sure all the parents will agree they want that to happen."

"Oh, right," Hannah says. Then she thinks about it. "You know, I heard Charlotte say something very weird. I better tell you about it."

---

Lilli has heard that I might show a documentary film about my parents to the class. I ask if Elinor and I can come to her house to talk about it.

When we're in Lilli's living room, there's not much chitchat. I tell her what the documentary film is about, and she says she's eager to see it.

I look at Elinor and she nods. I say, "Lilli, Hannah told us she overheard Charlotte tell some other kids her great-grandfather was Hitler's bodyguard."

"Oh my God!" She is shocked. "Hitler's bodyguard? What does that even mean?"

"The SS was kind of symbolically that. SS stands for *Schutzstaffel*. Doesn't that mean ...?"

"Protection Squadron," she says. "Charlotte said it, like, how? Bragging about it?"

Elinor says, "She couldn't know what she was saying, Lilli. I think she just wanted to feel ..."

"Special," I say. "She wanted to feel special, Lilli. That's all I think it was."

"There's more to it," Lilli says. "Charlotte saw somethin', I guess—overheard somethin'."

"About your grandfather?" Elinor asks her.

"I been gettin' emails from fans of his for years. They want pictures, memorabilia, whatever I got."

I am taken aback. "*Fans* of his?"

"I know. Neo-Nazis, white supremacists. That kind of scum. I never answer 'em."

"Lilli," I say, "all the parents in the class will get a copy of the documentary that I want to show the class, but ..."

"We wanted to talk to you about this first," Elinor adds.

"You think I'll say no?"

"No, I think *we* might say no," I tell her. "I'm not sure it's right to show it with Charlotte there."

Lilli is genuinely confused. "Because of my grandfather? She won't make a connection. We've never talked about it."

"Right," Elinor says quietly. "You never talked about it. Thing is, after Saul shows the documentary, the plan is for the class to take part in a Personal-History Week."

Now Lilli gets it. We can see it in her eyes. "Oh."

"So if Saul shows it, and Charlotte is left out …"

"Right," she says, looking into the distance. She seems devastated.

"So I don't think I can show it at all."

"That's not right either. You should show it. And Charlotte should be there. But I guess I gotta talk to her first."

I look at Elinor for a moment and then say, "Lilli, do you know what your grandfather did during the war?"

"No." She is on the verge of tears and struggles to contain her emotions. "I can't do it. I never could do it. Never looked him up. I just could never bring myself to do it. I'm forty-two, I guess it's time for me to open all the doors and windows in my life—what kind of wife I am, what kind of mother I am. What kind of woman. My whole life, I never asked any questions. Why my mother always fought—screamin' fights—with her father. Why my grandfather's only son, my uncle, lives alone somewhere in Germany, no contact with any of the family, in and out of mental institutions all his life. Why my grandmother died of a heart attack right after the war, in her forties. I never asked why."

We are all silent for a while. Then Lilli looks at me. "Would you do it? Look him up?"

"You want *me* to …?" Lilli nods and gestures to a computer in the room.

She spells out his name. I tap through a few sites. And find it. "Lilli, there's good news and bad news. Good news is, he was never a wanted war criminal."

Lilli says, "Bad news is, … he shoulda been?"

I don't answer, I can see she knows it's true.

"I'll talk to Charlotte," she says. "I'll tell her everything."

A week later, Charlotte, the great-granddaughter of a perpetrator, and Hannah, the granddaughter of survivors, sit side by side in their classroom and watch the documentary about my parents.

When the film ends, I can see many of the students are emotional. I'm exhausted but exhilarated. I feel it's taken me most of my life to get here, to share this story with these young people, and if the film has left out exactly how my sister died, well, it's a promise I made to my parents, and so be it.

I say to the class, "I asked you earlier to raise your hands if you think that what happened to my family is more important, or somehow more dramatic than what happened to your family, to your people. Most of you raised your hands. Maybe after seeing this film, you still think that's true."

I look at all the young faces in front of me, and I suspect that's what they believe—and maybe even more strongly now. And I look at Charlotte sitting beside Hannah. She's looking down, not meeting my eyes. Of course, it's not true for her.

I turn back to the class. "In your own family history, I believe that you can find great romance, miraculous coincidence, betrayal, murder, lives saved at the last minute, cowardice, and courage, as dramatic as any of the greatest novels ever written. You can find victims and perpetrators, heroes and bystanders. All in your own family history. If you ask the right people the right questions."

After that, Mrs. Schmidt tells the students about the Personal-History Week idea. For the next week of classes, the students share something about their own family histories: a short interview with a grandparent or another relative, a song, a poem, photographs, letters, or artifacts—each one telling the story of a different family journey.

During that week, Charlotte is upset. She talks to Hannah about it. Everybody is sharing cool stories, funny stories, even heroic stories about their families. Before her mother talked to her about her great-grandfather being in the SS, all Charlotte knew was that her mother's side of the family came from Germany. They have beer festival parties in October, and they have her great-grandfather's beer stein sitting on a shelf in their house. But now, how can she tell others this horrible story about her family?

Hannah says, "You don't have to. There are other stories in your family. What your great-grandfather did in the war does not define your whole family. You're not your great-grandfather. And I'm not my grandmother."

"Easier for you than for me," says Charlotte. Hearing that, Hannah takes a breath, holding onto her anger. *Easier? Nothing easy about finding out most your family was murdered.* She takes a few seconds to calm down, and then says, "Charlotte, do you think anybody in our class is being told horrible stories by their family? And even if they are, they're sure not sharing those secrets with us. I think we're all in the same boat."

Charlotte, her eyes shining from the tears ready to flow, says, "Hannah, if, somehow, everybody could share their stories, wouldn't genocide be impossible?"

---

Darkness, and then it's annihilated in a terrifying, overwhelming rush of white.

I wake up, my hand covering my mouth, stifling a scream. Elinor is still asleep beside me. It's the first time in months the nightmare has come back.

I get out of bed as quietly as possible and go into the kitchen for a glass of water. I sit at the table, head in my hands.

"Trouble sleeping?"

Rachel sits across from me, a sympathetic smile on her face.

"That old nightmare," I tell her.

"Oh no," Rachel says. "Well, I guess just 'cause you figured out why it exists, kiddo, doesn't mean it goes away forever."

I look at her, knowing that's true about her too. "She keeps coming for me, Rachel. She won't stop."

"The cuckoo woman."

"Yeah."

"With cream."

"With something, Rachel. Something bad. Something that'll kill me."

I go back to bed, afraid to fall asleep.

Hey, as Orson Welles once said, "If you want a happy ending, it depends, of course, on where you stop your story."

---

# WHAT'S TRUE AND WHAT'S NOT

THIS BOOK IS TITLED *All in the Telling: a somewhat true story*. I'll explain.

My friend Rick Cleveland is a playwright and an Emmy Award-winning television writer. I've known him for thirty years. I've shared a lot about my life with him, and he's done the same with me. In 2016, after I told Rick about my conversation with my cousin, Gérard, Rick suggested I might not be finished with the story about me and my family.

I reacted defensively and with some hostility: "I took my parents back to Poland! I wrote a book! I made a documentary film! I'm done!"

Rick had read my book, *So Many Miracles*, a few years earlier. He was far more experienced than I with the struggles of being a writer, and he was patient with me. He said, "You told your parents' story. You have not told *your* story. You haven't told the true story of your sister—how she really died and how she's been a presence throughout your life. And you have not told the story about Hannah and her friend Charlotte."

Rick said there was a play there, and if I wanted to write it, if I was willing to go on that journey, he would accompany me to be my dramaturge, to help me as I wrestled with the material.

I felt he was right, but how could I do that? First of all, there were too many stories. How could I choose which stories to put into a play? What would the thing be about?

The thought that I wasn't done with this story gnawed at me for a year. And then I started to write the play. With Rick's help, it took me around three years to complete the first draft. I called it *All in the Telling*.

Just before COVID-19 broke out in February 2020, I held the first reading of the play with actor friends in my living room in Los Angeles. I invited an audience of about twenty people—individuals I knew would provide honest and constructive criticism.

To remain faithful to the truth, the first draft of the play featured two separate women in my life—Kate and Elinor—as does this book. After the play reading, there was a common consensus that I somehow had to combine the two women characters into one, otherwise, it would be too confusing. I asked Elinor what she thought about this idea. She agreed it was the right thing to do, but she said I really shouldn't call the new character either Kate or Elinor. Instead, she suggested her middle name, Ann, since there was truth to her part of the story. I then sent the play to Kate, and she, too, agreed the two women characters should be combined. Subsequent drafts of the play included the character named Ann. I retitled the play *All in the Telling: a somewhat true story*.

However, in writing this book, I remained closer to reality: both Kate and Elinor appear here. I realized that in book form, I have much more room to avoid confusion than I had in a play.

So why do I still call this book "a somewhat true story"? A few reasons.

In real life, Kate and I began living together in late 1975, not in 1984. I condensed the timeline of events by a few years in order to make the story more concise.

I was in rehearsal and performance for several plays during my ongoing lie of pretending to write a book. I was not in rehearsal for the play *Terrible Advice*. That play was actually written by me and was performed both in London in 2011 and, in German, in Berlin in 2013. I never acted in it, but I included it in the book as an example of the kind of stress I was going through while working on other plays during that time period.

Agnieszka (not her real name) was our translator while filming the documentary in Poland, and she really was a spy for the Polish government. Agnieszka and I exchanged letters after the documentary aired on Polish television. She told me about the Censorship Committee and what happened in that room. However, although I based what I wrote on her letters, I invented almost all of the dialogue in those scenes, and the two characters Kosevich and Radzik are pure inventions on my part. According to Agnieszka, the Polish Ministry of Culture was indeed worried about a possible accusation of murder—an accusation they thought I would make, possibly to the press, about what happened on the Bania farm while my parents were in hiding.

When Hannah graduated college, she told me she wanted to work on a new version of the book *So Many Miracles*, one that would have the full version of the family stories. The excerpts in this book (and in my play) of my parents talking about their experiences are a result of Hannah's extraordinary talent in editing the original material.

I have always felt the presence of my older sister. I really did name her Rachel, but I never told my parents about that. And it's true, I did not find out how my sister really died until 1986, when we were filming a reenactment of my mother giving birth in Poland.

*So Many Miracles*, my original book, was published in 1987 by Penguin. It contains the complete transcripts, edited by me, of the conversations I recorded with my parents on my cassette player. That book has very little of me in it.

In my play, and in this book, I tried to follow Rick's wise suggestion that I include my own story. In order to get at what I believed would be a deeper truth than an act of journalism chronicling true-life events, I wrote something that is "somewhat" factually accurate. That's why the title is *All in the Telling: a somewhat true story*.

A couple more things are true: I could not have written this without the wise and loving support of my wife Elinor Reid and our children, Hannah and Sam. Also true is my gratitude to my good friend and brilliant editor, Laura Ross, who was with me every step of the way getting this book published.

Except for what I have told you happened in real life, everything else in this book is true—at least, as true as I know how to write it.

If you would like to see the documentary film **So Many Miracles**—in which I take my parents back to Poland in the summer of 1986 to have a reunion with with the Polish farmer Zofia Bania, and her son Maniek, who hid my parents for two and half years during the Holocaust—you can purchase it here:

https://bit.ly/SoManyMiracles

**SAUL AND ELINOR**
(1989)

**HANNAH**
(Elinor and Saul's daughter,
age fourteen)

**SAM**
(Elinor and Saul's son, age ten)

www.ingramcontent.com/pod-product-compliance
Lightning Source LLC
LaVergne TN
LVHW092012090526
838202LV00025B/2627/J